AMERICA IN THE ANTARCTIC TO 1840

University of Illinois Press, Urbana, 1959

AMERICA IN THE

ANTARCTIC TO 1840

BY PHILIP I. MITTERLING

TO MY FATHER AND MOTHER

ACKNOWLEDGMENTS

In a sense, this study of Antarctic exploration and the conditions contributing to the use of federal funds for overseas researches was a cooperative work, because many individuals contributed their knowledge and time to ease my labors. To acknowledge their assistance in a small measure expresses my gratitude.

Countless librarians answered inquiries, particularly the reference staffs at the University of Illinois Library, University of Pittsburgh Library, New York Public Library, American Philosophical Society, American Geographical Society, Historical Society of Pennsylvania, Maryland Historical Society, Albany, New York, Public Library, New Bedford, Massachusetts, Public Library, and the Wilmington, Ohio, Public Library. In Washington, D.C., Mr. Nelson M. Blake of the Naval Records Section, National Archives, and Messrs. Solon J. Buck, David C. Mearns, and C. Percy Powell of the Manuscripts Division, Library of Congress, helped with the searches in their collections, while Mrs. Leila F. Clark, of the Smithsonian Institution, generously gave of her knowledge of the hollow earth theory. The Yale University Library and the Adams Manuscript Trust, Massachusetts Historical Society, gave permission to publish excerpts from the journal of Lieutenant George F. Emmons and the diary of John Quincy Adams. The Controller of Her Britannic Majesty's Stationery Office and the Hydrographer of the Navy allowed me to reproduce the chart of Edward Bransfield's voyage to the South Shetlands and the Antarctic Continent, while the *Mariner's Mirror, Journal of the Society for Nautical Research*, Greenwich, England, permitted me to copy the facsimile of this manuscript published earlier in that journal. Permission to publish the late Colonel Lawrence Martin's map of Captain Nathaniel Palmer's voyage to Antarctica was granted by the *Geographical Review*. The outline map of Antarctica was provided by the Hydrographic Office, Department of the Navy, and microfilm copies of the John Cleves Symmes Papers in the Draper Manuscripts, Wisconsin Historical Society, were made available by the Historical Survey of the University of Illinois.

Other individuals gave information and assistance of a special nature. Miss Mary E. Cooley, of Ann Arbor, Michigan, allowed me to use her microfilm of the Emmons journal and to examine the manuscript of her unpublished study, "Charles Wilkes and the U.S. Exploring Expedition." Mr. Carl C. Cutler, former Curator of the Marine Historical Association, Mystic, Connecticut, provided valuable information concerning the sealers generally and Nathaniel Brown Palmer particularly. The distinguished Arctic explorer, Vilhjalmur Stefansson, opened his magnificent polar library to me. And Mr. Fenley Hunter, of Flushing, New York, directed my attention to the John James Audubon drawing of John Cleves Symmes, Jr., which is owned by the New York Historical Society.

Professor Victor L. Johnson, of Muhlenberg College, originally suggested the subject of United States overseas exploration to me. Professors Arthur E. Bestor, Jr., Frederick C. Dietz, Raymond P. Stearns, and Edward H. Davidson, all of the University of Illinois, Robert E. Carlson, George B. Fowler, and James A. Kehl, of the University of Pittsburgh, and Maynard Smith, Hobart and William Smith Colleges, read the manuscript in whole or in part and offered thoughtful criticism. Professor Donald D. Jackson, of the University of Illinois Press, made important editorial suggestions. Professor Charles E. Nowell, of the University of Illinois, provided so much inspiration and guidance that to attempt to recount his suggestions and to describe his counsel would be endless. Suffice to say, that this study would not have been prepared without his help. Finally, my wife, Doris Davenport Mitterling, alternately performed the duties of proofreader and critic, while, at the same time, amusing an active young daughter and a baby son so Daddy could work.

PHILIP I. MITTERLING

CONTENTS

chapter one

CONCEPTIONS OF THE
ANTARCTIC BEFORE 1800

The six ships of the United States Exploring Expedition were gently riding at anchor in the Navy Yard at Norfolk in August, 1838. Each was ready to be taken to sea. Repairs and alterations had been made, provisions and equipment stowed. But the picture of tranquillity presented by the idle ships was not in accord with the feelings of the officers, seamen, and scientists attached to the expedition. All were restless. All were anxious to unfurl the sails and begin their trek southward to the bottom of the world, even though they had earned repose after the backbreaking labor of preparing the ships for service. Conflicts over the expedition in past months were still fresh in their minds. Many had thought, in fact, that this important undertaking might never be sent to sea, as politicians had argued over appropriations and Navy administrators had haggled over the objectives and size of the squadron. But now the difficult problems had been solved and all the explorers, especially the ebullient young commander of the expedition, Lieutenant Charles Wilkes, were impatiently awaiting a messenger from Washington bearing orders for sailing from Secretary of the Navy James Kirke Paulding.

In the dispatch Wilkes received, the explorers were ordered to proceed southward into the extreme southern latitudes. Their initial objective was to investigate the theory of a British sealer, James Weddell, who maintained he had sailed as far as 74° S., between the meridians 25° and 50° W., without being retarded by either ice or land. Weddell's claim that an open polar sea existed in the Antarctic contradicted the discoveries of American seal-hunters who had seen land about ten degrees to the west and had surmised that it was part of a southern continent.

This first penetration of the storm-tossed seas of the Antarctic actually was to be of short duration, since the extended search for territory was planned for a more propitious time when the entire Antarctic summer could be utilized. The planners of the expedition knew Wilkes and his men would not reach the high latitudes of the south until much of the warm weather had passed, and they cautioned the explorers to avoid becoming frozen in. There were many islands in the Pacific to be explored before the fleet was moved to Sydney, Australia. This city had been chosen as the base where the ships would be refitted and repaired in preparation for a wide-ranging exploration of the Antarctic on the other side of the world.[1]

Antarctic exploration was not the sole objective of the expedition, for Wilkes had been instructed to survey islands in the South Pacific and to determine the existence of all doubtful shoals and reefs which lay in the common track of American whalemen. Furthermore, significant scientific observations and collections were to be made. On the other hand, exploration in the Antarctic was not a secondary aim, since existing geographical knowledge of that section of the world was no more than sketchy, and the propagandists who pressed for exploration financed by the federal government were primarily interested in discovering an Antarctic continent.

Knowledge of the Antarctic at the beginning of the nineteenth century was a link in the evolving chain of geographical knowledge. From the time of the Greek geographers to the British explorer James Cook, all ideas regarding the size of the world and of the amount of land on its surface entailed speculations about territory south of the ecumene or known world.

Many philosophers during ancient and medieval times conjectured about the problem of the earth's size, and a variety of

----

[1] James Kirke Paulding to Lieutenant Charles Wilkes, Navy Dept., Aug. 11, 1838, in Charles Wilkes, *Narrative of the United States Exploring Expedition, During the Years 1838, 1839, 1840, 1841, 1842* (5 vols., Philadelphia, 1845), I, xxvi, xxvii. For the details of Weddell's open polar sea theory see his *Voyage Towards the South Pole, Performed in the Years 1822–'24* . . . (London, 1825).

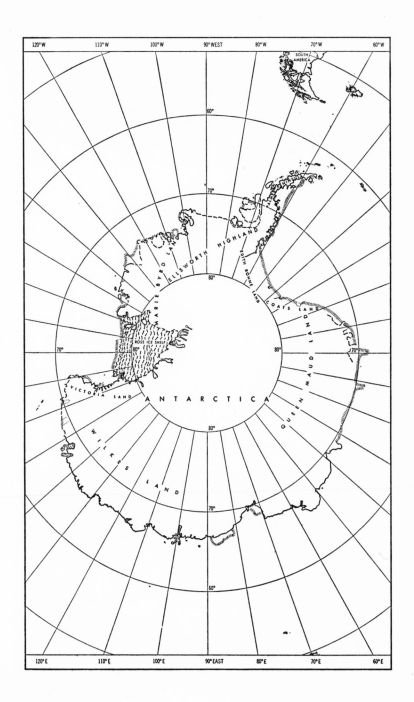

unreliable conclusions were reached. By far the most significant of these speculations were those carried out by the Roman geographer Claudius Ptolemaeus or Ptolemy. This man, living in Alexandria during the second century, considerably influenced later geographers because his work was authoritative. Ptolemy painstakingly analyzed and evaluated the work of earlier writers and prepared a map of the world much more comprehensive and detailed than any offered before.

Regarding the existence of lands south of the known world, Ptolemy departed from the Greek theory of an Africa encompassed by water. Instead of an ocean south of the ecumene he drew an immense southern land mass—an area he labeled *Terra Incognita*. This land of continental proportions connected Africa with the Malay Peninsula in the east, making the Indian Ocean a closed sea. Ptolemy himself regarded his southern continent merely as a probability, but as late as the sixteenth century it was being used as the basis for most scholarly and popular geographies while serving also as a source of speculation. In fact, this Roman geographer's conception was not disproved until the Portuguese captains Bartholemew Diaz and Vasco da Gama rounded the Cape of Good Hope during the last years of the fifteenth century and proved that Africa was not connected to lands in the east by a southern continent.

Thus, at the dawn of the great Age of Geographical Discovery most informed geographers did not believe there was an Antarctic continent south of Africa. But in attempting to reach Cipango or Cathay by sailing through or around Christopher Columbus's Indies, the Spanish inadvertently discovered land, which gave rise to further speculation concerning an Antarctic land mass. Every Spanish explorer who charted the east coast of South America probed all sizable indentations for a passage until Ferdinand Magellan, a Portuguese captain in the service of Spain, in 1520 discovered the 360-mile strait which bears his name. In so doing he not only proved that China and Japan could be reached by sailing westward, but also strengthened belief in the existence of a southern continent by reporting that the fiery land he had seen to the south, Tierra del Fuego, was part of it.

This discovery was the great contribution of Spanish explorers to geographical knowledge concerning land south of the known world. None of the mariners who explored islands in the South Pacific during the sixteenth century made any important discoveries or ventured south of Magellan's Strait, but this did not prevent other Spaniards, notably Pedro Fernando de Quiros, Alvaro de Mendana, and Juan Luis Arias, from indulging in extravagant visions of a great habitable land somewhere south or west of Chile which would fall into Spanish hands through exploration and colonization. Quiros gave the impression he had seen it, but he never realized his dream of finding a second empire for Spain. The memoirs he published nevertheless served as an important motivating force behind Dutch, French, and British explorations in the seventeenth and eighteenth centuries.[2]

Late in the sixteenth century Dutch ships began plying the two sea routes to the East Indies. In 1598 a fleet of five ships under the command of James Mahu sailed southwestward to enter the Pacific through Magellan's Strait. Misfortune befell this squadron almost from the start. Not long after leaving Rotterdam the commander died and Sebald de Wirt became leader of the fleet. A pilot named Dirck Gherritsz took command of one of the vessels. When the ships reached the Strait in April, 1599, the Dutchmen decided to spend the southern winter in Tierra del Fuego rather than risk navigating the hazardous passage during the stormiest season. But fate was against them. After making their way through safely in the spring, they were met in the Pacific by a furious storm which separated the ships and ended the voyage. According to reports, one vessel returned to Rotterdam, two reached Japan, one was captured by the Portuguese, while the fifth, under the command of Gherritsz, surrendered to the Spanish.

This ill-fated expedition would have been of no significance in the annals of exploration had not the Spanish historian Antonio de Herrara published a book in 1602 entitled *Historia de los hechos de los castellanos en las islas i tierra firma del mar oceano* which was translated into French, Dutch, and Latin. In the French edition Dirck Gherritsz was credited with discovering land in the

---

[2] James Burney, *A Chronological History of the Discoveries in the South Sea or Pacific Ocean* (5 vols., London, 1803–17), II, 180–81, 268–326; and R. H. Major, ed., *Early Voyages to Terra Australis, now called Australia* . . . (London, 1859), pp. lxx–lxxvii, 19. See also Edward Heawood, *History of Geographical Discovery in the Seventeenth and Eighteenth Centuries* (Cambridge, 1912), pp. 71–74.

vicinity of latitude 64° S. His ship was said to have been blown south and east of Tierra del Fuego by the storm, accidentally encountering unknown terra firma. Although this story is based on rather unsubstantial evidence, some explorers and geographers of the nineteenth century believed Gherritsz had discovered the South Shetland Islands.[3]

Some years after the Mahu expedition a Dutch company deliberately set out to discover territory in the southern latitudes. Motivation for this exploration came from the memoirs of Pedro Fernando de Quiros. The Spaniard had published glowing accounts of the immense riches of this continent as well as enticing pictures of the potential profits of trade which could be established there. The Dutch adventurers organized a squadron under the leadership of Willem Corneliszoon Schouten and Jacob Le Maire. These men set out in 1615 to discover not only the southern continent but also a passage to the Far East south of Magellan's Strait.

When Tierra del Fuego was reached, the explorers sailed southward and found the strait which separates that land from a small island to the east. The strait was given the name Le Maire, and the island was called Staten Land in honor of the States-General of the Netherlands. When the explorers reached the southernmost point of Tierra del Fuego, they sighted a cape which they labeled Hoorn, after the town in Holland whose merchants had sponsored their voyage, and sailed westward into the Pacific. Now the insularity of Tierra del Fuego was established. It was not part of a southern continent as Magellan had reported.

For two decades after Schouten and Le Maire's voyage, Dutch navigators concentrated their efforts in the western Pacific. From the beginning of the sixteenth century Dutchmen had been adding to the geographical knowledge of the Malay archipelago, New Guinea, and Australia while searching for islands which bore gold and silver. Yet the idea of the mysterious southern continent had not entirely left their minds. It was too much for money-hungry traders to completely forget the prospects of additional productive commerce which Quiros had forecast. Consequently, the powerful

----

[3] See Edwin Swift Balch, *Antarctica* (Philadelphia, 1902), pp. 40–45. One of the nineteenth-century authors who accepted the Herrara account of Gherritsz's voyage was James Burney. See his *Chronological History*, II, 198, 204.

Dutch East India Company resolved to assemble an expedition to search for a passage between Eendrachtsland (Australia) and this continental land mass. By finding such a passage, the company governors supposed they could open trade with Chile. Obviously, knowledge of the explorations of Schouten and Le Maire had not been made available to them. Also they wanted their explorers to circumnavigate New Guinea to determine whether it was part of a larger territory to the south. The command was given to Abel Janszoon Tasman.

Tasman, with the ships *Heemskerk* and *Zeehahen*, left Batavia in Java in August, 1642, steering westward toward Mauritius. From this island he varied his course, sailing south-southeast until he reached the 45th parallel of latitude, where signs of land were observed. Tasman directed his pilots to steer eastward. When the ships reached latitude 42° 25′ S. and longitude 145° 52′ E. on November 5, a high, mountainous land was discovered. This land was the southwest coast of the island now called Tasmania. Tasman called it Van Diemen's Land in honor of Anthony Van Diemen, governor of the Dutch East Indies and sponsor of the voyage.

During the month which followed the discovery, Tasman and his crews occupied themselves exploring bays, inlets, and capes. Then they planted a standard signifying possession by the Dutch East India Company and sailed eastward.

Tasman's explorations were not satisfactory to the authorities of the Dutch East India Company. He had discovered no southern continent nor had he encountered any natives with gold to trade. The masters of the company were not interested in finding barren islands; they wanted income and Tasman's explorations had yielded none. During the remainder of the seventeenth century they were apathetic to exploration, devoting themselves to their profitable trade in Java, the Moluccas, New Guinea, and the Celebes.

It was the Dutch West India Company that made the next attempt to solve the Antarctic problem. In 1696 a man named Roggeveen had submitted a plan to the Company in which he detailed a project for the discovery of the southern continent. At that time the company was engaged in other more lucrative activities, but promised to take up the proposal as soon as practicable. An expedient time did not come for twenty-five years, and only then because Jacob Roggeveen, the son of the original planner, resubmitted the scheme. This time the company agreed to support an expedition, and a fleet of three vessels was detailed for Roggeveen's use.

The course of Roggeveen's ships took them southward in the Atlantic where the explorers touched the Falkland Islands, naming them Belgia Australia, and rounded the Horn via the Strait of Le Maire. As was frequently the case, they encountered dirty weather while sailing into the Pacific, but even when the skies cleared, the Dutchmen were unable to perceive a large continent between New Zealand and Staten Land. The voyage was not completely fruitless, however, for they discovered Samoa and some other islands in the Pacific. Roggeveen was the last of the Dutch navigators who attempted to find the habitable southern continent. The search was taken up next by the French and the British.

The history of early French explorations in the southern hemisphere follows the same pattern as the Dutch voyages of Schouten and Le Maire and of Roggeveen. They had their own pioneer, like Quiros, in Binot Paulmier de Gonneville. This sixteenth-century merchant and voyager followed Vasco da Gama's track southward in 1503. While rounding the Cape of Good Hope, his ship was driven off course during a storm and fell in with a large island, undoubtedly Madagascar, which Gonneville named Southern India. On the return voyage, the explorers were captured by an English privateer who confiscated their personal effects, including their journals. Gonneville thus lost the written proof of his discovery, but a native prince whom he had kidnapped provided an elaborate description of Southern India.[4] The prince's account was widely circulated to influential Frenchmen, among whom was a French East India Company captain, Bouvet des Loziers. Following the Dutch pattern, Bouvet took the memoir to company officials and asked to be given command of a fleet to rediscover and reclaim Southern India for France. The company, envisioning the profits which could be gained, granted Bouvet the *Aiglé* and the *Maria*, which were provisioned for a voyage of eighteen months.

[4] See Major, *Early Voyages to Terra Australis*, pp. xx–xxi; and John Callander, ed., *Terra Australis Cognita: or Voyages to the Terra Australis, or Southern Hemisphere during the Sixteenth, Seventeenth, and Eighteenth Centuries* (3 vols., Edinburgh, 1766–68), I, 63–72.

Contrary to Dutch practice, the French company's plans did not call for Bouvet to explore as he pleased. Company officials were certain Southern India lay between latitude 44° and 55° S. in a longitude roughly corresponding to the Cape of Good Hope, so they instructed their explorer to concentrate his surveys in that area. If Southern India was not located there, Bouvet was to search along the 44th parallel of latitude as far as 80° east of Paris. The company governors left nothing to chance. In case the glory of discovery was not incentive enough, Bouvet and his crew were guaranteed a bonus if they sighted land.

The French fleet sailed south from Lorient in July, 1737. Five months later it was south of the Cape of Good Hope, where floating ice was met somewhere in the vicinity of 48° 50′ S. As the ships pushed southward, no land was sighted, but the icebergs increased in size and number. Bouvet was convinced that Southern India must be nearby, since icebergs and ice islands break off from land. Finally, on New Year's Day, the Frenchman's convictions were justified when a high snow-clad mountain was sighted. For several days Bouvet and his crews attempted to land, but rough water kept them off. When they gave this up, they charted their land as being approximately 55° south and 28° east of Teneriffe. Because of its steep coasts, the Frenchmen named the land Cape Circumcision, even though they had seen enough to know it was an island and not a very large one. Bouvet had not found Southern India, but he had discovered the small island which bears his name, and supplied additional evidence that the mythical southern continent did not exist immediately south of Africa. Some thirty-one years later, another Frenchman, Yves Joseph de Kerguelen-Trémarec, performed the same service for the east section of the South Indian Ocean.

Kerguelen's motivating influence also was Gonneville, but he was sponsored by the French royal court. Since Bouvet had not located Southern India in the South Atlantic, he concluded it must lie to the east in the same latitude. His voyage was not entirely unsuccessful, for he discovered a small island in 49° 40′ S., which he named La France Australe. This sub-Antarctic islet did not match its discoverer's description, because Kerguelen said his new land was part of the central mass of the Antarctic Continent. It would serve as a naval station to command the sea routes to India, and as a supply outpost where French voyagers could obtain needed wood and vegetables, as well as valuable diamonds and rubies. The French court received this information enthusiastically, but many members of the nobility scoffed at the zealot's statements. After all, mariners had been sailing in the Indian Ocean for centuries and none had reported a fertile continent. Kerguelen was sent out again to survey his discovery more thoroughly. When he saw the island a second time he changed the name from South France to the Isle of Desolation. No colony was established there, and this unhappy expedition rang down the curtain on eighteenth-century French attempts to discover the southern continent.

The final chapter in the history of eighteenth-century Antarctic exploration was written by the English commander, James Cook. On three successive voyages during the years 1768 to 1779, this explorer made contributions to geography which changed men's knowledge of the earth. Cook rose from the ranks of the merchant service to prominence as Britain's most important explorer. The son of a Northumbrian farm laborer, he enlisted in the Royal Navy at the beginning of the Seven Years' War and early became identified with hydrographic surveying. During the siege of Quebec, he helped make soundings in the St. Lawrence River, and later he was assigned to the coast survey of Newfoundland. Because of this experience, Cook was given command of an expedition to observe the transit of Venus on the island of Tahiti and to make explorations in the South Pacific.

This expedition resulted from the exertions of the influential Royal Society and of one member in particular, Alexander Dalrymple, a successful merchant, scientist, voyager, and propagandist. Astronomers in the Society wanted to observe the solar parallax during the transit of Venus in order to calculate the sun's distance from the earth. They knew this phenomenon could be seen best in the South Pacific and convinced the Admiralty of the need for a naval expedition.

When they began drawing up plans, the ambitious Dalrymple took a great interest in the work. For some years he had been studying the early Spanish voyages in the Pacific, having read and translated Quiros's memoirs as well as accounts of the voyages of Magellan, Mendana, and Juan Fernández. From his research, he had not only become convinced of the existence of a southern continent, but also obsessed with a desire to search for it. His desires meshed with those of the scientists, and the astronomical expedition became an exploring expedition as well.

Dalrymple was the Society's choice for commander, but he did not receive the position. He was a civilian, and the lords of the Admiralty did not favor giving a king's ship to civilian command. They remembered, no doubt, that seventy years earlier, Sir Edmund Halley, another Royal Society luminary, had commanded a similar expedition which was adjudged unsuccessful from a naval standpoint. James Cook was the Navy man they selected.

On his first voyage, Cook contributed to the solution of the Antarctic problem by finally making a legend of Pedro Fernando de Quiros's immense, temperate southern continent. After observing the transit of Venus at Tahiti, the explorers circumnavigated New Zealand, proving it was not a continent, and investigated the strait between Australia and New Guinea. But unfortunately Cook's own version of the voyage never reached the British public. After the return of the expedition, his logs were given over to Dr. John Hawkesworth, an essayist, editor, and translator, to be transformed into story form for public consumption. They ultimately were published in a volume with narratives of the voyages of Byron, Wallis, and Carteret.

While Cook was at sea, Alexander Dalrymple was not idle. He published an edition of his Spanish voyages which also included accounts of the explorations of the Dutch. In it Juan Fernández was credited with having discovered the southern continent in 1552 while searching for a suitable track between Peru and Chile. About ninety years later, Dalrymple added, this land mass had been seen on its west side by Abel Tasman. Yet both the Spanish and the Dutch had neglected their discoveries.

To Dalrymple the existence of a great southern land mass could not be denied. Since there were large bodies of land in the north, he reasoned, territory of similar extent must exist in the south; a southern continent was absolutely necessary to balance the earth on its axis and to maintain conformity between the northern and southern hemispheres. He estimated this land in the south to be equal in size to all the civilized part of Asia, from Turkey to China, and to be inhabited by at least fifty million people. A continent of such proportions offered extraordinary opportunities for trade. The English, Dalrymple demanded, had to follow the *"sublime conception"* of Pedro Fernando de Quiros and establish commercial relations with this land.[5]

Hawkesworth's literary edition of Cook's voyage seemingly refuted Dalrymple's assertions. The land Tasman had seen in 1642 had been circumnavigated by more recent explorers and had been proved not to be of continental proportions. Nevertheless, Dalrymple was convinced of the accuracy of his conclusions. Rather than attack the Admiralty or their explorer, James Cook, he lashed out savagely at John Hawkesworth for endeavoring to cast doubt on his veracity and on the validity of his allegations. Hawkesworth replied in kind, and a lively literary battle ensued with other literary and scientific figures taking part. Dalrymple's sentiments, incidentally, were echoed by groups in France and Spain who believed the reports of Kerguelen and Quiros.

While this was going on, Dalrymple appeared before the Admiralty and asked to be given command of an expedition to prove his contentions. When his appointment was not forthcoming, he wrote letters to the Prime Minister, Lord North, urging consideration, but none was given. Nonetheless, Dalrymple's propaganda, to which was added a fear that France or Spain might locate and colonize the southern continent, caused the Admiralty to authorize James Cook to continue his explorations.

Cook's second expedition was better prepared than any prior one, largely because the commander was given charge of all arrangements. When he was not satisfied with any of the ships in the Royal Navy and insisted on having specially constructed exploring vessels, two were built under his supervision for the expedition's use. The *Resolution*, of 462 tons, and the *Adventure*, of 336, were ideal since they had no great draft and could run close to shore where larger ships would become stranded in shallow water. They were also easily maneuverable and had sufficient capacity to accommodate crews totalling about 200 men and to carry adequate provisions. Cook commanded the *Resolution*, and Tobias Furneaux, who had sailed with Wallis, was given the mastership of the *Adventure*.

-----

[5] Alexander Dalrymple, *An Historical Collection of the Several Voyages and Discoveries in the South Pacific Ocean* (2 vols., London, 1770–71). See particularly I, 53, xxiv, 95–144, 17 in Appendix.

The plan of exploration also was drawn up under Cook's direction. The expedition was to sail to the Cape of Good Hope and from there to 54° S., 11° 20′ E., where a search for Bouvet's Cape Circumcision was to be undertaken. If the Cape proved to be a continent, the explorers were to survey its shores; if it turned out to be an island, the expedition would sail southward and eastward in high southern latitudes until a continent was found. The return to England would be around Cape Horn. Cook's ships were provisioned for two years, and carried livestock and vegetable seeds to be planted on the islands the explorers discovered. The German scientist, John Reinhold Forster, and his son, accompanied the expedition as naturalists.

The *Resolution* and the *Adventure* left the Thames in June, 1772. After a leisurely voyage they reached Table Bay at Cape Town in October. Since his crews were in excellent health, Cook spent little time attending to their needs and soon began the voyage southward. Not many days elapsed before icebergs became an impediment to travel. As they threaded their way farther, the *Resolution* and *Adventure* passed within ten leagues of Bouvet's Island, but the explorers failed to sight it. In 57° S. they encountered a barrier of ice and sailed west-southwest in order to skirt it. Cook now was confident Cape Circumcision was not a continent, for he could see clearly seventy miles north and south. Besides, the masses of ice would not be drifting northward if a continent blocked them.

On the second day of the new year Cook instructed his crews to head the vessels toward the southeast. During the course of this cruise the squadron crossed the Antarctic Circle. The English explorers had gone farther south than any humans before them. When they reached 67° S., the commander felt compelled to turn back because of the ice and the lateness of the season. Actually Cook was in the Antarctic during the best season, for the months of January and February are the high months of the Antarctic summer. On their northward voyage the ships followed the 60th parallel of south latitude eastward until reaching Queen Charlotte's Sound, New Zealand. By so doing they proved again that no habitable continent existed in the South Indian Ocean.

The explorers spent the late summer of 1773 surveying the coast of New Zealand and cruising the Pacific before heading their ships southward again on a southeasterly track in November. Huge ice

islands soon made progress risky, but the *Resolution* was pushed
onward to 67° 31′ S., in 147° 30′ W. At this point several factors
forced Cook to give up the cruise. Many members of the crew
were afflicted with a slight fever, an impenetrable barrier of ice
prevented further progress southward and eastward, the *Adventure* and the *Resolution* had been separated during a storm and
the commander was anxious to re-establish contact with Furneaux,
and, lastly, time could not be wasted searching for a passage
through the icy barrier when there was a vast sea to be explored.

After several weeks of zigzagging across the Pacific between
145° and 105° W. without finding land, Cook steered the *Resolution* southward again. This last assault on the ice carried him south
of the Antarctic Circle to 71° S., 106° 54′ W. Again the ship met
an impenetrable barrier. Cook was convinced the ice extended to
the pole, and further attempts to penetrate it would be the height
of folly. Even though he saw penguins and other Antarctic birds,
signifying the proximity of land, he concluded they came either
from a small ice-encased island in the immediate vicinity or from
a larger territory lying at the pole and hence unexplorable. His
mission now was accomplished and he could return home.

Since his crew had enjoyed extraordinarily good health, Cook
determined to make a hasty final search for the continent whose
discovery Dalrymple credited to Juan Fernández, and which
Quiros had supposedly seen. By the time he reached latitude 37°
54′ S., longitude 90° W., he was satisfied at last that this continent
could have been nothing more than a small island, and he sailed
westward with Tahiti his destination.

After a pleasant month at Tahiti where the explorers feasted on
fresh fruits, vegetables, and meats, Cook explored in the Central
Pacific, where he discovered New Caledonia and the New Hebrides Islands. In October, 1774, he was back at New Zealand stor-
ing provisions before embarking on the final lap of his circumnavigation of the world. These preparations were completed by
mid-November, and the *Resolution* was steered on a southeasterly
course toward Tierra del Fuego. The explorers rounded the Horn
late in December, heading eastward until they reached what is
now called South Georgia Island. Cook was elated with this insignificant discovery inasmuch as it was the only ice-capped island
he had sighted. After surveying its coasts, he turned to the south

again, where he found a high, rocky coast in latitude 59° 13′ S. which he named Southern Thule. This name was changed later to Sandwich Land when the coast proved to be one of a group of islands. From there the explorers bore northeastward toward Cape Town and home.

James Cook returned to England to witness his triumph. The royal court proclaimed its satisfaction with the results of his cruise, and the Admiralty raised him to the rank of post-captain. The honor he cherished most was his election to fellowship in the Royal Society. Now Cook was considered important enough to write his own account of the voyage. The journal he published in 1777 established Alexander Dalrymple's Spanish memoirs as fables. The illusion of a *Terra Australis Incognita* which could be opened to commerce and colonization was now finally dispelled, and a shadow of doubt was cast upon the existence of an Antarctic continent.

From ancient times to the late years of the eighteenth century, ideas concerning the existence of a sizable land mass south of the ecumene ranged widely from Ptolemy's view of an immense *Terra Incognita* connecting Africa with the Malay Peninsula, and Quiros's idea of a habitable southern continent, to the conception that no continental territory existed in the extreme southern latitudes. Portuguese, Spanish, Dutch, French, and English explorers had found only insignificant polar and subpolar islands—Bouvet's Island, Kerguelen Island, South Georgia, and Sandwich Land. Yet the explorer who journeyed farthest south did not completely discount the presence of sizable terra firma close to the pole. James Cook observed too many indications to state conclusively that no land was there. But his penetrations to 67° and 71° S. in different longitudes did not allow him to visualize a territory of continental proportions, a territory which in fact does exist.[6]

Antarctica still is the least known of all the continents on the globe. For centuries the secrets of this bleak land at the bottom of the world have been hidden under millions of cubic miles of ice, and only in recent months have scientists successfully probed beneath this icy surface to study the terrain. These scientific inves-

....

[6] Recent Russian explorers claim Antarctica is an ice-covered group of islands, but this is contrary to the results of other investigations. See the *New York Times,* Aug. 31, 1957, 32; and Dec. 9, 1957, 25.

tigations and studies of the recent International Geophysical Year will revise old conceptions of Antarctica just as explorations during the first half of the nineteenth century altered ideas that prevailed at the time of Captain Cook.

On modern maps the Antarctic Continent is shown as a pear-shaped territory about twice as large as the United States. The large base is east of 0° longitude and is surrounded for the most part by the Indian Ocean. The top is bounded by the Pacific on one side and the Atlantic on the other, while the stem is the rugged, mountainous peninsula stretching northward toward Tierra del Fuego, and is a continuation of the Andean chain. But this conception of the size and shape of the continent will be modified because the outline on maps conforms to the contour of the continental ice shelf and not to the coastline. Explorers have discovered recently that this shelf extends out to sea as far as 500 to 1,000 miles and is 1,000 to 1,200 feet thick in some places. Furthermore, it is now believed that Antarctica is partly ringed by a chain of islands lying under the shelf.[7]

The ice in Antarctica distinguishes it from other continents. It is the only land mass almost completely covered with a moving sheet of ice which changes little during the seasons of the year. Conditions in Antarctica, in fact, are much the same as conditions in North America and Europe during the Ice Age. Huge glaciers, with surfaces broken by deep crevasses, grind their way to the ocean. Temperatures are uncommonly cold. During 1957, for example, the South Pole had an average temperature of −55° F. The summer average was −13°; the winter −73°. Such extreme weather is not common to the whole of Antarctica, however. In coastal areas it is warmer, especially in the summer, when gigantic sections of the ice shelf break off, forming tabular icebergs or ice islands.[8]

Recent estimates show that approximately 3,000,000 cubic miles of ice cover the continent—about 90 per cent of the ice in the world. So great is the weight of this ice that scientists believe it has

----

[7] *New York Times,* Dec. 11, 1957, 17; Feb. 20, 1958, 11. The most authoritative study of postwar Antarctic explorations has been prepared by a journalist who accompanied the expeditions. See Walter Sullivan's *Quest for a Continent* (New York, 1957).

[8] *New York Times,* Jan. 2, 1958, 10; and Sullivan, *Quest,* pp. 2, 3.

caused the continent to sink below sea level in some places.[9] Moreover, this sheet of ice obscures a rugged terrain characterized by scraggy fjords, deep canyons, and towering mountains. Completely submerged mountains at least 7,000 feet high have been discovered, and other more lofty ranges, whose highest elevations only protrude through the sheet, have been explored. This ice is thickest in the interior, where depths of 10,000 feet have been recorded and where it is believed thicknesses of at least 14,000 feet will be found. But this sheet recedes as it flows toward the sea until it is about 2,000 feet thick along the coast.[10]

The Antarctic Continent is unrelated to other continental land masses by reason of more than its tremendous sheet of ice, however. It is isolated by distance also, being separated by hundreds of miles of deep, storm-tossed waters. Cape Horn, the nearest continental point, is over 600 miles away. But here the dissimilarity with the rest of the world ends, for the Antarctic, like every other region, contains animal life of various forms.

Beautiful snow petrels, which protect their young by vomiting a foul-smelling liquid at their attackers; giant fulmars, known to attack and kill men; penguins, which cannot soar in the air but can fly in the water, and other forms of bird life dot the landscape. Of these, the penguins are the most interesting, especially the Emperors. These majestic birds stand three to four feet high and often weigh as much as eighty pounds. They are believed to be the most primitive of birds because of their adaptation to an Ice Age existence. The Emperors seek the coldest climes even in the winter when they lay and hatch their eggs during violent storms. Other penguins, the numerous Adélies for example, breed in the spring.[11]

Besides these birds, other animals are Antarctic residents—animals which are and were of commercial value. Different species of whales, particularly the mammoth blue whales, often 100 feet long and weighing 150 tons, have become of great value to twentieth-

---

[9] Scientists believe that the crust of the earth floats on molten underlayers which have compressed under Antarctica owing to the weight of the ice. See *New York Times*, May 5, 1957, 1, 46.

[10] *Ibid.;* Feb. 9, 1958, 1; and March 10, 1958, 25.

[11] Walter Sullivan, "Animal Mysteries of Antarctica," *New York Times Magazine* (March 24, 1957), pp. 14, 42. See also his *Quest*, pp. 10–14; and Admiral Lord Mountevans, *The Antarctic Challenged* (New York, 1955), pp. 8–11.

century Antarctic whalers. The other animals, various Antarctic members of the seal family—fur seals, crabeater seals, Weddell seals, sea leopards, and sea elephants—are not hunted commercially at present, but the pelts and oil of these beasts were of inestimable value to American traders in the early days of the nineteenth century and enticed intrepid American sealing captains into the Antarctic south of Cape Horn in quest of rookeries.

chapter two

SEALERS IN THE SOUTH

After Captain James Cook completed his very successful second voyage in the South Pacific and the Antarctic, the logical step in British overseas exploration was to employ their most famous explorer to make surveys in the north. Such an expedition to the northern hemisphere would contribute greatly to the geographical knowledge of that section of the world, and at the same time satisfy long-standing British economic ambition, scientific interest, and national policy. This was finding a solution to the problem of a northwest passage linking the Atlantic with the Pacific. Cook was commissioned with such an objective in 1776.

On his voyage northward in the Pacific from New Zealand, the explorer located the Hawaiian Islands, discovered King George's or Nootka Sound, surveyed the northwest coast of North America, and determined that any ocean passage around or through the continent in the Arctic was blocked by a barrier of ice. In Nootka Sound and along the coast north to Bering Strait, Cook's ships were visited by scores of natives with a great variety of furs to trade. The Englishmen especially prized the pelts of the sea otter, buying quantities of them with "trifles"—beads and iron trinkets.

When the explorers visited Canton, China, on their voyage home, they found the Chinese placed great value on these particular furs. One seaman sold his stock for $800, while another disposed of a few prime skins for $120 each. In all, at least £2,000 sterling was gained by Cook's officers and men for their pelts, most of which were spoiled, having been worn by the Indians and used by the Englishmen as bed-robes. Captain Cook himself did not live to see these transactions, which foretold a profitable North

19

Pacific fur trade for the British East India Company, since he was assassinated by natives during a return visit to Hawaii. But his successor as commander, Captain James King, urged the Company to send out each of its China ships with a quantity of unwrought iron and a blacksmith to make tools, as well as supplies of knives, woolen cloth, and trinkets to barter for furs with the aborigines on the western coast of North America.

News of the English explorers' good fortune was disseminated to the people across the Atlantic not only in the published journal of the expedition, but by a much-traveled New Englander, John Ledyard, who had sailed with Cook in a minor capacity. This man had been a member of Captain King's company, who were "not far short of mutiny" in their predilection to return immediately to the North Pacific, and he undertook to induce an enterprising merchant to finance a voyage there under his command. In New York he was unsuccessful. Merchants there viewed his scheme as visionary, "bearing the marks rather of a warm imagination, and sanguine temperament, than of sober and mature judgment." [1] But in Philadelphia, Robert Morris, financier of the American Revolution, and a merchant who rarely overlooked an opportunity for profit, agreed to furnish a ship and provide an outfit. Since a suitable vessel was not available in the Pennsylvania city, Ledyard was sent to Boston to purchase one. None was found there, nor was he able to locate a ship in New London, Connecticut. After a year's search, Morris's patience was exhausted, his interest turned elsewhere, and in the end John Ledyard's fur-trading expedition did not materialize.

But at the time intelligence of the Cook expedition's dealings was being diffused, a Boston ship, *The States*, was sent to the Falkland Islands off the coast of Argentina, ostensibly on a sea elephant voyage. The crew members of the *States* were nominally whalemen, but hunting elephants was far less hazardous than chasing whales, and their oil was of the same quality. When they reached their destination, however, instead of filling the hold of their vessel

---

[1] Jared Sparks, *Life of John Ledyard, the American Traveller; Comprising Selections from his Journals and Correspondence* (Cambridge, Mass., 1828), p. 133. See also Captain James Cook and Captain James King, *A Voyage to the Pacific Ocean. Undertaken by the Command of his Majesty for making Discoveries in the Northern Hemisphere* . . . (3 vols., London, 1785), III, 434–35.

completely with barrels of oil, they stowed some 13,000 fur seal pelts, which they delivered to a New York merchant.

This voyage of the *States* is the first known sealing expedition from the United States, and it was the first step in proceedings ultimately inaugurating the fur trade with China. The New York tradesman bought the skins for $6,500, fifty cents each. He then shipped them to Nantucket, where they were loaded on board the brig *Eleanora,* commanded by a Captain Metcalf, and were subsequently carried to Canton. In that city Chinese merchants rewarded the owner by paying $5.00 per skin or $65,000 for the cargo! [2]

Other American China traders in Canton when Metcalf made his sale did not fail to hear about it, and they hastened home to broadcast the news. Soon ships from New York, Massachusetts, and Connecticut ports, loaded with salt, lances, knives, pegs, and other sealing implements, were heading southward to the Falklands. A new maritime industry was born.

After leaving their ports the sealers usually sailed to Port Egmont or, as the Americans called it, West Point Harbor, in the bleak, wind-swept Falklands. There, besides slaughtering seals, they could obtain fresh water and a store of geese and wild hogs. With part of their holds filled with skins they rounded the Horn through the Strait of Le Maire and sailed northward toward the Juan Fernández Islands, hugging the coast of Chile. Amasa Delano tells us that very few American sealers sailed into the Pacific via Magellan's Strait. Rounding the Horn was definitely the lesser of two evils. The Strait was filled with shoals on which the timbers of a small wooden vessel could easily be torn, and in many places the water was too deep to offer a safe anchorage. [3]

---

[2] See "The Diary of Mr. Ebenezer Townsend, Jr., the Supercargo of the Sealing Ship 'Neptune,' on her Voyage to the South Pacific and Canton," *Papers of the New Haven Colony Historical Society,* IV (1888), 27. See also Edouard A. Stackpole, *The Voyage of the Huron and the Huntress: The American Sealers and the Discovery of the Continent of Antarctica* (Hartford, Conn., 1955), Appendix B, 75; and Edward H. Raymond, "The Fur-Seal Fishery and Salem," *Essex Institute Historical Collections,* LXXII (July, 1936), 184–85.

[3] Amasa Delano, *Narrative of Voyages and Travels, in the Northern and Southern Hemispheres: Comprising Three Voyages Round the World; Together with a Voyage of Survey and Discovery, in the Pacific Ocean and Oriental Islands* (Boston, 1817), p. 265.

On their voyage northward the sealers invariably skirted the Chilean coast. On the islands there, particularly Chiloe and La Mocha, they could add to their precious cargoes and procure more fresh meat. La Mocha was a favorite stopping place because its wild horses were easily slaughtered and not entirely unpalatable. At Mas Afuera, of the Juan Fernández group, more seals were skinned to complete the cargo. When the Americans first stopped at these islands early in the 1790's, it was estimated that at least three million seals lived there. Reckless killing soon decimated the population. It was not uncommon for one sealer, over a period of five years, to remove 100,000 seals.[4]

Since seals resort to land only during the months of November and December when their young are born, the sealers had to contend with all members of the herd. The large bulls, for whom they had a healthy respect, were either shot or stabbed with a lance, while the wigs (younger males), clapmatches (females), yearlings, and pups were killed by crushing their skulls with a club. The favorite method of taking them was to station a party of men armed with guns, lances, and clubs, between the herd and the water. The hunters formed columns through which the seals were driven. It was often unnecessary to drive these complacent animals, who seemed resigned to their fate and did not attempt to escape. Those only stunned were stabbed in the breast before their skins were removed. Then all hands began skinning. An expert sealer, it was said, could skin sixty seals in an hour. After the flesh and fat were removed, the pelts were stretched and pegged to the ground to dry.

While part of their crews were occupied at Mas Afuera, the sealing captains often sailed into one of the Chilean harbors frequented by sperm and right whales, usually Valparaiso or Coquimbo, where the remaining seamen were employed in offshore whaling. From these ports or from the Juan Fernández Islands the seal hunters sailed northward, sometimes anchoring at the Galá-

----

[4] Delano, *Narrative of Voyages,* p. 306; and Edmund Fanning, *Voyages Round the World; with Selected Sketches of Voyages to the South Seas, North and South Pacific Oceans, China, etc., Performed under the Command and Agency of the Author* . . . (New York, 1833), p. 118. Fanning estimated that the seal population of Mas Afuera in the late 1790's was between 500,000 and 700,000.

pagos, before crossing the Pacific with the help of the trade winds.

On their crossing to Canton, the usual ports of call were in the Sandwich (Hawaiian) Islands and the Ladrones (Marianas), where valuable additions to their cargoes such as sandalwood, mother-of-pearl, beche-de-mer, and edible birds' nests were collected. All these commodities brought fancy prices. The Chinese used the wood to manufacture sacred objects and furniture because of its sweet smell. The mother-of-pearl was used for decoration, while the others were delicacies only the rich could afford. Beche-de-mer, large marine worms measuring six to eighteen inches in length, were eaten after they were thoroughly dried. The birds' nests were about the size of a barn swallow nest and were made with a gummy thread. After the feathers and other dirt were removed, the nests were used to flavor soups and stews and as a tonic.

On their arrival in Canton the sealers visited the Hong Merchants, government appointees delegated to take responsibility for the ships' crews and for the collection of all tariffs and duties. Relations had to be established with them before any business could be carried on. All transactions were made with individual merchants, however. Sometimes days were spent haggling over prices. During good years the Americans received as much as $5.00 per pelt, but usually they had to be satisfied with $3.00 to $4.00.[5]

For unknown reasons the bottom fell out of the China sealskin market in 1793. Knowledge of this was heralded by Captain William R. Stewart, who received only $16,000 for 38,000 skins he transported to Canton on the ship *Eliza* of New York. When this information became common knowledge in ports all along the Atlantic seaboard, not a sealer departed from the United States for Canton during the next two years. The sealskin trade, however, did not disappear completely, for whaling captains who engaged in sealing as a side line continued to sell their pelts in Canton. By 1796 they were bringing back reports which forecast a rise in prices, and voyages to locate rookeries were begun again. The South Atlantic and South Pacific seals were used principally in this

[5] Raymond, "The Fur-Seal Fishery and Salem," *Essex Institute Historical Collections,* LXXII, 191.

revived trade, for the Pribilof rookeries in the north were not successfully exploited until the formation of the Russian-American Fur Company in 1799.

One of the first American captains to participate in the flurry of activity accompanying the price rise in Canton was Edmund Fanning, first of Stonington, Connecticut, then of New York. In May, 1797, he was introduced to Captain John Whetten, recently returned from China on the ship *Ontario*. Whetten was so enthusiastic about getting a voyage together that he volunteered to act as agent for the sealers when they arrived in Canton with their cargoes. He said that skins were in great demand and prices could be gained which promised handsome profits. The ambitious Fanning responded by searching for a merchant who would match a small sum he had saved while serving in various capacities from cabin boy to master on voyages to the West Indies, South Pacific, and England. He was readily successful, for an old friend and former benefactor, Elias Nexson, subscribed the necessary money and provided his own 93-ton brig, *The Betsey*, for use.

Less than a month after Whetten met Edmund Fanning, the *Betsey* left New York, bound for Stonington to enlist seamen. In June, 1797, she was headed southward by her crew of twenty-seven Stonington boys. The master was Captain Fanning, aged twenty-seven years, who was senior in age as well as rank. From the standpoint of exploration, Fanning's voyage in the *Betsey* is important, for he reported the discovery of Fanning's and Palmyra Islands in the South Pacific. But economically the cruise was a landmark in American sealing. On an initial investment of $7,867, Fanning, Whetten, and Nexson gained a net profit of $52,300. The captain probably earned more than $10,000 himself. Fanning was inspired to report: "The amount paid into the national treasury as duties on our China cargo, was more than three times the cost of the ship and her outfits." [6]

When news of this voyage and of other similarly profitable ones reached the Atlantic ports, the sealing business took on all the aspects of a gold rush. West Point Harbor in the Falklands was a boom town, while an area along the Patagonia coast used by the sealers to dry skins was named New Haven Green. During 1799

----

[6] Fanning, *Voyages*, p. 282.

sixteen sealers were reported at Cook's South Georgia Island, while some thirty more were working in the Pacific from Australia and New Zealand, as well as from the islands off their shores.

Like all booms this one came to an end. Its demise can be credited to the sealers' own avariciousness, for they destroyed their means of sustenance while contending for profits. By 1805 only stragglers and pups were left on the familiar resorts of herds in the Falklands and the Juan Fernández group. The remains of their innumerable inhabitants were gracing the backs of wealthy members of Chinese, European, and American society, as well as covering the walls and floors of their homes. More enterprising sealers began searching for new areas of endeavor.

Edmund Fanning, voicing appeals from all members of the sealing industry, petitioned the President of the United States to commission an exploring voyage to locate new seal islands. In the spring of 1812 President James Madison provided the *Volunteer* and the *Hope* to explore in the southern hemisphere and to sail around the world. Fanning was named commander and was given letters of introduction to officials in the navy departments of the principal nations of Europe. The value of these letters to the commander of an expedition charged with exploring principally in the southern hemisphere was never demonstrated, for the exploration was suspended owing to the war with England.[7] During this conflict the woefully unprepared United States Navy granted letters of marque to sealing vessels as privateers, while others were kept at home by their owners, who feared losing their investments to the enemy.

When the Peace of Ghent was concluded, Edmund Fanning was back in his native Stonington, a thriving sea community of about 5,000 people. This Connecticut town stands on a point of land called Long Point, directly opposite the eastern end of Fisher's Island in Long Island Sound. The anchorage there was a roadstead rather than a port, and in later years the townsmen were forced to build a breakwater to shelter their ships.

Fanning was a man of stature in his home town—a three-time circumnavigator of the world, and a successful, moderately wealthy maritime promoter. He had come home to interest some

[7] Fanning, *Voyages,* pp. 492–94.

of his friends in a sealing voyage to islands supposedly lying in the South Atlantic. The Stonington boys who had accompanied him on the voyage of the *Betsey* were now veterans of the sea engaged in activities such as shipbuilding, whaling, and the commercial trade. They expressed no great interest in Fanning's proposals. During the years immediately before its disappearance, sealing had been a risky business. The war, moreover, had caused a dislocation of all ocean trade, and those gainfully employed could not afford to risk several years' wages on a sealing voyage.

But Fanning's promise that new seal rookeries would be found and the formerly lucrative business revived was too tempting to go unanswered indefinitely. A veteran sealer, James Sheffield, agreed to undertake a cruise and was given command of the brig *Hersilia,* a fine new vessel of 130 tons, "coppered and fitted out in the best manner." She had been built in Mystic, Connecticut, in 1819, and was registered to William A. Fanning, son of Edmund. A mere youth, Nathaniel Brown Palmer, signed on as second mate.

When Nat Palmer associated himself with Fanning and Sheffield, he was just nineteen years of age, but a proved navigator. From early childhood he had been associated with seafaring men. When Nat was quite young, his father gave up his law practice to turn shipbuilder, while his Uncle Jonathan was the so-called collector of the port of Stonington, because he assessed duties and tonnage fees when he received cargoes in his bonded warehouse. Young Nat probably overheard the sea stories of his father and uncle with no little interest.

During the War of 1812 Palmer had manned the tiller of a blockade-runner between New York and Boston. To complete this voyage required more than a little skill, as well as considerable luck. British blockaders lay off New London in order to intercept any ships sailing to Boston on either side of Long Island, and American sailors had to run the blockade on dark nights without lights. They were as familiar with this stretch of ocean as Mark Twain's riverboat captains were with the Mississippi. It was said that blockade-running skippers could "smell their way from Hell Gate to Providence with their eyes shut." When the war was over, Nathaniel entered the coasting trade and became a full-fledged master before his nineteenth birthday. No doubt he was both

proud and excited when invited to join the veteran sealers Fanning
and Sheffield in a search for new sealing grounds in the south.

It is possible Edmund Fanning had heard of reputed American
voyages to islands southeast of Cape Horn,[8] but he asserted in his
autobiographical *Voyages* that knowledge of the Aurora Islands,
of Dirck Gherritsz's supposed discovery of land in the 64th parallel of south latitude, and observations made at South Georgia
Island had motivated him to plan the expedition. The Auroras had
come to his attention through an account of a survey of them in
1794 by Alejandro Malaspina in the Spanish corvette *Atrevida*.
These islands had been seen for the first time twenty-two years
earlier by the officers and seamen of the Spanish ship *Aurora*,
hence the name. Between 1769 and 1794 commanders of other
vessels reported sighting them and for this reason the captain of
the *Atrevida* made a search on his voyage to the Río de la Plata
and round the Horn. The officers of this ship presumably reported
the Aurora group as consisting of three small islands lying in the
vicinity of 53° S., and 48° W.

During his circumnavigation of the world in the corvette-built
ship *Aspasia*, 1800–1802, Fanning had stopped at the island of
South Georgia in the spring of 1801 to procure sealskins. There he
observed the breaking up of winter ice. A gale which blew up from
the west-southwest carried along "fleets" of ice islands, "giving
decisive evidence that extensive land did exist in that direction,
for as numerous ice islands had formed at South Georgia, and
drifted away to the eastward in these gales, it was certain that the
ice islands . . . must have had land to form at, or they could never
have been in existence." [9] Fanning maintained he was convinced
important discoveries could be made in the region between 60°
to 65° S., and 50° to 60° W., a conviction strengthened by his belief in the validity of the Gherritsz discovery.

....

[8] When the British announced the discovery of the South Shetlands in
1820, articles appeared in United States newspapers claiming American
sealers had been going there for years, but had kept their voyages secret
because of the great competition for seals. See, for example, the *Daily National Intelligencer*, Washington, D.C., Sept. 30, 1820, 3; Oct. 3, 1820, 3;
and *Niles' Weekly Register*, Baltimore, XIX (Sept. 16, 1820), 43–44;
(Sept. 30, 1820), 65; and XX (May 19, 1821), 192.

[9] Fanning, *Voyages*, p. 428.

Edmund Fanning apparently instructed his commander to sail to the Falklands, where water and fresh meat were to be procured. Then he was to follow an easterly track while searching for the Auroras. If they were located, and proved to be the home of numerous seals, all hands were to go to skinning. If not, Sheffield was to take the *Hersilia* to Staten Island, from whence he was to stand southward in the longitude of Cape Horn until he reached 63° S. Fanning said he was certain land lay to the eastward along this parallel. Even if they were unfortunate enough not to find the Auroras or Gherritsz's land, they could not return to Stonington empty-handed. A cargo had to be procured in order to pay for the voyage, and three alternative methods were proposed. They could hunt seals in the Pacific; at the islands about Cape Horn; or at the Falklands.

Two different accounts of the voyage of the *Hersilia* exist, differing in important details. The one, Fanning's account, follows the instructions the author asserted he gave to Sheffield almost to the letter. After stopping at the Falklands, the captain headed his ship eastward and successfully located the Auroras in latitude 52° 58′ S., longitude 47° 51′ W. Sheffield and his crew sailed around and between these islands, "each in form of a sugar loaf, but having no landing places, even for amphibious animals, on them." [10] The only living creatures they saw were birds.

Since the sealers did not find their prey, they turned their vessel westward for Staten Island according to instructions. After procuring necessary water, fuel, and provisions, they again headed south, bearing east until they arrived near the 63rd parallel of latitude, where appearances of seals and numerous birds "gave strong hopes of being in the vicinity of land." As they bore eastward they came upon a "high and round mountain island" which was covered with snow. This discovery, which they named Mount Pisgah (Smith) Island, soon proved to be one of a group. The other islands explored carefully were called Fanning's Islands and Ragged (Rugged) Island.

Sheffield was able to find an anchorage for the *Hersilia* in a cove on Rugged Island and the sealers made it ashore. When they climbed a high point they "discovered more land to the eastward,

[10] Fanning, *Voyages*, pp. 429–30.

but as the season was drawing to a close, and they were anxious to hasten home and report the discovery of such vast numbers of seals to their friends in time for the next season, they had no leisure to visit or make a survey of it." [11] After filling the hold of the *Hersilia* with several thousand choice skins, they hastened home, because they did not have enough salt to cure the skins of all the seals they saw.

The other account, presumably related by Palmer, maintains that Sheffield hunted for the Auroras because all commanders at that time searched for the "fabulous" islands. During the exploratory voyage, Young Nat, as he was known, and another sailor were left at the Falklands to slaughter bullocks. Not long after the *Hersilia*'s departure, another vessel, the *Espirito Santo,* of English registry out of Buenos Aires, came into sight, and Palmer piloted her into the harbor. Her captain informed the Americans that he was " 'bound to a place where there were thousands of seals, but [he] refused to divulge the situation.' " [12]

Three days after the *Espirito Santo* departed, the *Hersilia* returned from a fruitless search for the Auroras. Palmer immediately told Sheffield the story of the seal islands and expressed the notion that he could find them by following the course of the ship. " 'Capt. Sheffield, having great confidence in his second mate, followed his advice, and in a few days discovered the South Shetlands, at that time unknown to the continent of North America.' " The crew of the vessel from Buenos Aires was surprised to see the Americans, " 'but their admiration of 'Young Nat's' skill was so great that they even assisted in loading the *Hersilia,* and she returned home with 10,000 of the finest skins.' " [13]

Factually, the Palmer account is the more plausible, even though it is hardly likely that the captain and crew of the *Espirito Santo* admired Young Nat's skill, which enabled him to find their sealing grounds, so much that they would assist in loading sealskins on the *Hersilia.* Sealing was a highly competitive business. British sealers, in fact, had attempted to keep Americans away from South Georgia when they began working there after Captain Cook's dis-

---

[11] Fanning, *Voyages,* p. 431.

[12] Edwin Swift Balch, "Stonington Antarctic Explorers," *Bulletin of the American Geographical Society,* XLI (1909), 476–77.

[13] *Ibid.,* p. 477.

covery of the island. It is also improbable that Nat Palmer's eye-
sight was good enough to enable him to watch the *Espirito Santo*
sail from the Falklands and thus establish her course to the South
Shetlands. These islands lie approximately four hundred miles
southeast of Cape Horn.

But Fanning's version is even more farfetched. In the first place,
it is doubtful he deliberately sent Captain Sheffield to locate the
South Shetlands. Conceivably he knew the Gherritsz story, or he
might have heard rumors of American voyages there, but his cap-
tain later reported that he himself "had heard a report of new
Islands and went to look for them." [14] It can be assumed that this
information was gained either at the Falklands or Staten Island.
Possibly the commander of the *Espirito Santo* told Sheffield or
Palmer of the South Shetlands' recent discovery by a British coastal
trader, William Smith, who visited Buenos Aires as a port of call.[15]
Secondly, it is beyond reason to believe the sealers located the
Auroras, because they do not exist. Sheffield might have misjudged
his position and sighted what are called today the Shag Rocks, between 53° and 54° S., in approximately 42° W., but it is doubtful
if the *Hersilia* could have sailed between them.

Both versions agree that the new seal beaches were on the South
Shetland Islands. This group, lying south and east of Cape Horn,
is composed of approximately ten major islands stretching in a
northeast-southwesterly direction for a distance of 250 miles. They
are rugged and mountainous with sharp, snow-covered peaks rising as high as 4,000 feet above the ocean. Most are of volcanic
origin. Although they are an independent geological unit, and lie
somewhat north of Palmer or Graham Land, which trends northward toward Tierra del Fuego, the South Shetlands are subject to
extreme polar conditions, having the same climate as the coastal
areas of Antarctica. Except for Deception Island, they are devoid
of vegetation. The best harbor of the group is provided where the
sea has entered this breached crater of a volcano. Since the ice is
broken up by steam issuing from the ground and by hot springs,
moss and lichens are able to thrive there.

....
[14] James Byers to General Parker, New York, Sept. 4, 1820, Records of the
Department of State, R.G. 59, Miscellaneous Letters, August–October, 1820,
National Archives. Hereafter cited as RDS.

[15] Stackpole, *Voyage of the Huron and the Huntress*, p. 12.

Unless the Gherritsz story or the protestations that American sealers visited there are credible, the South Shetlands were discovered in 1819 by William Smith on a voyage from Montevideo to Valparaiso in his brig *Williams*. Smith, hoping to find better weather, allowed himself to be driven southeastward by strong head winds. On February 19 he fell in with one of the South Shetlands, probably Livingston Island. Only a cursory examination was possible before he sailed on to Valparaiso, where he told English authorities about his discovery. These officials scoffed, being unconvinced he had seen anything more than a large iceberg. They did nothing. On his return voyage to the Río de la Plata, the trader attempted to reach the land again, but was held up by floe ice. In Montevideo and Buenos Aires, Americans showed much more interest in Smith's discovery than the British naval officers in Chile. They offered him large sums of money for the location, but he refused because he had not taken possession in the name of his king. After he picked up another cargo for Chile, he pushed southward again and successfully proved his contention. Smith named his land New South Britain, but later this was changed to New South Shetland, because the islands were in the same longitude as the Shetland Islands off the coast of the British Isles.[16]

After the Stonington sealers returned home, Captain Sheffield announced his discovery in a letter to a former employer, the New York merchant and sealing entrepreneur, James Byers. In this letter he described his success and offered to undertake a voyage to exploit the new sealing grounds further. That Sheffield should do this is curious since he had been in the employ of Edmund Fanning. At any rate, his letter must have been as devoid of details as a sealer's logbook, because Byers sent his partner, Walter Nexson, to get the particulars of the voyage from the *Hersilia's* captain.

Nexson learned that the sealers had coasted the "Great New Island or Continent" for a distance of fifty miles and had discovered no end. But they had seen myriads of seals—"at one view" 300,000. Such a sight only frustrated Sheffield, because he had gone out with half a cargo for Spanish colonial markets, and carried only a small quantity of salt, a necessity for the preservation

---

[16] Lieutenant Commander R. T. Gould, R.N. (ret.), "The Charting of the South Shetlands, 1819–1828," *Mariner's Mirror, The Journal of the Society of Nautical Research*, XXVII (July, 1941), 210–13.

of sealskins. His crew had taken 9,000 pelts in the short period of fifteen days, but he estimated they could have filled ten vessels like the *Hersilia.*

This was important information. It was a simple matter to forecast possible profits. Thoughts concerning them undoubtedly were exhilarating to the investors in sealing enterprises, for James Byers and his partners began making large plans. Their schemes centered in the preparation of a sealing fleet not only to take skins, but to take possession of the South Shetlands as well! They knew such plans were problematical, unless they could gain the protection of the United States Navy. As a result, Byers sent an appeal to General Daniel Parker, Adjutant and Inspector General of the United States Army, on August 18, 1820, asking that he urge the Monroe administration to support their activities by sending an armed vessel to the South Shetlands.

The plan outlined in this letter included occupation of the islands, since *"absolute occupancy"* was the sole basis for taking possession of territory. The American sealers were prepared to "cheerfully remain as long as . . . necessary" on the islands. In fact, the ships being provisioned were to carry timber, nails, and other materials needed to construct a building. A member of the party was to establish a settlement as an agent of the United States government. Possession was necessary, Byers reiterated, because "the new islands or Continent may prove as profitable to our country as Nootka Sound trade to England. Depend on it, this business [is] well worth the serious attention of Govt." [17]

General Parker sent Byers's plea to Secretary of State John Quincy Adams, who undoubtedly replied that the government would give the project serious consideration. But he requested additional information concerning the discovery before discussing it with the President. Byers complied by describing the islands and by presenting Sheffield's predictions concerning the size of the seal population. He added the observation that "it is quite fashionable . . . among a certain class of citizens, to accuse our Administration of lukewarmness in regard to the Mercantile interest" and "it would afford great satisfaction to every American if our Government was the first to survey and name the new World." [18]

....

[17] James Byers to General Parker, New York, Aug. 19, 1820, RDS.
[18] James Byers to General Parker, New York, Aug. 25, 1820, RDS.

The sealers' project interested Adams, long-time friend to mercantile and fishing interests, and he transmitted Byers's letter to President Monroe with a request that Byers be allowed to confer with the Secretary of the Navy regarding it. Byers had said the New York sealers would reach the islands before the English, but Adams was doubtful. If they did, however, the Secretary was certain the State Department would hear of it. He asked Monroe to give the affair his "particular consideration." After all, "the British Government just now have their hands so full of Coronations and Adulteries, Liturgy, prayers and Italian Sopranos, Bergamis and Pergamis, High Treasons and Petty Treasons, Pains, Penalties and Paupers, that they will seize the first opportunity they can to shake them all off, and if they can make a question of national honour about a foot-hold . . . upon something between Rock and Ice-Berg, as this discovery must be, and especially a question with us, they will not let it escape them." [19] The possibility of having a controversy with Lord Castlereagh, the Foreign Minister, was "quite fascinating" to the Secretary of State.

President Monroe, though he thought the South Shetlands were in the Pacific, supported Adams, agreeing to communicate Byers's information to the Secretary of the Navy, who should then consult with the Secretary of State on a course of action. But Navy Secretary Smith Thompson was in New York, and no consultations took place until a third letter from James Byers was delivered to the State Department.

This contained news that the American sealing fleet had departed with orders to reach the islands by the first of October. "If the British Govt. send an armed vessel, they will not, I think, like to approach the high latitudes till about Dec.—We Yankees you know, do not fear cold Weather — There is not the least doubt . . . the British will attempt to Drive our Vessels from the Islands — Not by open hostility & blows—but by blustering & threats— The vessels from this quarter, all went out armed for their own safety against pirates or robbers of any other description—and we will make—a bold defence over against John Bull." [20] Byers be-

[19] John Quincy Adams to James Monroe, Washington, Aug. 26, 1820, in "The First American Discoveries in the Antarctic, 1819," *American Historical Review*, XVI (July, 1911), 797. Adams was alluding to the trial of Queen Caroline.

[20] James Byers to General Parker, New York, Sept. 4, 1820, RDS.

lieved the appearance of an American ship-of-war would prevent any such injury to the voyage. Adams agreed and instructed Parker to see the Chief Clerk of the Navy Department, B. Homans.

On September 11, Adams sent for Homans, and inquired if the Navy had two ships it could employ soon, "one to protect the Sealing and Whaling Settlement on the Newly discovered land South of Cape Horn, and the other to go to the island of St. Thomas [in the Caribbean] and bring home four American mutineer seamen. . . ." Homans stated that the return of the mutineers could be carried out easily, but he opposed sending a Navy ship to protect the sealers because of the distance, "the dangers of an unexplored coast in that extreme latitude," and finally because of the threat of "a collision with the British." [21] The Secretary of State refused to agree that the dangers of distance, unknown waters, and battle with the British in a remote section of the world were sufficient reasons for failing to support the sealers' project. But the Chief Clerk was in no position to act. He responded that the Navy Department would have to wait for the return of a ship from the Mediterranean squadron before any plans could be made.

That Homans was procrastinating became obvious. Nothing was done subsequently even though the Secretary of State maintained a continuing interest in the subject. When a fourth appeal arrived from James Byers, he promised to mention it to Homans again, and told Parker he had been studying an extract from the London *Morning Chronicle* stating that the land seen by William Smith had been discovered in 1599 by Dirck Gherritsz. Adams had examined several collections of maps and found no traces of such land on English ones, but he did find a territory labelled Port of Drake on those made by the French. This caused him to read the articles on Francis Drake in Dobson's and Rees's *Encyclopedias*, but he found no mention of Drake's Port. Both encyclopedias testified that Drake had passed through the Strait of Magellan and had returned to England via the Cape of Good Hope. The Secretary of State gave up this study because he had no books supplying additional information.

In the middle of October, at about the same time John Quincy Adams halted his study, James Byers and his partners ended their

---

[21] John Quincy Adams, MS Diary, Sept. 11, 1820, in the Adams Papers, Massachusetts Historical Society, Boston, Mass.

efforts to gain protection for their sealers from the United States Navy. Part of the American fleet was in the South Shetlands and the sealers were competing for skins. No Navy ship arrived and no efforts to take possession of the islands were made.

chapter three

NAT PALMER—
DISCOVERER
OF ANTARCTICA?

Sealing, virtually a dead industry even before President Jefferson's embargo and the War of 1812 interrupted overseas trade, was speedily revived when it was learned that Captain James Sheffield had seen hundreds of thousands of seals on the new islands in the South Atlantic and that his half-cargo of furs had been sold for more than $22,000. Ships were immediately coppered and repaired for their voyages into Antarctic seas, while suppliers had a run on salt meat and dried vegetables, as well as vinegar, flour, tea, coffee, rum, gin, and wine needed to satisfy their crews. In Stonington, captains led by Edmund and William Fanning assembled and equipped a fleet of five ships: the brig *Frederick,* Captain Benjamin Pendleton; brig *Hersilia,* Captain Sheffield; schooner *Free Gift,* Captain Thomas Dunbar; schooner *Express,* Captain Ephraim Williams; and the sloop *Hero,* under Captain Nathaniel B. Palmer. Pendleton, a veteran sealer who had been associated with Edmund Fanning on earlier voyages, was made commander of the expedition.

In view of her later importance, the *Hero* merits special attention. Palmer's little sloop was built wide and flat, with a length of 47 feet, 3 inches, a breadth of 16 feet, 10 inches, an over-all draft of not more than 7 feet, and a capacity of slightly over 44 tons. She had been built in Groton, Connecticut, in 1800, and because of her construction it is probable she never was used in the overseas trade or as a sealer or whaler. It is likely her employment had been confined to the New England coastal trade, but she was

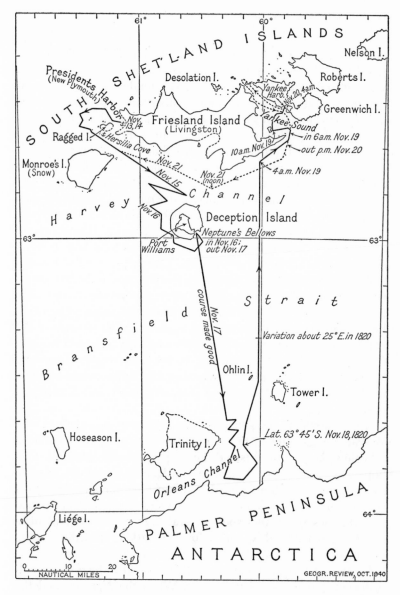

Colonel Lawrence Martin's map of Captain Nathaniel B. Palmer's voyage to the Antarctic Continent in November, 1820. The calendar dates are shown.

added to the Fanning fleet because she had qualities useful to the expedition. The *Hero* could be employed as an exploring vessel to seek out undiscovered seal beaches, as a tender or shallop to collect skins, and as a supply ship to distribute provisions to the skinners encamped on shore. For this work of exploration, collection, and distribution, she was ideal, since she could enter most harbors and inlets, running close to shore where larger vessels would become grounded. Many sealing fleets included ships with the *Hero*'s capabilities.

The *Frederick* and her tender, the *Free Gift*, departed from Stonington more than two months before the *Hersilia, Express,* and the *Hero* got underway late in July. Possibly Pendleton and Dunbar took their vessels to the Cape Verde Islands to take on essential salt. When the other ships got underway, the *Hersilia* took the lead, while the *Hero* and *Express* made the voyage together even though Palmer's was the faster vessel. Their cruise to the Falklands was accomplished without mishap, and by October 21 Palmer and Williams had anchored their ships in West Point Harbor, where they met a Salem sealer, Captain William B. Orne, on the ship *General Knox*. Later, two vessels of a second Stonington fleet, the brigs *Emeline* and *Catharine*, commanded by Captains Jeremiah Holmes and Joseph Henfield, were anchored nearby.[1]

After slaughtering water fowl and collecting eggs, Palmer and Williams turned their ships southward again toward their next stopping place—Staten Island. During this cruise, while the captains were closing in to converse, the *Hero* rammed the *Express*, carrying away two timber heads. This accident fortunately did not require immediate repairs and late in October the sealers reached Port Hatches, where they spent several days sealing and replenishing their wood and water before embarking for the sealing grounds.

On the journey southeastward, Palmer's little sloop easily outdistanced the slow-sailing *Express*. When the *Hero* crossed the 61st parallel of south latitude on November 9, her captain was certain he was near his destination because he saw the usual

---

[1] Edouard Stackpole has clarified the facts concerning the ships at the South Shetlands during the 1820–21 sealing season. See his *Voyage of the Huron and the Huntress*, pp. 15–16.

indications of land—the presence of whales, albatrosses, and sea gulls. The next day Palmer sighted the South Shetlands, and on November 12 his sloop was anchored in the harbor on Rugged Island near the *Hersilia*.[2]

The master of the *Hero* undoubtedly was eager to hear the latest news from his old friend, James Sheffield. He learned the *Hersilia* had arrived at Rugged Island twelve days earlier, some weeks after the *Frederick* and *Free Gift*, which were anchored in Presidents' Harbor across the strait separating Rugged and Frezeland (Livingston) Islands. These ships must have reached the South Shetlands at least a month before the *Hero,* for their crews had already taken a quantity of skins. In fact, after the *Hero* and the *Hersilia* put in at Presidents' Harbor on November 13, Palmer was immediately employed transporting pelts from the skinners' camps to the larger vessels where they were stowed.

The shallop was next used to distribute provisions to the encampments before Nathaniel Palmer turned her toward Deception Island on November 15, 1820. Undoubtedly this was an exploring cruise, since three days earlier there were "no seal up" at Presidents' Harbor. Palmer followed the southeast coast of Deception Island, which lies somewhat south and east of Livingston, without finding a safe anchorage until he entered the opening called the Dragon's Mouth by the sealers. He stood in, finding a spacious harbor with water fifty to sixty fathoms deep. Safe anchorage was located about a mile and a half from the mouth and the crew was sent ashore to collect eggs. Palmer spent most of the next day exploring this discovery, where the water is frequently disturbed by subterranean heat, and he found "it to be an Excellent Harbor secure from all wind." Deception Harbor later became the favorite rendezvous for sealers and whalers who worked in the South Shetland area.

By 10 A.M. on the ship's day of November 16, Palmer had completed his surveys of the interior of Deception Island and was once again at the harbor entrance. The *Hero* soon was clear from the Dragon's Mouth and "stood over for the Land," following a

....

[2] The only manuscript document in which this voyage to the South Shetlands is described in detail is the logbook of the *Hero,* Captain Nathaniel B. Palmer, Master, in the Papers of Nathaniel B. and Alexander S. Palmer, Manuscripts Division, Library of Congress.

course south by east ½ east. In this manner Nathaniel Brown
Palmer recorded his sighting of the Antarctic Continent or the
coast of Trinity Island lying off the peninsula which bears his
name. He had probably noticed the highlands of Antarctica from
Deception Island before venturing south to explore, although he
does not expressly say this in his logbook. At 8 P.M. on the following day Palmer "got over under the Land" only to find the sea
filled with ice islands and bergs. Since the land was inaccessible
at this point, where he hoped to land, he "sailed off & on until
morning." By 4 o'clock in the morning of the seventeenth, Palmer
made sail once again for the shore and discovered a strait "trending S S W by N N E" which was "Literally filled with ice." Rather
than risk the destruction of his tiny vessel among the ice floes, he
decided against entering this passage and returned to the South
Shetlands. The explorer located the strait's entrance at 63° 45′ S.[3]

From the information in Nat Palmer's logbook it is possible to
reconstruct his voyage to the Antarctic Continent from Deception
Island. Since he mentions sailing toward the "Land" on the six-
teenth of November, it is probable he sighted the highlands from
Deception Island, or on a lookout point from the mainmast of the
Hero. Even though the continent lies some fifty miles south of
Deception, it is not an extraordinary feat to see that distance on a
clear day in high latitudes.

After sighting the land, he probably sailed in search of seal
rookeries. His track, recorded as south by east ½ east, no doubt
took him to the coasts of Trinity Island off Palmer Peninsula in
about 63° S. The strait he sighted and investigated must have
been Orleans Channel, separating Trinity Island from the mainland, because its entrance, as Palmer recorded it, is 63° 45′ S.
Orleans Channel, moreover, is the only strait or passage trending
northeast-southwest between the 63rd and 64th parallels of south
latitude near where Palmer's course from Deception Island took
him.[4]

----

[3] All quotations are from the logbook of the *Hero*, entries for November
16 and 17, 1820, Palmer Papers. A ship's day began and ended at noon.
Palmer actually left Deception at 10 A.M. on the calendar day, November 17.

[4] The late Colonel Lawrence Martin, who was Chief of the Maps Division
and incumbent of the Chair of Geography in the Library of Congress, brought
to light the many significant details of Palmer's November cruise in his
article, "Antarctica Discovered by a Connecticut Yankee, Captain Nathaniel

Nathaniel Palmer's logbook shows he sighted and coasted the shores of the Antarctic Continent on November 16, 17, and 18, 1820, but is he the discoverer? The answer to this question must be negative, for satisfactory evidence proves a British surveyor, Edward Bransfield, sighted the continent on January 20, some ten months earlier than Palmer did. Bransfield's log is not extant, but his manuscript chart does exist among the documents of the Hydrographic Office in London. The facts this chart provides are substantiated in two published journals of the voyage—one in the *Edinburgh Philosophical Journal* of April, 1821, and the other in the London *Literary Gazette, and Journal of Belles Lettres, Arts, Sciences, &c.,* November 3, 10, and 24 of the same year. The latter is more complete, and from it the course of Bransfield's voyage can be reconstructed in a reasonably accurate manner.

Edward Bransfield had been instructed to survey the South Shetlands after William Smith's second voyage there. He was at the time master of H.M.S. *Andromache,* Captain William H. Shirreff, commander. Shirreff was one of those officers who had ridiculed Smith's first report of his discovery, but he had become convinced of the need for a survey when he read the journal of the discoverer's second visit to the islands. Smith's brig, the *Williams,* was chartered in the name of the King, her owner was named pilot, and Bransfield was given command. In addition, three midshipmen from the *Andromache,* as well as a surgeon from H.M.S.

....

Brown Palmer," *Geographical Review,* XXX (Oct., 1940), 531–35. See also his "The Log of Palmer's Discovery of Antarctica," *Science,* 87 (Feb. 18, 1938), 165–66, and "Palmer's Instrumental Observations in Connection with the Discovery of Antarctica," *Science,* 87 (May 20, 1938), 465–66.

Edouard Stackpole disagrees with Martin's interpretation. He believes the log indicates Palmer sailed along the southern coast of Livingston Island rather than the mainland of Antarctica during his November cruise. On November 15, he entered Ereby's Bay, "a spacious harbor with very Deep water 50 to 60 fathoms," and the next day he discovered the harbor labelled Palmer's Bay on the chart of James Weddell, the English sealer. This was the "excellent Harbor secure from all winds." It was from this harbor that Palmer followed a course south and east ½ east, "got over under the Land" and found the sea filled with ice. The "Land" was not the Continent, but Livingston Island, while the strait was the one separating Livingston and Deception. Since there is no evidence in the log that Palmer took a sight or even kept his position by dead reckoning on November 16 and 17, Stackpole concludes he undoubtedly was incorrect when he placed the mouth of the strait at 63° 45′ S. See his *Voyage of the Huron and the Huntress,* pp. 28–32.

Slaney, accompanied the expedition. It is believed one of the midshipmen wrote the journal published anonymously in the *Literary Gazette.*[5]

Bransfield received orders from Shirreff to proceed to latitude 62° S. and longitude 62° W. in order to ascertain the extent of the land Smith had seen there. He was to determine whether it was an island or part of a continent. If it proved to be the latter, his instructions were to follow its coast to the eastward, proving whether it was connected to Cook's Southern Thule or Sandwich Land. On "each quarter of the land" Bransfield was told to take possession in the name of His Majesty King George III.

After leaving Valparaiso, the *Williams* reached Livingston Island in the South Shetlands on January 16, 1820. A few days were spent there while the surveyors examined the coastline before sailing northward and eastward skirting the coasts of Greenwich, Roberts, Nelson, and King George Islands. These Bransfield charted as a continuous coastline because the straits separating them were partially closed with ice and the constant fog hid them from view. On January 19, the explorers rounded the northeast coast of King George's Island and sailed south and west until they found a suitable anchorage, which they named George's Bay. There Bransfield and his party went ashore and planted "the Jack," taking possession for His Britannic Majesty.

Bransfield, Smith, and their surveyors spent approximately a week exploring King George's Island. They then steered the *Williams* on a west-southwest course, sailing along the southern extremities of the South Shetlands before bearing sharply to the southwest past Deception Island. When they reached 63° 16′ S., 60° 28′ W., the explorers headed directly south on account of the weather. It appeared as if they were running from the land owing to the haze in front of them, which blotted out the area to the south. But when the mist and fog cleared, they unexpectedly sighted land to the southwest and were soon among a chain of islands running from northeast to east. "The whole of these formed a prospect more gloomy than can be imagined, and the only cheer

[5] Gould, "Charting of the South Shetlands," *Mariner's Mirror,* XXVII, 220. See also his "First Sighting of the Antarctic Continent," *Geographical Journal,* LXV (March, 1925), 220–21.

the sight afforded was in the idea that this might be the long-sought Southern Continent, as land was undoubtedly seen in latitude 64°, and trending to the eastward." [6] A round island they passed was named Tower Island, latitude 63° 29' S., longitude 60° 34' W., while the land beyond it was called Trinity Land in honor of the Trinity Board.

Bransfield directed the *Williams* north and east skirting his discovery, but he was unable definitely to determine its extent. The ice-filled sea and foggy weather obscured its coast. His chart indicates he thought the land might trend northeastward until it reached Elephant Island, one of the northeastern members of the South Shetland group named for the sea elephants which inhabited it. Only the northern coast of this island was explored, and therefore its insularity was not determined.

After circumnavigating Clarence Island, almost due east of Elephant Island, he sailed northeastward searching for additional territories. When in 61° 31' S., 52° 23' 45" W., the "brig made a dash to the southward, determined to enter the Antarctic Regions." After sailing some forty miles into the Weddell Sea, huge ice islands were encountered and floe ice stopped their progress. Since further penetration would have been hazardous, the explorers headed north and returned to Valparaiso.

Additional confirmation of Bransfield's discoveries was provided later by William Smith in a memorial presented to the Admiralty by way of obtaining remuneration for his discovery of the South Shetlands. Smith became bankrupt during his third voyage to the islands because his partners in the Argentine-Chilean coastal trade lost their money. According to the laws of the era he became indebted along with them. All his assets, including the *Williams,* were seized by creditors, and he was left penniless; so he appealed to the Admiralty, hoping to get payment for the exploring he had done. To accompany this plea, Smith sent a chart, drawn by a William Henry Goddard, showing his discovery, as well as the coasts of Bransfield's Trinity Land. This map differs from Bransfield's chart only insofar as the South Shetlands are depicted as a chain of islands, not a continuous land mass. Trinity Land is sketched where Bransfield recorded it on

---

[6] "New Shetland," *Literary Gazette,* X (Nov. 24, 1821), 746.

his chart, making it apparent Goddard used the discoverer's own sketches of his discovery.[7]

It is evident therefore that Edward Bransfield sighted the Antarctic mainland approximately nine months before Nathaniel Brown Palmer. His chart, the narrative of his voyage in the *Literary Gazette,* as well as Smith's memorial and chart present substantial proof of this.

After his voyage of reconnaissance, which took him to the coast of Antarctica, Nathaniel Palmer explored Yankee or Macfarlane Strait between Livingston and Greenwich Islands, discovering the well-protected harbor in Greenwich the sealers named Yankee Harbor. Today it is called Hospital Cove. When he reported this discovery to Pendleton, the sealers decided to move from Presidents' Harbor to the safer anchorage, because their ships were not sheltered sufficiently. The *Frederick,* in fact, had been driven from her moorings by heavy gales from the southwest. Throughout the remaining weeks in 1820 Palmer was occupied transporting skins from the shore camps to the larger vessels. Sealing was good and the skinners took more than 40,000 pelts.

According to the extract from a journal Jonathan Pendleton kept of the *Frederick's* voyage, Nathaniel Palmer was dispatched on another search for seal beaches on January 14, 1821. He supposedly completed this cruise and returned to Yankee Harbor on January 28, after exploring north, east, and southwest.

Even though the protagonist does not mention such a voyage in his logbook, this bit of information, together with other evidence,

....

[7] Memorial of William Smith, Discoverer of the South Shetland Islands, to the Lords Commissioners of the Admiralty, in the Public Records Office, Admiralty, Secretary, Letters 5029, for 1821. The chart is among the documents of the Hydrographic Office and is marked Ael S91. See the facsimile of it in Gould, "Charting of the South Shetlands," *Mariner's Mirror,* XXVII, 226.

Both Colonel Martin and the late William Herbert Hobbs, professor of geography at the University of Michigan, attempted to discredit Bransfield's discovery. See Martin, "Antarctica Discovered by a Connecticut Yankee," *Geographical Review,* XXX, 538; and Hobbs, *Discoveries of Antarctica within the American Sector, as Revealed by Maps and Documents* (Philadelphia, 1939), pp. 37–38. Hobbs is answered in Gould, "Charting of the South Shetlands"; A[rthur]. R. H[inks]., "On Some Misrepresentations of Antarctic History," *Geographical Journal,* XCIV (Oct., 1939), 309–30; and by R. N. Rudmose Brown, "Antarctic History; A Reply to Professor W. H. Hobbs," *Scottish Geographical Magazine,* XLV (May, 1939), 170–73.

has been construed to mean that Palmer circumnavigated the South Shetlands and investigated the coast of Palmer Land again. Of the supporting data, only a letter written from the sealing grounds in February, 1821, by Daniel W. Clark, mate of the *Hersilia*, to the editor of the *New Haven Journal*, is contemporary with Pendleton's log. In it Clark asserted that the sealers had been as far south as 66° south latitude. Although he does not mention Palmer specifically, and probably was discussing the explorations of another sealer, this information has been purported to be a confirmation of this cruise. The remaining evidence is the product of recollection and reflection directed toward proving Palmer "discovered" the mainland of Antarctica during the month of January, 1821, rather than November, 1820. The story of this "discovery" had been told many times and in various forms.

In 1828, while collecting information for the Navy in New England ports regarding the discoveries of sealers and whalers in the South Sea and Pacific Ocean, Jeremiah N. Reynolds, during an interview with Edmund Fanning, was told the story of Palmer's sighting of the continent. He published an account of it in the Washington *National Intelligencer*, December 13, 1828, and later described it for a Washington audience in the Hall of Representatives on April 3, 1836. Fanning himself related a closely similar version in his *Voyages* (1833).

This Fanning report, as well as the Reynolds rendition, is generally in accord with accounts of the cruise appearing after 1833, but in comparison they are decidedly devoid of details. In these later versions, supposedly based on Palmer's own description, many interesting facts are added. Here is Palmer's story as related by Frank T. Bush, former U.S. consul in Hong Kong, to whom it was told in 1844.

While exploring Deception Island, Palmer sighted the highlands of the Antarctic Continent and sailed to investigate. On the return voyage to join the other sealers he encountered almost constant fog. One night when the mist was unusually thick, the captain of the *Hero* came on deck to take the watch, struck one bell, and received an answer. He was startled, but soon regained his composure. When Palmer struck two bells to announce the first hour of the day and was answered by "a human hand," he was incredulous. He thought he was dreaming. Phineas Wilcox, the

first mate, insisted the sound was "tricky," refusing to believe
other humans were nearby. At seven bells voices were heard, and
when the fog lifted, the Americans found themselves between a
frigate and a sloop-of-war flying Russian colors.

Needless to say, the sealers were astonished at this sight. An
officer from the Russian frigate soon was sent to the *Hero* with
a message from his commander requesting Palmer to join him.
The American had been cordially welcomed when the following
conversation ensued:

> What is your name?
> Nathaniel B. Palmer.
> Where are you from?
> Stonington, Conn., U.S.A.
> The name of your boat?
> *Hero,* Sir.
> What are you doing here?
> On a sealing expedition.[8]

When the Russian commander learned Palmer's business was
sealing, he asked for an account of the voyage, tonnage of the
ships, number of skinners, and other details. Answers to these
questions brought further interrogation concerning Palmer's explorations. He declared that he not only gave his southernmost
position, but described his discovery as well. The commodore
then "arose much agitated" begging Nat to produce his logbook
and chart. Palmer immediately obliged and the Russians sent a
boat to the *Hero* to get them.

While luncheon was served, many additional questions were
presented concerning the seal fishery and the town of Stonington.
Afterward the sealer's map and log were laid upon the table and
the Russian commander carefully examined them. Presently he
rose from his seat and exclaimed: " 'What do I see and what do I
hear from a boy in his teens: that he is commander of a tiny boat
the size of a launch of my frigate, has pushed his way towards the
pole through storm and ice and sought the point I in command of
one of the best appointed fleets at the disposal of my august master
have for three long, weary, anxious years, searched day and night
for.' " Placing his hand on the young American's head, the Russian
continued in a downcast manner, " 'What shall I say to my master?

---

[8] Balch, "Stonington Antarctic Explorers," *Bulletin of the American Geographical Society,* XLI, 480.

what will he think of me? but be that as it may, my grief is your joy. Wear your laurels. With my sincere prayers for your welfare, I name the land you discovered in honor of yourself, noble boy, Palmer's Land.'" [9] The proud young master of the *Hero* then returned to his sloop and sailed northward to join his companions from Stonington.

The commander of the Russian fleet was Fabian von Bellingshausen, who undertook an extended voyage of exploration in the ships *Vostok* and *Mirnyi* to the south polar regions in 1819 to enhance the prestige of the Russian navy by emulating the exploits of the British explorer, James Cook, and by training seamen in the perilous seas of the Antarctic. His duty was to circumnavigate the globe, following a course in high southern latitudes as Cook had done. Commanding the *Mirnyi* was Lieutenant Mikhail Lazarev, who also served as interpreter.

Throughout his voyage Bellingshausen conscientiously avoided following Cook's track, however. He chose a southeasterly course after proving Sandwich Land in the South Atlantic was a chain of islands, and on January 15, 1820, he crossed the Antarctic Circle without mentioning it in his journal. The ice did not impede his progress until the following day, when he fell in with the barrier in 69° 21′ S., 2° 15′ W. Actually he had reached the coasts of the Antarctic Continent. The "ice-hillocks" he saw beyond the shelf were undoubtedly ice-covered mountains.

These events of January 16 were characteristic of the Russians' voyage eastward on a course which frequently took them south of the Antarctic Circle. On many occasions they skirted the continent without sighting land. This may be credited to the extreme caution and reluctance of their commander, who steadfastly refused to label any suspicious ice formation as terra firma. He was hesitant because he did not get soundings on the continental shelf of Antarctica which would have indicated the proximity of a land mass. The voyage southeastward through the South Indian Ocean was barren of discovery.

After refitting at Port Jackson (Sydney, Australia), Bellingshausen and his crews surveyed and explored some Pacific islands before sailing southward to search for land again. On January 10,

----

[9] *Ibid.*

1821, after almost completing their circumnavigation of the Antarctic Continent, the explorers saw "a black patch through the haze to the east-north-east." Their position was 69° 22′ south latitude, 92° 38′ west longitude. Bellingshausen described the scene:

The sun coming out from behind the clouds lit up the place and to our satisfaction we were able to assure ourselves that what we saw was land covered with snow. Only some rocks and cliffs, where the snow could not hold, showed up black. Words cannot describe the delight which appeared on all our faces at the cry of 'Land! Land!' Our joy was not surprising, after our long monotonous voyage, amidst unceasing dangers from ice, snow, rain, sleet and fog. We had no reason to suppose that we should find land in this quarter, because we had not encountered the usual signs of it, such as floating seaweed and penguins.[10]

An examination of the coast soon proved the land was an island about nine miles long and four miles wide. The Russians gave it "the great name of the founder of the fleet of the Russian Empire —'Peter I Island.'" Bellingshausen was the first explorer definitely to sight land within the Antarctic Circle.

The Russian explorers threaded their way through the ice filling the sea along the Antarctic mainland for another week before making an additional discovery. On January 17, land was seen again in latitude 68° 29′ S., longitude 75° 40′ W. "One of its headlands stretched to the northward and ended in a high mountain which was separated by an isthmus from another mountain chain extending to the south-west." [11] Their path to its coast was through submerged, drifting ice floes. While they initially attempted to close in, danger forced them back. What appeared to be avenues quickly closed up, and they were prevented from getting closer than forty miles.

The explorers were convinced nevertheless that they had sighted land rather than an island, because its southern limits disappeared beyond their range of vision. Since they were exploring in high southern latitudes at the instance of Czar Alexander I, Bellingshausen thought it his duty to name the land after his emperor. It was his opinion that time destroyed monuments of

---

[10] *The Voyage of Captain Bellingshausen to the Antarctic Seas, 1819–21* (2 vols., trans. from the Russian, ed. by Frank Debenham, London, 1945), II, 410.

[11] *Ibid.*, II, 419.

stone, but Peter I Island and Alexander I Land would inde-structibly stand forever in commemoration of the czars. Three days after this coastline was discovered, the Russians rounded Cape Horn, destination the South Shetlands, to prove whether they were part of the supposed Southern Continent.

By January 24 the ships were off Snow or Monroe's Island, where the explorers saw eight or nine American and British sealing vessels lying at anchor. Proceeding southeastward, Bellingshausen sighted a "high Island, with steep cliffs" which he called Teille Island in honor of Major-General Baron de Teille von Seraskerken. This was Deception Island, and in the strait separating it from Snow and Livingston Islands the Russian explorer met Nathaniel Palmer in the *Hero*.

At 10 o'clock we entered the strait and encountered a small American sealing boat. I lay to, despatched a boat, and waited for the Captain of the American boat. The lead did not touch bottom at 115 fathoms. Soon after Mr Palmer arrived in our boat and informed us that he had been here for four months' sealing in partnership with three American ships. They were engaged in killing and skinning seals, whose numbers were perceptibly diminishing. There were as many as eighteen vessels about at various points, and not infrequently differences arose amongst the sealers, but so far it had not yet come to a fight. Mr Palmer told me that the above-mentioned Captain Smith, the discoverer of New Shetland, was on the brig *Williams*, that he had succeeded in killing as many as 60,000 seals, whilst the whole fleet of sealers had killed 80,000. As other sealers also were competing in the destruction of the seals there could be no doubt that round the South Shetland Islands just as at South Georgia and Macquarie Islands [south of Australia] the number of these sea animals will rapidly decrease. Sea elephants, of which there also had been many, had already moved from these shores farther out to sea. According to Mr Palmer the bay in which we saw the eight ships lying at anchor is protected from all winds and has a depth of 18 fathoms, thin mud. Owing to the peculiar nature of the bottom the vessels frequently got adrift even with two anchors out. Two British ships and one American one had dragged their anchors and been wrecked. Mr Zavadovski [second in command of the *Vostok*] shot a tern with blackish feathers above the neck, light grey on the back. The beak and claws were of a bright red colour. Round about us birds were diving, penguins were calling, albatrosses, gulls, pintades, blue petrels and cormorants were flying about in all directions. Mr Palmer soon returned to his ship, and we proceeded along the shore.[12]

....

[12] *Voyage of Captain Bellingshausen,* II, 425–26.

Bellingshausen's account of his voyage and the meeting with Palmer makes it all too apparent that exaltation of their hero is the central theme of the stories told by Americans. Some differences in the American and Russian versions undoubtedly are due to faulty translations of the conversation, although this point seems to be stretched beyond comprehension when many of the highly ornamented speeches attributed to Bellingshausen are judged on this basis. Besides, Lazarev had served in the British Navy and probably knew English well. Notwithstanding, two important statements supposedly made by the Russian commander become mythopoeic when examined in the light of evidence in his journal. First of all, Bellingshausen would not have inquired about the South Shetlands because he was acquainted with the Smith discovery, and had already sighted Snow Island. Besides, he was cruising in the area in order to survey them. He tells us the Russian ambassador to the Portuguese court at Rio de Janeiro informed him of the discovery while he was in Australia. "It was . . . February of the year 1819 that the island [sic] was unexpectedly discovered by Captain Smith, the captain of a British merchant brig."

The second statement is even wilder than the first. Picture an august, senior commander of an expedition which had discovered land 400 miles south of Palmer Land placing his hand on the young American's head while reflecting on the humiliation that would be his cup of hemlock when he faced his emperor. In such a performance Bellingshausen would have been entirely out of character. Allowing for discrepancies in translation, it is extremely doubtful if Palmer and Bellingshausen talked about anything except the sealing business. Had he known of Palmer's discovery, doubtless he would have mentioned it. Throughout his journal Bellingshausen lauded all discoveries by other explorers.[13]

Obvious attempts at ostentation, such as these, make the American stories of Palmer's voyage of January, 1821, more fiction than fact. By keeping in mind the information in his logbook, an examination of the various American versions brings into focus certain distinct facts. From the log it is possible to deduce that Palmer was sent out on a voyage of reconnaissance for seal

[13] See Frank Debenham's introduction to Bellingshausen's journal, I, xxv–xxvii.

beaches on November 15, 1820, because two days earlier no seals were up at Presidents' Harbor. He sailed southeastward, reaching Deception Island. There he sighted the Antarctic highlands and stood over to investigate. After reaching the land, he coasted its shore long enough to determine that there were no seal rookeries, and with his mission thus accomplished, he sailed northward again. These facts also are contained in the later versions of Palmer's supposed voyage of discovery when he met Bellingshausen.

From the Russian's journal we know the meeting took place on January 24, 1821, but no specific dates are recorded in the American accounts. Since Palmer remembered he had coasted the mainland of Antarctica and had conversed with Bellingshausen, it is evident that a faulty memory caused him to dovetail the two accounts, making it appear he was returning from the continent when he fell in with the Russian ships. Attempts to substantiate this imperfect evidence, as well as efforts to prove Nathaniel Palmer discovered Antarctica, have obscured the real accomplishments of Palmer, Bransfield, and Bellingshausen. The names of all three deserve a place on the map of Antarctica.

chapter four

DAVIS AND BURDICK,
PALMER AND POWELL,
BENJAMIN MORRELL

Competition for seal pelts was great at the South Shetlands during the Antarctic sealing season of 1820–21, with approximately forty American, English, Scotch, and Australian ships contending. From the United States, almost every important port between New York City and Salem was represented. James Byers of course sent a fleet, consisting of the brig *Jane Maria*, brig *Aurora*, and the schooner *Henry*. A second Stonington group, in addition to the one organized by the Fannings, composed of the ship *Clothier*, brig *Catharine*, and brig *Emeline*, made the voyage, as did the schooners *Huntress* and *Harmony* from Nantucket; the ship *O'Cain* and the brig *Stranger* from Boston; the ship *General Knox*, brig *Nancy*, and the schooner *Governor Brooks* from Salem; the ship *Huron* from New Haven; and the brig *Gleaner* out of New Bedford. These Americans were in competition with an equal number of English and Scotch sealers, as well as a vessel from Botany Bay, Australia.

Of the American sealers, Benjamin Pendleton and his Stonington group were the most successful, and much of their good fortune resulted from the discoveries of Nathaniel Palmer in the *Hero*. His locating Yankee Harbor and the immense rookery on the northeastern coast of Livingston Island in Blythe Bay enabled the Fanning fleet to be the first to slaughter seals there. While the other Americans ultimately moved their ships to Yankee Harbor and established camps nearby, they had to be satisfied with the seals left by Pendleton and his men. By January, 1821, with the end of the Antarctic summer and the sealing season in sight, the other

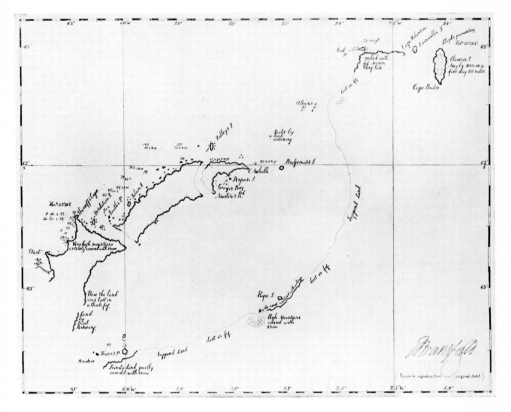

Facsimile of Edward Bransfield's chart of the South Shetlands and Trinity Land

seal hunters were forced to find additional populated beaches or return home with partial cargoes. Some ranged to the north and east, exploring islands adjacent to Greenwich, while others cruised southwestward, where they sighted the highlands of Palmer Peninsula.

Captain Robert Johnson, commander of Byers's New York fleet, completed an extensive, twenty-two-day exploring cruise to the southwest on January 27. According to Captain Christopher Burdick, who reported this voyage in the logbook of his Nantucket schooner *Huntress,* Johnson had sailed to 66° S., 70° W., and sighted elevations he thought were land, but which proved to be islands of ice and snow.[1] Johnson unfortunately saw no dark patches which would have indicated he was near territory, but if his reckoning and Burdick's reporting were accurate, the New York master probably had reached a position near the shores of Adelaide Island off the Antarctic Continent.

The failure of James Byers's commander to find seals might have influenced the decision of Captain John Davis of the New Haven ship *Huron* to take her shallop, the *Cecilia,* into the same region. Davis was skinning in company with Burdick, whom he had met in the Falklands during his voyage to the South Shetlands. His partner already had investigated the southern shores of Livingston, while Davis himself had explored the coasts of Nelson and Roberts Islands without notable results. Few weeks remained for the sealers to work with any degree of safety, because the Antarctic winter with its hurricane gales and fierce blizzards was coming. Davis hoped he would have more success finding populated beaches in the southwest than Johnson.

After leaving Morton Strait, which lies between Livingston and Snow Islands, the tiny shallop was steered by compass on a southwest by ½ west course into Bransfield Strait on January 31. The sealers put Snow Island to the northwest, Deception to the northeast, when they sighted Low or Jameson Island. Since Captain Davis was searching for seals, he decided to investigate the southern coast of Mount Pisgah (Smith) Island before exploring the discovery. This visit proved unrewarding because an Australian sealers' camp already was there, but a survey of Jameson Island

---

[1] See the logbook of the *Huntress* as quoted in Stackpole, *Voyage of the Huron and the Huntress,* p. 47.

disclosed seals, and the crew of the *Cecilia* took almost 700 skins on its north shore. When these pelts were loaded, the shallop was headed southeastward on February 7 toward another island seen in the distance.

This small body of land, Hoseason Island, did not long occupy the sealers' attention, because a much larger territory was perceived on the horizon. They ignored the island, in fact, closing in near the coast of the land mass in latitude 64° 01′ S., where the *Cecilia* was anchored. A whaleboat was lowered, and a party rowed ashore, only to make a disappointing investigation for seals. When the hunters returned, the shallop was steered up a large bay, " 'the Land high and covered intirely [sic] with Snow.' " But a thick snowstorm forced them to tack away from the coast into open water for the protection of their vessel. Davis had seen enough to conclude, " 'I think this Southern Land to be a Continent.' " [2]

The location of the sealers' landing is difficult to determine. Their course and recorded position, 64° 01′ S., placed them somewhere at sea east of Liege Island and north of the Island of Two Hummocks. Undoubtedly the *Cecilia* had reached a position several minutes farther south. Captain Davis was a mariner whose experience precluded his mistaking a small island for a sizable land mass, so it is not probable he had anchored off one of those in Gerlache Strait. His southeastward course past Hoseason Island, moreover, would have taken him east of the large Brabant Island, between Liege and Intercurrence Islands, into Hughes Bay. The first known landing on the Antarctic mainland, accomplished by the New Haven sealers, probably was made on the shore of this capacious body of water. [3]

The heavy snowstorm that had caused Captain Davis to tack away from the Continent was accompanied by fierce gales from the north, and made the return voyage to Yankee Harbor hazardous. Every degree of latitude was gained with the utmost difficulty. Northeast of Bransfield's Trinity Island, the sealers sighted Antarctica again, but did not approach the shore, owing to the strong wind and the heavy seas. On February 10, after the wind

---

[2] The logbook of the *Huron*, Feb. 7, 1821, quoted in Stackpole, *Voyage of the Huron and the Huntress*, p. 51.

[3] *Ibid.*, pp. 53–54.

had changed its direction and moderated, Captain Davis was able to anchor the little shallop in Yankee Harbor near the *Huron*.

A few days after Davis's return, his partner, Captain Christopher Burdick, nosed the *Cecilia* out of the sealers' haven bound for Jameson Island again. This voyage was undertaken not only to slaughter seals, but to gather skins as well. A stop was made at a camp on the south shore of Livingston Island where some 470 pelts were loaded. Burdick then headed his craft directly south toward his destination. In 63° 17' south latitude, he sighted the highlands of Palmer Peninsula. Like Nat Palmer and Captain Davis, the master of the *Huntress* was able to perceive these mountains because of the remarkably clear atmosphere. He too believed the land was a continent.

The logbooks of Captains John Davis and Christopher Burdick contain the first known reference to Antarctica as a continent which was written by explorers who saw the mainland. Yet it is presumable that in employing this term both were speculating. After all, neither had coasted the land far enough to determine definitely that it was of continental proportions. Furthermore, almost from the time the *Hersilia* had returned to Stonington with news of the existence of the South Shetlands, notices containing conjectures about a southern continent had appeared in newspapers. Some of these articles suggested that the South Shetlands themselves might be part of a continent.[4] The Russian, Captain Bellingshausen, surveyed them to prove the truth of such a supposition. It is likely therefore that the masters of the *Huron* and the *Huntress* were using the word continent merely to designate a body of land larger than a small island.

Though crews from approximately forty sealing vessels from the United States and Great Britain had been slaughtering fur seals in the South Shetlands during the Antarctic summer of 1820 and 1821, the sealers' faith in the gainfulness of their business, as well as their own capabilities to make it profitable, appears to have been boundless. The next season the Fannings not only sent a fleet to the South but increased it by one ship, the 80-ton sloop *James Monroe*, which was given over to Nat Palmer. This voyage enabled him to make a final contribution to Antarctic discovery before giving up

---

[4] See, for example, *Niles' Weekly Register*, XIX (Sept. 16, 1820), 43–44; and the *Daily National Intelligencer*, Oct. 3, 1820, 3.

sealing for shipbuilding, commercial shipping, and the clipper ship trade to China.

Edmund Fanning and Benjamin Pendleton, agents for this expedition, instructed Palmer to take his sloop to East Harbor, Cape St. John, in Staten Island with the brig *Alabama Packet,* William A. Fanning, commander. Then these captains were to proceed to their final place of rendezvous, Deception Harbor in "New South Iceland." At all times and under all circumstances, Palmer was to consider his vessel as mated to the brigs *Alabama Packet* and *Frederick,* the schooners *Express* and *Free Gift,* as well as the sloop *Hero.* But it was especially important that he arrive at Deception Island with the *Frederick* and *Alabama Packet,* for the *James Monroe* was to be used as a shallop or tender, as was the *Hero.*[5]

Nathaniel Palmer carried out his instructions to the letter. Throughout his voyage to Staten Island he was in company with the *Alabama Packet.* The fleet left Stonington on July 25, 1821, reaching Staten Island on October 27. There, as was common, the sealers cut wood and stored water before setting out for the South Shetlands. By November 6, all the ships were anchored off Deception Island and preparations were being made to begin work.

Almost from the start the sealers experienced difficulty fulfilling their mission. The devastating slaughter of the previous season had taken its toll, and for the most part only stragglers and pups were found on the beaches once heavily populated. To locate new seal haunts, the *James Monroe* and the *Hero* were put into service as exploring vessels. From Deception they sailed northeastward to the coast of Livingston Island and began an examination of the southern coasts of the islands composing the central group of the South Shetlands. Palmer and Jonathan Pendleton, captain of the *Hero,* found no substantial herds of seals or elephants, for they continued their searches northeastward until they reached the tiny Penguin Island off the southern shore of Bransfield's King George Island. There they halted the voyage to collect eggs and fuel before Palmer extended his investigations to Elephant Island and the other bodies of land making up the South Shetlands' eastern group.

When the *James Monroe* arrived at Elephant Island, Palmer ordered his crew ashore to search for seals or elephants, and they

----

[5] E. Fanning and B. Pendleton to N. B. Palmer, Stonington, July 21, 1821, Palmer Papers.

were thus engaged when the British sloop *Dove* arrived. George Powell, the *Dove's* commander, invited Palmer to join in an exploring cruise to the northeast, since he was certain any new islands would be inhabited by seals and elephants. Palmer readily agreed, for he knew "the danger that would be attending one vessel." Besides, the *James Monroe* and the *Dove* were built along similar lines and their commanders believed they would perform well as a team.

Palmer and Powell moved their sloops northward around Elephant Island, reaching Cornwallis's Isle, north of the strait separating Elephant from Clarence Island. When nothing of interest was found there, they stood over for Clarence, which was examined with similar results. On December 4, 1821, the *James Monroe* and the *Dove* were steered into unknown seas to the northeast where the South Orkney Islands eventually were discovered. This voyage was not without incident.

From Cape Bowles, Clarence Island, Palmer and Powell sailed 148 miles before encountering foul weather and drifting ice, which caused them to drop anchor. They did not wish to risk passing land in the fog or damaging their ships. While they were idle, the seamen of the *Dove* supplied the *James Monroe* with 120 gallons of water. The sun broke through the haze during the afternoon of the sixth of December, and the explorers continued their course for another 32 miles before large bodies of ice blocked their passage. Shortly after they veered to the southeast for clear water, "the man at the masthead" of the *Dove* sighted what appeared to be land. Because the *James Monroe* was about four miles astern of the British ship, Powell hailed his consort before continuing. Palmer apparently did not notice the object until he was close to the *Dove,* and then he "doubted whether it was land or ice." Notwithstanding, he promised to follow Powell and they sailed toward the discovery, "which proved to be three spiral rocks quite inaccessible, without the least sign of vegetation." [6] The Englishman used his chronometer and ascertained their position as 60° 32′ S., 46° 52′ W.

Late on December 6, the explorers sighted what appeared to be a considerable territory "bearing by compass E. by N." They

[6] George Powell, *Notes on South-Shetland, &c. Printed to Accompany the Chart of these Newly Discovered Lands, which has been Constructed from the Explorations of the sloop Dove* (London, 1822), p. 8.

opened their sails to the wind, but encountered great difficulty getting close "owing to the vast quantity of ice that was drifting in every direction." Early the next day they maneuvered their ships in sufficiently to see that the discovery was a cluster of islands forming a bight or open bay. Powell decided to take a party ashore, but Palmer refused, saying "it would not be worthwhile, for they could see no prospect whatever of any seals." [7] The Englishman was interested in more than sealing, however, so the seamen from the *Dove* set out in their whaleboat. They took possession of the islands in the name of King George IV, naming the largest Coronation Isle, believing it was the first land discovered since their King's coronation, and the one next in size Laurie Isle, probably in honor of the London chartmaker, R. H. Laurie.

Throughout the week following December 7, Powell and his crew surveyed the northern coasts of Coronation and Laurie Islands, while Palmer and his men searched for seals. From Powell's account it appears as though Palmer was scornful of the islands when they were uninhabited by seals. The Americans did little exploring and went on shore only to gather eggs and capture sea leopards, which may have been why the Englishmen failed to complete their surveys before a shortage of provisions forced both ships back to the South Shetlands. The *Dove* anchored in Clothier Harbor, Roberts Island, on December 22. Powell's printed journal does not indicate when he separated from Palmer, but it does disclose that he visited other sealers who provided data concerning the southern coasts of the South Shetlands he was unable to survey before returning to England.

Late in 1822 George Powell published a chart of the South Orkney Islands which included sketches of the South Shetlands and Palmer Land. This outline of Palmer's discovery does not conform to the details he recorded during his voyage of November, 1820. Powell admitted his knowledge was limited, since it had not been "sufficiently explored." It had been described, "as very high, and covered with snow, with inlets, forming straits, which may probably separate the land, and constitute a range of islands, similar to those of South-Shetland; at least, such is the appearance of the northern side, which alone has yet been seen." [8]

---

[7] Powell, *Notes*, p. 8.
[8] Powell, *Notes*, p. 12.

Some vague evidence suggests that Nathaniel Palmer re-ex-plored the coast of Palmer Land during his search for seals in 1821–22. Since it is linked with information regarding the South Orkneys, it appears as though Palmer's voyage with Powell has been mistakenly reported as an exploring cruise to the coast of the Antarctic Continent. On April 24, 1823, a story appeared in the New London *Connecticut Gazette* which stated that Palmer had "proceeded in the James Monroe from the Shetland Isles to the continent, and coasted it, from abreast of the Isles to the eastward, as far as 44 degrees West Longitude." The explorer, the story said, cruised as close to the shore as possible, but at some points he was unable to approach nearer than five or six leagues "owing to the firm and fast ice." In 61° 41′ south latitude, 45° 27′ west longitude, he discovered a fine harbor "lying about one mile within the en-trance of Washington Strait, which harbour was named Palmer's Harbour, where he came to anchor." The land was barren and inhabited only by sea leopards. It was proclaimed as being part of a *"South Continent,"* and the conclusion was offered that Captain Cook's Sandwich Land was attached to it. "Captain Palmer could discern the mountains with snow, in the interior, as he sailed along the coast." [9] A similar story was printed later in Edmund Fanning's *Voyages.*

The positions designated in this article are in the vicinity of the South Orkneys, indicating that the report of the voyage is either erroneous or that Palmer regarded those islands and Sandwich Land as an eastern extension of the peninsula which bears his name. If the latter is the case, the American sealer was no better an observer than Edward Bransfield, whose chart suggests that Elephant Island might be a continuation of Trinity Land. Wash-ington Strait appears on Powell's chart between Coronation and Laurie Isles.

Nathaniel Palmer's experience of finding leopards instead of seals was shared by many sealers who worked the South Shetlands during 1822 and 1823. In one short sealing season the large seal population of these islands was all but wiped out. Fanning's and Pendleton's Stonington fleet collected an insignificant 1,000 skins and 1,100 barrels of elephant oil. Late in January, 1822, the *Fred-*

---

[9] See the article as reprinted in the *Daily National Intelligencer*, May 10, 1822, 3.

erick, Alabama Packet, and the *Hero* rounded the Horn to complete their cargoes on islands off the coast of Chile. Even then they were not entirely successful, having to be satisfied with sea lion pelts, which were far less valuable than those of the fur seal.

Although all sealers were affected by the disappearance of the fur seal herds, they did not forsake their business immediately. More intrepid skinners began investigating other islands in the South Atlantic, Kerguelen's Isle of Desolation in the South Indian Ocean, as well as islands south of Australia. One of these was a Stonington citizen, who sailed out of the port of New York, Benjamin Morrell, Jr.

To Benjamin Morrell belong distinctions no other Antarctic explorer from the United States can claim. By some historians he has been designated the "Baron Munchausen of the Antarctic"—a plagiarist, forger, and a fake—by others a bona fide explorer. The opprobrious epithets were applied because of his descriptions of an ice-free south polar sea, and an Antarctic land mass, New South Greenland, in his *Narrative of Four Voyages* (1832).

On his initial sealing voyage, Morrell served Captain Robert Johnson as first mate on the schooner *Wasp,* one of James Byers's ships that left New York for the South Shetlands in June, 1821. Late in September the sealers sighted Snow Island and initiated a hunt for seals and elephants which took them toward Yankee Harbor. The crew of the *Wasp* found no appreciable number of fur seals, but took 700 barrels of elephant oil, before reaching the Seal Islands off the southern coast of Elephant Island. A cursory examination proved the island's name was inappropriate, so Johnson altered his course toward the east and south. On December 2, the sealers discovered an island "bearing east-half-south, distant five leagues; not noticed on any chart." [10] Morrell led an exploring party ashore, but found neither seals nor elephants. Only sea lions inhabited its shores. Captain Johnson concluded that sealing in the South Atlantic would be unrewarding, so he steered his vessel toward Staten Island, where Morrell was given command of the *Jane Maria,* bound for New York. Johnson meanwhile took his ship into the Pacific.

....

[10] Capt. Benjamin Morrell, Jun., *A Narrative of Four Voyages, to the South Sea, North and South Pacific Ocean, Chinese Sea, Ethiopic and Southern Atlantic Ocean, Indian and Antarctic Ocean* . . . (New York, 1832), pp. xxiii–xxiv. Hereafter cited as Morrell, *Four Voyages.*

After the *Jane Maria* reached her home port, Byers acknowl-
edged Morrell's services by promising him the command of the
Wasp when she returned. His immediate duty was supervising the
refitting of the schooner *Henry*, which was to become Johnson's
command. Later the two sealers were sent on a two-year voyage to
the Antarctic and Pacific.

Morrell disclosed that he had long believed the great object of
this cruise was to acquire knowledge of the Antarctic regions, and
if circumstances permitted, to ascertain the possibility of sailing
to the South Pole. Many navigators had attempted to penetrate
south polar seas, but all had stopped "at a certain point, timidly
shrinking from the farther prosecution of what they deemed an
impracticable project. Some, . . . have even been deterred by a
superstitious notion that an attempt to reach the South Pole was a
presumptuous intrusion on the awful confines of nature,—an un-
lawful and sacrilegious prying into the secrets of the great Creator;
who, . . . has guarded the 'ends of the earth' with an impassable
bulwark of indissoluble ice. . . ." [11] Morrell knew this icy barrier
existed. Only a miracle could open a passage through it, but a
combination of "genius, science, and energy" could work miracles.
Scientific knowledge and intelligence, in fact, could melt an avenue
through solid ice to the center of the earth.

These thoughts in mind, the captain of the *Wasp* headed his
schooner southward from New York Harbor on June 20, 1822. This
voyage was not unlike previous ones, with the sealers following a
course prescribed by necessity, via the Falklands and Staten Island.
After gathering eggs and slaughtering wild cattle on New Island,
in the Falklands, Morrell searched for the Auroras, even though
Captain Johnson had devoted the better part of six weeks to such
exploration. For fifteen days, the master of the *Wasp* sailed north
and south, east and west, between the 50th and 53rd parallels of
south latitude, and the 40th and 44th degrees of west longitude,
but the "tantalizing Auroras" eluded him. He concluded they must
have been gigantic ice islands mistaken for land.

When this was abandoned, the sealers stood over for South
Georgia to find seals. On arrival, part of Morrell's crew used a
whaleboat to circumnavigate the island, but discovered no animals.
Since the sole object of their visit was thus beyond accomplish-

----

[11] Morrell, *Four Voyages*, p. 29.

ment, they weighed anchor on November 24 and proceeded eastward toward Bouvet's Island southwest of the Cape of Good Hope.

Although not completely compensating, the sealers' stop at this
dot on the map proved more rewarding than the one at South
Georgia. Morrell's reconnaissance crew skinned about 80 fur seals
which were "perfectly tame; so much so, that they would come up
and play among the men who were skinning their companions."
Their luck did not continue, however. After clearing the beach
where the first seals were found, they were unable to locate another strand along the steep coasts where seals could get ashore.
The sealers continued their eastward course until the schooner
was anchored in Christmas Harbor at Kerguelen Island on the last
day of 1822.

Again a seal hunting circumnavigation was unproductive. Morrell then steered his vessel southward and eastward on January 11
with nothing more in mind than penetrating the Antarctic ice. In
62° 27' S., 94° 11' E., an extensive ice field stretching for 150 miles
east and west restricted their progress and caused them to alter
their course rather than hazard their vessel. They stood to the
northeast until they reached the 58th parallel of latitude, where
the *Wasp* was headed directly eastward.

From the day the *Wasp* departed from Kerguelen Island until
the end of January, the explorers had only one clear day. Early on
February 1, they "took the wind fresh from the north-east" and at
midday reached latitude 64° 52' S., longtitude 118° 27' E. In Morrell's words, "The wind freshened to an eleven-knot breeze, and
we embraced this opportunity of making to the west; being, however, convinced that the farther we went south beyond lat. 64° the
less ice was to be apprehended. . . ." The sealers pushed southwestward until they crossed the Antarctic Circle, reaching 69° 11'
S., 48° 15' E. "In this latitude there was *no field ice,* and very few
ice-islands in sight." [12]

In a clear sea the explorers pushed due west, crossing the meridian of Greenwich on February 23. It was a cloudless day, but Morrell was forced to retreat northward to the Sandwich Islands because of a desperate need for fuel. Five days later the cheering
shout of "Land, Ho!" came from the masthead. They had reached

[12] Morrell, *Four Voyages,* p. 65.

Candlemas Isles, one of the more northerly groups making up Cook's discovery. These were small, but both were burning volcanoes. In Sandwich Land Morrell noticed "nine burning volcanoes—fire in abundance, but no fuel for the Wasp." Because of their vain search for wood, the Captain had to limit the galley fires to one per week. But despite the obvious danger, the sealers pushed into the Antarctic again.

From March 6 to 14 the fast-sailing *Wasp* was steered almost 800 miles south of Sandwich Land to 70° 14′ S., 40° 03′ W., in the Weddell Sea. This section of the South Atlantic was entirely free of ice fields. The temperatures of both the air and water, Morrell testified, were substantially warmer than in the area five or ten degrees to the north. This observation, combined with his knowledge that few territories existed in the Antarctic where ice islands and bergs could form, caused the sealer to conclude that "the antarctic seas must be much less obstructed by ice than is generally supposed; and that *a clear sea is open for voyages of discovery, even to the south pole.*" [13] With neither fuel nor water for such an extended voyage, the intrepid Morrell was constrained to steer his schooner northward on March 15.

Soon the sealers sighted the northern cape of a sizable body of land—New South Greenland—discovered earlier by Captain Johnson.[14] Tacking southeastward along its coast to latitude 67° 52′ S., longitude 48° 11′ W., they saw myriads of birds, as well as elephants, lions, and leopards. Snow-covered mountains could be perceived seventy-five miles to the south. But owing to their short supplies they "bade adieu to the cheerless shores of New South Greenland" on March 19, 1823, steering a course toward Staten Island. Captain Benjamin Morrell's voyage to the open south polar seas was thus completed.[15]

Does this sealer deserve the epithet, "Baron Munchausen of the Antarctic"? A cursory examination of his narrative shows it is not

----

[13] Morrell, *Four Voyages,* p. 69.

[14] Edmund Fanning states that New South Greenland and Palmer Land were one and the same, but the positions given by Morrell for the former are in the Weddell Sea considerably east of that territory. See Fanning, *Voyages,* p. 437n.

[15] The theory of an open polar sea in the Arctic long occupied explorers in that region. See John K. Wright, "The Open Polar Sea," *Geographical Review,* XLIII (July, 1953), 338–65.

entirely inappropriate, for Morrell was guilty of exaggeration and inaccuracy. After leaving Kerguelen Island, the position he attained where no field ice and few ice-islands existed was several degrees south of the coast of Enderby Land, which was not discovered until 1831 by the Englishman John Biscoe. An open polar sea was encountered again when the sealers reached 70° 14′ S., 40° 03′ W., this time in the Weddell Sea. Only a shortage of fuel and water prevented their invasion of the pole itself. Later, during the sealer's voyage to warmer climes, Morrell rediscovered New South Greenland.

Benjamin Morrell was not alone in believing land could be found between 63° and 68° S., 48° W., however. In 1842, Sir James Clark Ross, an experienced British explorer, saw what appeared to be land in the same area.[16] For many years, moreover, Ross's notice was accepted as conclusive proof that New South Greenland existed, even though the French explorer, Dumont d'Urville had taken soundings he thought proved the nonexistence of land where Morrell had placed it. The distinguished Scottish geographer and explorer, Sir William Bruce, even plotted New South Greenland on his bathymetrical map of the South Atlantic.

In 1902, Otto Nordenskjöld, commanding the Swedish Antarctic Expedition, on a voyage into the Weddell Sea reached a position in 48° W., without making a discovery. Still, many geographers refused to believe Ross's and Morrell's land was mythical until Sir Ernest Shackleton convincingly disproved its existence. On August 17, 1915, Shackleton made a sounding which "gave 1676 fathoms, 10 miles west of the charted position of Morell [sic] Land. No land could be seen from the masthead, and . . . [he] decided that Morell Land must be added to the long list of Antarctic islands and continental coasts that on close investigation have resolved themselves into icebergs." [17]

In terms of more recent findings, part of Morrell's narrative is fallacious, but modern discovery is only one standard by which

---

[16] Ross omits this information from his popular printed narrative, but Sir William Bruce, who examined his manuscript journal, supplies the material. See "The Weddell Sea: An Historical Retrospect," *Scottish Geographical Magazine,* XXXIII (June, 1917), 244.

[17] Sir Ernest Shackleton, *South: The Story of Shackleton's Last Expedition, 1914–1917* (New York, 1920), p. 60.

journals like his can be judged. It is impossible to expect the accuracy of modern explorers from early nineteenth-century sealers,
who usually lacked all navigation instruments except a magnetic
compass. It is entirely possible Morrell did not know his true position when he reported an open polar sea where land was later
discovered, and described lands which did not exist. For example,
when he reached 69° 11′ S., 48° 15′ E., and saw an open polar sea,
he could have been far from that location. He had had only one
day of clear weather from January 11 to 31, during which he could
have fixed his position by observing the situation of the sun. In
addition, he might have incorrectly determined his direction, since
his compass would have been affected by the magnetic pole.

Although Morrell said he considered the variation of his compass in locating New South Greenland, his position set by observation still could have been incorrect. On the other hand, he might
have thought barrier ice, clouds, or even fog was land. Many de-
pendable explorers have suffered similar delusions. When Nordenskjöld was near the position of Morrell's land, his men began to
think they "stood on the brink of an important discovery." Their
pathway toward the "land" lay "right through the midst of the
pack-ice." The crew was "warmly interested," but no one dared
venture an opinion on what they saw. Nordenskjöld stated:

Opinions change from minute to minute; sometimes it looks so won-
derfully like land—a wide expanse of rolling snow-clad landscape,
with a few hills, which are snow-clad too, and in one place we
imagine we see a lofty snow-free peak—and then again, when it is
revealed in a new light, it seems to be merely an immense ice-fell. We
are evidently coming near, although at first we can scarcely mark the
fact. . . . We see now that it cannot be very large, but still, at the
very last moment the excitement and our hopes are raised to the very
highest pitch. The great difference between the dark parts and the light
since the sun went down, the perfect resemblance to land, the gently-
rounded forms by the side of the highest peak—it could scarcely be
possible for it to appear as it does were it merely an ordinary iceberg.
At last we found ourselves close beside the supposed island and rounded
it, only to find that it consisted of a lofty, peculiarly-formed iceberg
which had been turned upside down, and that the patches we had taken
for projecting points of land were merely compact, snow-free ice.[18]

----

[18] Dr. N. Otto G. Nordenskjöld and Dr. Joh. Gunnar Andersson, *Antarctica,
or Two Years Amongst the Ice of the South Pole* (London, 1905), p. 88.

Since Morrell was prone to exaggerate, it is possible that this supposed landfall was not nearly so extensive as he portrayed it.

The *Narrative of Four Voyages* is colored by redundant statements and this is beyond doubt Morrell's greatest reportorial weakness. Writing to Nathaniel Palmer in 1834, Jeremiah N. Reynolds said Morrell always saw through a "glass dimly" and his descriptions were more poetry than truth. It is likely he amplified a sea which was passable into an open polar sea free of pack-ice and ice islands. A British sealer, James Weddell, whose veracity has not been seriously questioned, experienced a similar phenomenon during the same year, and later Antarctic explorers reached positions as far south as Morrell. Polar ice does shift, and it is possible the Weddell Sea was reasonably free of ice during the Antarctic summer of 1823.

chapter five

HOLES IN THE POLES?

When New England sealers were becoming interested in the Antarctic, a former captain of the United States infantry, John Cleves Symmes, declared, "the earth is hollow, habitable within; containing a number of concentrick spheres; one within the other, and that it is open at the pole [sic] twelve or sixteen degrees."[1] This pronunciamento, delivered in April, 1818, accompanied by a certificate of Symmes's sanity, was sent to some 500 institutions of learning, as well as important government officials, in the United States and Europe. The author pledged his life in support of this "truth," spending his energies attempting to gain recognition and the command of an exploring expedition to prove everlastingly he could enter the earth.

John Cleves Symmes claimed discovery of his theory through extended and meticulous observations of the constellations in the heavens, together with deep reflection. Nothing in his career suggests he might have perused the works of the British scientist Edmund Halley, who suggested the earth might be composed of internal, but not hollow, spheres. Halley's idea, offered as an explanation of magnetism, was not readily available to a soldier who had spent most of his adult life in frontier army camps.

The author of the theory of concentric spheres was born in Sussex County, New Jersey, on November 5, 1780. His father, Timothy, named him after his brother, who gained significance as the purchaser of the Miami Territory in Ohio. The young

---

[1] See Symmes's pronouncement in the *Daily National Intelligencer*, June 18, 1818, 3.

John Cleves, like many boys of moderately well-to-do parentage, received a good common school education, which he himself augmented through wide reading and self-teaching. The physical sciences early occupied his attention, and he demonstrated his precociousness by explaining the movements of the earth to mystified playmates.

A few months before his twenty-second birthday, Symmes entered the United States Army as an ensign and gained successive appointments until he became a captain shortly before the War of 1812. On Christmas Day, 1808, he was married to Mrs. Marianne Lockwood, the widowed mother of five daughters and one son. Captain Symmes was more than a stepfather to the young Lockwoods. They were treated as his own, growing up in "perfect harmony" with the five children born to Symmes and their mother.

All of Symmes's army career was spent in such frontier outposts as Fort Coupee, Louisiana, Fort Adams (a Mississippi Territory fort south of Natchez), and New Orleans. While stationed at Fort Adams he engaged in a duel with a fellow officer who attempted to defame his character. This incident left Symmes with a stiff left wrist, but it did not impair his efficiency as a fighter. He later acquitted himself in a creditable manner during the War of 1812 in the Battle of Lundy's Lane, and in a sortie at Fort Erie, where it was said he singlehandedly spiked some British cannon after leading a charge against their position.

In 1816, when peace with Great Britain was restored, Symmes resigned from the army and moved his growing family to St. Louis. There he spent two unprofitable years as a Fox Indian trader and supplier of United States troops on the upper Mississippi. He next took up residence in Newport, Kentucky, devoting his life to constructing proofs for the theory he had earlier presented to the citizenry of the world.

Symmes, the theorist, believed the earth was composed of at least five hollow concentric spheres, with spaces and an atmosphere between, which were habitable on both their concave and convex surfaces. The earth, however, was not unique in the universe, for all the "celestial orbicular bodies . . . visible and invisible, which partake in any degree of a planetary nature, from the greatest to the smallest, from the sun down to the most blazing meteor or falling star" were also hollow. Even the most minute particles of matter in the atmosphere were similar. As Symmes explained, "every portion of infinite space, . . . is filled with an aerial elastic fluid, more subtile than common atmospheric air; and constituted of innumerable small concentric spheres, too minute to be visible to the organ of sight assisted by the most perfect microscope. . . ." [2] The elasticity of these minute particles accounted for atmospheric pressure, since they continually pressed on one another even though frequently changing their relative situations.

After publishing the outline of his theory on April 10, 1818, Symmes drafted a memoir in which he explained the formation of planets. It was his notion that the earth in a formless state began to rotate, and projectile force threw the matter outward from its axis. Gravity held it together or in form. A balance between projectile force and gravity, in fact, sustained all parts of the revolving mass at a certain distance from the axis. This fact also explained the irregularities on the face of the earth such as mountains, hills, rivers, islands, and continents.

In its fluid state, the earth was composed of elements of different densities. When it began to revolve, the heaviest masses were thrown out first and farthest, rising above the surface of the ocean. Mountains and islands were formed; clusters of islands massed together to become continents. If the substances composing the continents did not harden immediately, the interaction of the sun and changing temperatures transformed them into solid rock. Symmes was convinced the peaks of the Alps and the Andes were formed in this manner. Also, when one continent emerged, "another would naturally be produced simultaneously on the opposite side of the sphere, as an equipoise to the first, to keep equal the earth's motion; until all the heavy substances . . . [were] thrown out and united in a compact sphere." [3]

....

[2] *Symmes's Theory of Concentric Spheres; Demonstrating that the Earth is Hollow, Habitable Within, and Widely Open About the Poles.* By a Citizen of the United States (Cincinnati, 1826), p. 25.

[3] *Ibid.*, p. 46. See also the Memoir on Geometry in the *Western Spy*, Cincinnati, Oct. 3, 1818, 2; *Daily National Intelligencer*, Aug. 10, 1818, 3;

But if force projected the heaviest elements outward, what would prevent the internal concentric spheres from coalescing into a solid body? Symmes believed these spheres were composed of a "very light and elastic fluid, rarified in proportion to the gravity or condensing power of the exposed surfaces of the respective spheres. . . ."[4] Between them were midplane spaces filled with another volatile fluid somewhat heavier than the one within the spheres themselves. Thus they were suspended in space. Besides, oceans, continents, islands, and other solid matter extended from the external crust through the internal globes, serving as braces to support the earth in its spherical form.

Having adopted the theory of projectile force as an explanation of the formation of the earth, Symmes next reasoned that it would throw the elements some degrees from the poles. Isaac Newton believed the globe was flattened at the poles. The author of the theory of concentric spheres went a step further by maintaining that rotation would not only flatten the poles, but would cause the matter to gravitate toward the equator. This would protrude the equatorial regions and create yawning openings at the ends of the earth. The earth was thus an oblate spheroid whose crust was thick and compact at the equator, and thin and receding at the poles. Its openings were large and did not follow any particular degrees of latitude.

Symmes estimated the northern opening was 4,000 miles in diameter, while the one in the south was at least 2,000 miles larger. The edges or verges of these openings were closer to the equator on one side of the globe than on the other. For example, the northernmost point of the southern opening, or the point closest to the equator, was southeast of Madagascar in 34° S., 50° E. From this location in the Indian Ocean the verge passed near the Cape of Good Hope, across the Atlantic and Argentina, to the southernmost point, 46° S., 130° W., in the Pacific. From there it crossed the south island of New

---

and Thomas Tufts to Dr. Samuel L. Mitchill, Le Roy, Genesee County, N.Y., July 22, 1819, *Daily National Intelligencer*, Aug. 12, 1819, 2.

[4] Americus Symmes, comp., *The Symmes Theory of Concentric Spheres, Demonstrating that the Earth is Hollow, Habitable Within, and Widely Open About the Poles* (Louisville, Ky., 1878), p. 43.

Zealand and the northern part of Tasmania. In the north the point closest to the equator was in the Pacific, 50° N., 160° W., near the northwest coast of America, while the most distant location was in Iceland not far from Mount Hecla.

Because of the great size of these polar openings, Symmes believed the concave and convex surfaces of the concentric spheres would be lighted by the rays of the sun. If the sun was sufficiently high in the heavens, and if one of the inner spheres did not block its rays, the inner world would be illuminated, much like a house. This was certainly possible, according to the theorist, for sunlight entering a room through a tiny hole in a window shutter projected a large spot of sunshine on the opposite wall. Because the sun would shine through the northern and southern openings at alternate times of the day, a convert of Symmes's, Hugh Steel of Brownsville, Illinois, reasoned the "inhabitants of the inner surface . . . [could] have but two nights in the year, and those of but short duration, viz: when the sun is near to and about crossing the equinoctial line." [5]

Throughout his life Symmes diligently searched for evidence to prove his theory. His study of scientific manuals, explorers' journals, and encyclopedias convinced him that many phenomena of nature proved the hollowness of the earth. Among these testimonies, those connected with heavenly bodies were most important. Since all the major planets exhibited their concentric circles, there was little reason to doubt that the earth was constructed in the same manner. Saturn, Mars, and Jupiter provided visible evidence of their concentricity. Through a telescope it was not difficult to perceive the rings of Saturn, belts of Jupiter, and the alternating dark and light rings on Mars. These Symmes knew were the verges of their concentric spheres. The concentricity and emptiness of Venus, the sun, and the moon, however, were not as easily observed, except by a student of his theory. On Venus the depressions around the horns or cusps were the openings to her internal surfaces, while the cavities on the moon and the spots on the sun un-

---

[5] Hugh Steel to John Cleves Symmes, Brownsville, Jackson County, Illinois, Sept. 21, 1819, in the *Western Spy, and Cincinnati General Advertiser*, Oct. 16, 1819, 4.

doubtedly were fractures in their crusts, showing their internal emptiness. The theorist believed this evidence was valid because fallen meteors displayed concave and convex shapes. He explained, "The phenomena are precisely such as would occur, supposing the fireball to have been a small satellite, or erratic planet, at first fluid, which had become so condensed by the increased action of terrestrial gravity, occasioned by its sudden approach, as to cause its fluid parts to crystalize [sic] and form into, at least, three concentric spheres. . . ." [6]

Besides the concentricity of planets, Symmes employed the aurora borealis and the Magellanic Clouds in his demonstrations. Since the brilliant twilight in the north and south called the aurora was not explained, it must be caused by the polar openings. The Captain thought it might be produced by the rays of the sun projecting into the inner world through the southern opening. By two refractions at each opening, and by reflections from the inner concave surface, these rays would be seen in the north over the verge as a brilliant twilight. The Magellanic Clouds, on the other hand, were merely reflections of New Zealand, Australia, and Tasmania across the verge, seen only at night in the regions south of Magellan's Strait. Symmes felt that these continental islands reflected light and their images were thus projected.

Although Symmes maintained that this celestial evidence offered the most conclusive proof of his theory, certain terrestrial manifestations also were very important. The dip or variation of a magnetic compass needle in high latitudes was not understood, so this problem was embraced as confirmation. The theorist knew the true magnetic poles were not at the point where the "line of no variation" terminated, but were equidistant from it, directly beneath the highest points of the verges. Conversely, the real line of no variation was halfway between these poles. "The needle while it does not vary along the line to the right or the left, yet as it goes northward or

[6] *Symmes's Theory.* . . . By a Citizen of the United States, p. 52. See also Americus Symmes, *The Symmes Theory*, pp. 24–28; John Cleves Symmes to Anthony Lockwood, Pass Christianne, Aug. 24, 1817, in the John Cleves Symmes Papers, Draper Manuscripts, 1WW77, Wisconsin Historical Society, Madison; *ibid.*, 2WW34; and the *Liberty Hall and Cincinnati Gazette*, Nov. 21, 1823, 3.

southward from the magnetic equator, it is attracted towards the true magnetic poles lying under the highest part of the verges; and so the dip is increased till it reaches the apex of the verge, where it is the greatest." [7] He believed the needle actually indicated the center of the polar opening rather than the axis of the earth.

Other unexplained terrestrial phenomena—volcanoes and earthquakes—were employed as testimony also. The rarefied fluid or gas escaping from the mid-plane spaces between the internal concentric spheres was responsible for both. Volcanoes were caused when gas, seeping into the atmosphere through a small aperture or crevice, burst into flame, while earthquakes resulted from expansion near the earth's crust. This expansion was sudden, creating fissures through which the gas escaped. When the crust settled again, the earth trembled, because the quantity of gas in the mid-plane spaces had been lessened substantially.

Certain conditions in nature provided additional authentication for the theorist. Some of this evidence was provided by proselytes and friends. Dr. Samuel L. Mitchill, the noted physician-scientist from New York, who encouraged the Captain, recognized that God, the Creator, displayed the highest possible degree of perfection in his world. His was a great system of creative economy, a system in which space was not wasted. Why then would the Creator have formed a solid earth? Many phenomena answered this question. Large bones, skulls, veins, arteries, the stomach, intestines, and the windpipe were hollow. But the foremost example of hollowness in nature was the egg, which often contained other eggs inside. Here indeed was visible proof of concentric spheres. "The egg, . . . has been called a microcosm, or 'little world,' and not without reason," Mitchill concluded. [8]

Even though Symmes overlooked these so-called "analogous proofs," he found much to corroborate his theory in the same quarter. Rees's *Encyclopedia* served as an indispensable source

----

[7] P. Clark, "The Symmes Theory of the Earth," *Atlantic Monthly*, XXXI (April, 1873), 475.

[8] Samuel L. Mitchill to John Cleves Symmes, New York, Sept. 19, 1819, in the *Western Spy, and Cincinnati General Advertiser*, Oct. 9, 1819, 4.

of this data. Its articles suggested that all migratory fishes and animals journey to the interior of the earth before winter sets in. Reindeer, for instance, head northward during the month of October, in herds of 8,000 to 10,000, choosing the nearest route to the fertile and habitable lands on the inner surfaces. In the spring they returned fat and healthy, having fed on lush grasses. Musk oxen, seals, and various fishes engage in similar migrations. Symmes's son Americus proclaimed: "If we were to judge . . . the internal surface of the sphere by its animal production . . . we should conclude that the internal region of the earth is . . . much more favorable to the support of animal life, as the reindeer is larger than our deer, and the white bear is larger than our bear, and, consequently, we must conclude that there are more salubrious climates and better countries within than any we have yet discovered without." [9]

This and additional evidence caused Symmes to postulate that the Indian races of North and South America originated in the internal world. When James Clark Ross was exploring the Arctic in 1818, he met Indians who told him they had come from the far north, obviously the interior of the earth, where many people lived. Indian mythology, moreover, tended to verify this assumption. In the account of Indian legends given by the Pennsylvania German Heckewelder, a Mohawk chieftain was credited with the story that one of his warriors accidentally found a hole, emerged from the interior regions, and discovered a deer which was fat and healthy. He returned to his people, described the advantages of living on the external crust of the earth, and brought some of them out from their internal haunts to the exterior, where they began a new life and planted corn. These facts led the theorist to assume that the inner world was composed chiefly of land "inhabited by human beings of various casts and of various grades of civilization, none, however, being much civilized. . . ." [10]

John Cleves Symmes considered these proofs as commanding

---

[9] Americus Symmes, *The Symmes Theory*, pp. 33–34. See also John Cleves Symmes to the Editors of the National Intelligencer, Newport, Ky., Jan., 1822, Symmes Papers, 2WW30.

[10] See the *Daily National Intelligencer*, Aug. 4, 1825, 2, and Sept. 13, 1819, 3; the *Western Spy, and Cincinnati General Advertiser*, Aug. 2, 1819, 4;

evidence, but much to his chagrin most scientists refused to recognize his theory even to the point of discussing it. He knew silence was not approval in this instance, and made frequent appeals to scientific societies asking their members to judge the merits of his thinking. After meeting little success with petitions to individual societies, a request was addressed to all the learned societies of the United States in March, 1822, requesting them "to record in their several journals—and ultimately anounce [sic] to the public their dissent to . . . [his] Theory of the System of the Earth (and of the System of other planets,) so far as they do or may reject it; or so far as they decline to approve it on a general scale. . . ." [11] He charged them to hand down undisputable evidence of the doubt and apathy with which they had received his theory. Symmes thus threw down his gauntlet, but no scientist picked it up.

The most serious criticisms were insensitive strictures published in newspapers by amateur scientists, many of whom merely relished an argument. The most persistent of these debaters was a man named Preston, who wrote under the initials "D. P.," and became the unsolicited leader of people who thought Symmes was a plagiarist and the creator of an outlandish theory which did not subscribe to the laws of gravity. "D. P." himself held the opinion that the Captain was the "humble copyist of the absurdities of Dr. Halley." His adherents went further by declaring that he might even have copied the German mathematician, Leonhardt Euler, who subscribed to similar views, or the hollow earth system presented in Eaton Stannard Barrett's satire, the *Heroine*. Symmes abruptly dismissed these allegations by declaring that he had not heard Halley's or similar ideas before he issued his pronouncement in April, 1818.

Regarding the law of gravity, "D. P." and his friends were convinced Symmes's hollow earth could not maintain its shape. It would cave in and become a solid sphere, since the poles were attracted to one another and nothing could keep them

The Commentator, Frankfort, Ky., March 5, 1819, 2; and *Symmes's Theory. . . . By a Citizen of the United States*, p. 83.

[11] "A General Request to the Learned Societies of America," Newport, Ky., March 25, 1822, in the Symmes Papers, 2WW38.

apart. Centrifugal force after all was not as great as centripetal, and could not prevent the poles from converging. A more serious criticism was offered by a person who invited Symmes to explain the reason the earth always cast a circular shadow on the moon. This would have been impossible if the earth was widely open at the poles. The Captain did not reply to this query, but he attempted to answer "D. P.'s" strictures. Rotary motion, he contended, would cause the earth to flatten at the poles "and project and accumulate towards the equator" much like "a whirling soap bubble." [12]

While "D. P." criticized the theory of concentric spheres because it did not conform to scientific laws, a citizen of Lynchburg, New York, who called himself "Galileo," claimed Symmes's ideas were based on principles which contradicted the Mosaic theory of creation as presented in the Book of Genesis. He was convinced the interior of the earth could not be lighted by the rays of the sun. For this reason it would be more suited for residence by perverse spirits than by beings who were thought to have a civilization and culture. "Galileo" argued that the earth was a solid sphere whose surface was changed by the great flood. If Symmes believed otherwise, he was an atheist.

Answers to "Galileo's" arguments were supplied not only by the theorist, but by several of his proselytes as well. Symmes challenged "Galileo" to present any passage in the Bible which contradicted his theory. After all, the first verse of Genesis reads, "In the beginning God created the heaven and the earth." Does this preclude any particular formation? Definitely not! He himself was reasonably familiar with the Bible, having learned to read from it.

Thomas S. Hinde, a proselyte of the theory from Newport, Kentucky, thought the Greek translation of the Book of Genesis actually supported the idea of a hollow earth. In the second verse of the first chapter, the Greek words *Theos* and *Beos* were translated as form and void. To Hinde, *Beos* or void could also have meant hollow or empty. Another adherent countered religious criticisms by dismissing them as unwarranted abuse of a scientific matter.

----

[12] *Western Spy, and Cincinnati General Advertiser*, Oct. 2, 1819, 2.

In answering his censors John Cleves Symmes always tried to keep his arguments on the highest possible level. For this reason he refused to answer ridicule and sarcasm. Many detractors derided the author personally. One capsuled the thoughts of many when he said, "If the captain is so much afflicted with the *cacoethes scribendi* that he must compose, and that composition must be published, it does appear to me, . . . that he is in duty bound to select subjects not entirely beyond his own comprehension, and so far to conform to the established rules of philosophizing, as to render himself intelligible if not conclusive." [13] But the most auspicious attempt to disparage the hollow earth theory was published in the form of a journal by a noted navigator, Adam Seaborn, who set out to discover the internal world in 1817.

To reach the south polar opening Seaborn employed a steam-driven vessel operated not unlike a Roman trireme. After entering the internal world, the explorers sighted an island they named Symzonia, inhabited by a race of men five feet tall. These strange personages were not unfriendly, and sent out a delegation to greet the Americans. "One . . . came to the threshold of the platform [where the ship was moored], and, raising his hand to his forehead, . . . brought it down to the point of his nose, and waved it gracefully in salutation." [14]

Seaborn and the others were not allowed to remain long in Symzonia, because only their excessive desire for profit had induced them to come there. Before they departed they learned the Symzonians had won their lands many years earlier from another internal race, the Belzubians. They had vowed then to bar all discordant elements from their possessions. Their government was headed by a chief with the title Best Man, who held office for life. They had a bicameral legislature composed of three orders of Worthies, the Good, Wise, and Useful, who enacted laws which were strict only insofar as they banished to the North Pole any citizens who practiced intrigue and backstairs influence. These people had developed a high culture largely because they were unencumbered with taxes. Seaborn ascertained that "the en-

[13] *Liberty Hall and Cincinnati Gazette,* Oct. 29, 1819, 2.
[14] Captain Adam Seaborn, *Symzonia; Voyage of Discovery* (New York, 1820), p. 107.

joyments of this refined people were intellectual and pure—not the debasing gratifications of animal passions and sensual appetites." [15] He was truly sorry to leave them.

Seaborn's *Symzonia* became sufficiently known to merit recognition in the *North American Review*, where the reviewer continued the satire. Symmes's views were authentic, he said, because "that which is good for much, whether in the unorganized, the vegetable, animal, or intellectual world, carries its merit within; and external beauties and superficial merits are proverbially transitory and worthless; either found to be unattended with interior worth, or at any rate far less permanent, and liable to rust, mildew, and decay." [16] He thought the earth should be viewed as a great fig with an unpromising black skin, but a nutritious pulp, and he facetiously urged his readers to give up their niggard support of the theory. The Captain's name was destined to go down in history ahead of Columbus's.

Throughout his career Symmes offered various proposals for an exploring voyage. He believed he could reach the northern opening by following the tracks made by reindeer in their migrations over the ice from Siberia, or by sailing in via the Arctic rivers whose sources were within the earth. The southern opening was even more accessible. It could be entered by water near Australia. Symmes suggested two expeditions should be equipped, one by sea to the south, the other by land to the north.

The suggestion of a Kentucky citizen that Symmes and his explorers utilize the facilities of the Mammoth Cave rather than make the hazardous journey across the ice from Siberia characterized the public reception of his pleas. In February, 1821, he called upon Senator William A. Trimble of Kentucky, a former army officer, to make application to the President, the Senate, or the House for an exploring outfit of two strong sloops-of-war and a steam vessel to sail into the northern opening. This request was made after the British explorer Parry had returned from the Arctic without discovering the internal world. His failure pleased Symmes, who believed a worthwhile trade could be opened there, and wanted American citizens, not British, to benefit from it.

The theorist's appeal reached Trimble when Congress was

---

[15] Seaborn, *Symzonia*, p. 182. See also pp. 124, 144, 197.

[16] *North American Review*, XIII (July, 1821), 136.

about to adjourn, and the Senator was reluctant to present it because of the depleted condition of the United States Treasury and the absence of support for a Symmesian expedition. A year later the Captain again presented a petition to the Senate, where it was tabled without debate and allowed to remain there.

These failures should have convinced Symmes that his task was hopeless, but they only caused him to work harder to advance his plans. On July 29, 1822, he addressed a circular to many newspapers asking their townspeople to subscribe memorials favoring an expedition and to send them to Congress. He called for "two vessels, well found for the purpose, furnished with suitable materials and preparations to enable the party to travel, when beyond the temperate parallels, either by land or on the ice, and provisioned for two years." It was his notion to take several "scientific and enterprising men," provided with suitable instruments and apparatus, to make investigations. Symmes now was confident he could find the true verge, which was "located within the civilized regions of Europe, and considerably to the south of some settlements of white people in America. . . ." [17]

Although the reception of Symmes's circular was halfhearted, he gained more subscribers than at any previous time. Enough citizens of Kentucky, South Carolina, Ohio, and Pennsylvania signed petitions to merit bringing the matter before the House. But these memorials suffered the same fate as earlier ones, and were tabled after a few wiseacres suggested they might be sent to the Committees on Foreign Relations or Commerce.

The years 1821, 1822, and 1823 were filled with disappointment for John Cleves Symmes. A lingering illness had sapped his strength, while his efforts to bring the petitions before Congress had cost him his savings and patrimony. In 1824, to live more frugally, he was forced to move his family to the few acres he held near Hamilton, Ohio. An unsuccessful attempt to get the Ohio Assembly to grant a resolution approving his theory was followed by a limited series of lectures around Cincinnati and Hamilton. Most of Symmes's converts, including several influential citizens, resided in southern Ohio. One, James McBride, was a trustee of Miami University in Oxford, a noted bibliophile, and a supervising commissioner of the Miami and Erie Canal, while

[17] *Liberty Hall and Cincinnati Gazette,* Aug. 3, 1822, 2.

another, Bellamy Storer, was a prominent lawyer and a justice in the Ohio Supreme Court. Both helped change Symmes's luck. McBride dedicated himself to the task of synthesizing and clarifying the theorist's unintelligible scientific hokum into an understandable book, which was published under the authorship of a "Citizen of the United States." Storer launched him on a successful lecture tour in February, 1824.

When Symmes's stock was lowest, Storer stepped forward and implored the citizens of Cincinnati not to judge anyone rashly, nor to doubt a person's views merely because of the skepticism of the age. He said, "If the falling of an apple suggested the doctrine of gravitation, why should we cavil at the system of a hollow globe, when its untiring advocate can exhibit a catalogue of facts to support it, numerous and plausible?" In Storer's opinion, Symmes was a man who had lived to partake of the ordeal by sarcasm inflicted by those denying the soundness of his principles. To his credit he had "passed the ordeal unhurt, and matured his system to a degree of comparative perfection." [18]

These elegant words did not fall on deaf ears. Late in March, 1824, the citizens of Cincinnati staged a benefit for the Captain in the Columbia Street Theatre. A company of amateur thespians enacted a five-act melodrama, while a poet, Moses Brooks, recited some verses he had written about Symmes's discoveries ending in these laudatory words:

> Has not Columbia *one* aspiring son,
> By whom th' unfading laurel may be won?
> Yes! history's pen may yet inscribe the name
> of SYMMES to grace her future scroll of fame.

Flushed with success, the Captain extended his lecture tour to the Kentucky towns, Frankfort, Lexington, Newport, Louisville, and Maysville, where he was met by large and enthusiastic audiences.

Early in 1825 a scathing rebuke rebounded in Symmes's favor. The narrative of Major Stephen Long's expedition to Lake Winnipeg and the Lake of the Woods was published. In it Major Long was credited with having described Symmes, whom he had met at Newark, Ohio, in 1823, as a man of partial sanity whose

[18] Elmore Symmes, "John Cleves Symmes, the Theorist," *Southern Bivouac: A Monthly Literary and Historical Magazine*, V, n.s. II (Feb., 1887), 562.

"unregulated mind" made him "pervert to the support of an evidently absurd theory all the facts, which, by close study, he has been enabled to collect from a vast number of authorities." [19] It was Long's contention that the people of the United States listened to this visionary only because they were sympathetic to a retired army officer who had served his country gallantly during the War of 1812.

When Symmes read Long's remarks, he addressed a public letter to his attacker, who thereby denied making the statements. To show his friendship he not only testified to the Captain's sanity, but also provided the information that Leavitt Harris, late consul of the United States in St. Petersburg, had said Count Romanzov, the Russian Chancellor, was interested in the theory. The Russians, in fact, were thinking of giving the American command of an expedition to the northern opening. Symmes immediately opened correspondence with Romanzov, pledging himself to Russia if the United States government failed to provide an appropriation for exploration.

The Captain felt the Russian offer could be used to turn the tide of opinion in his favor and he determined to visit Washington after lecturing on his theory in the Atlantic states. The editors of the *Liberty Hall and Cincinnati Gazette* were happy to hear of the tour, for they believed it would have one good effect —convincing the "eastern doubters" that John Cleves Symmes was of perfectly sound mind. In September, 1825, the author of the theory of concentric spheres departed from Hamilton with his stepson, Anthony Lockwood, and an enterprising young proselyte, Jeremiah N. Reynolds.

....

[19] William H. Keating, comp., *Narrative of an Expedition to the Source of St. Peter's River, Lake Winnipeek, Lake of the Woods, &c. Performed in the Year 1823* . . . (2 vols., London, 1825), I, 45.

chapter six

REYNOLDS BEGINS
THE CAMPAIGN

In 1826, an aging and infirm John Cleves Symmes confided to his wife, Marianne, "My mistake was in taking a stranger into my confidence. The lesson has been learned too late." [1] This confession concerned the conduct of Jeremiah N. Reynolds, a stocky man of medium height, who shared the platform with Symmes on his lecture tour of 1825 and 1826. Before a year had gone by, Reynolds had taken the center of the stage and the author of the theory of concentric spheres had assumed the stand-in role before their national audience.

From the time his family was taken from Cumberland County, Pennsylvania, to Clinton County, Ohio, the attainment of public notice was an obsession with Reynolds. The year was 1808, and he had recently acquired a stepfather, Job Jeffries. This man, a product of the frontier environment, thought a mastery of the tasks associated with farming was the principal goal in life, and he steadfastly refused to help his stepson gain a common school education. Reynolds's legacies were a deep-rooted sense of inferiority and an abiding dislike for Job Jeffries.

Before his fourteenth birthday, Jeremiah Reynolds had left his parental home in order to attend school. This required many disheartening hours of menial labor, which augmented his sense of inferiority. His dislike for Job Jeffries likewise increased. Every association with him was viewed as personal condemnation. Reynolds particularly hated being referred to as one of "Job's

---

[1] Elmore Symmes, "John Cleves Symmes," *Southern Bivouac*, V, 685.

oxen." During a log-rolling, when he was unable to do his share
of the work, his associates gleefully testified that "Job's ox" was a
calf. Reynolds answered defiantly: "Gentlemen, I have no father
to guide and protect me in life, and you have had your fun with
me to-day. Many of you are old enough to be ashamed of thus
rallying a young and unprotected boy; but, . . . you know little
about him of whom you are making fun to-day, for I assure you
the time is coming when you will feel proud that you ever rolled
logs with Jeremiah N. Reynolds. . . ." [2]

The fulfillment of this promise was begun when Reynolds obtained employment as a schoolteacher in Wilmington, Ohio,
where some of his pupils undoubtedly were children of those
who had previously derided him. In 1818, he was made a Master
Mason in the Wilmington Lodge, and the next year he became
a student in Ohio University at Athens. A lack of funds forced
Reynolds to leave the university after three years without receiving a degree, and he returned to teaching. In less than a year,
however, he gave this up to become editor of Wilmington's only
newspaper, the *Spectator*, an esteemed position in a small western
town. John Cleves Symmes provided Reynolds his first opportunity to leave Ohio, and it is probable Reynolds accepted the offer
to accompany the theorist as a lecturer with no misgivings. "Job's
ox" was escaping the mediocrity he so greatly feared.

Symmes and Reynolds lectured in some of the larger Ohio
towns—Lebanon, Xenia, Springfield, Chillicothe, Zanesville, and
Newark—before carrying their campaign for recognition and an
exploring expedition into western Pennsylvania, where they took
different routes toward Philadelphia. It is difficult to trace
Symmes's course because ill-health forced him to lecture sporadi-
cally, and most of the newspapers reported the plaudits Jeremiah
Reynolds was receiving.

From the time Reynolds delivered his first lecture in Washington, Pennsylvania, late in October, 1825, his tour in that state was
charted by public appeal. Much of his success resulted from
depositions of the Reverend Mr. Andrew Wylie, President of
Washington (now Washington and Jefferson) College, who

------

[2] *History of Clinton County, Ohio, Containing a History of the County;
Its Townships, Cities, Towns, Schools, Churches* . . . (Chicago, 1882), p.
581.

thought Symmes's theory opposed no law of nature. In Reverend Wylie's estimation, it was "in the strictest accordance with the economy of Nature," for the character of divine wisdom throughout the universe was the production of the greatest variety by the "fewest elements and the simplest means." [3]

The approbation of this esteemed clergyman and educator brought Reynolds invitations to lecture in Pittsburgh, Greensburg, Uniontown, and some of the smaller towns nearby. Symmes's partner proved a capable speaker. "His delivery was monotonous, but what he said was solid, and his air in a high degree respectful and earnest and withal very sad, as though some great sorrow lay upon his heart, which won . . . sympathy, and this without knowing anything of his history." [4]

Reynolds remained in western Pennsylvania longer than he had planned, for large and enthusiastic audiences presented him with acclaim and substantial collections at each stop. The report of a Pittsburgh writer reflects the climate of opinion this ambitious young man had created for Symmesian views. He thought it was "really amusing to witness the progress of public opinion," for in the beginning Symmes was laughed at and considered a madman. Now, however, almost every intelligent man in Pittsburgh seemed anxious to show he was a proselyte. Reynolds, he asserted, had created a new light by provoking "the inquisitive feeling which characterizes alike the savage and the sage, and which prompts to the investigation of new principles. . . ." [5] He urged the young lecturer to present his views in Washington in order to acquire government sponsorship of an expedition. Even if the theory was proved untrue, important discoveries could be made which would reflect on the national character. Reynolds left Pittsburgh in January, 1826, to join Symmes in Philadelphia.

The lecturers had planned to celebrate their success or decry their failure in Philadelphia. There was ample reason for celebration, but before Symmes and Reynolds prepared their toasts,

[3] See Andrew Wylie to J. N. Reynolds, Washington, Pa., Nov. 1, 1825, in the *Daily National Intelligencer,* Nov. 18, 1825, 3.

[4] Henry Howe, *Historical Collections of Ohio* (3 vols., Columbus, Ohio, 1891), I, 432.

[5] See the extract from the Pittsburgh *Mercury* in the *Liberty Hall and Cincinnati Gazette,* Dec. 27, 1825, 3.

they came into open disagreement over the destination of the expedition. Symmes had centered his attention on north polar exploration, while Reynolds had become interested in the South Pole.

During the many months spent formulating intelligible lectures from the scientific conglomeration Symmes called his theory, Reynolds concluded that an Arctic expedition lacked the appeal of one to the Antarctic. Symmes had found many of his proofs in journals of Arctic explorers like Cook, Parry, and Hearne, mainly because similar evidence did not exist concerning the polar regions in the south. Obviously the Antarctic had been neglected and remained unknown.

Reynolds was definitely not circumspect in his dealings with Symmes, who was appalled at the effrontery of his young partner. In spite of Reynolds's entreaties, the author of the theory of concentric spheres refused to alter his views, because he had never seriously considered an expedition to the Antarctic. Besides, the now sickly Symmes viewed any reorganization of his ideas as an insurmountable task.

The first public statements regarding the argument came from Reynolds, who announced the split occurred because Symmes's folksy style of lecturing had little appeal for city audiences whose support was needed for exploration. This was undoubtedly an attempt to divert attention to Symmes rather than to his theory, since Reynolds probably feared the consequences an open disagreement on Symmesian views would create. His effort to build a smoke screen was short-lived, however, for the hot-tempered former captain reported the true nature of the dispute to the public while expressing his intention of publicly denouncing Reynolds. In a fit of anger he even suggested reconciling their differences in a duel, but saner minds prevailed and the lecturers went their separate ways.

Surprisingly, neither Symmes nor Reynolds was badly injured by their clash. The opponents of the theory chose to satirize rather than malign. These attacks were epitomized by the editors of the New York *National Advocate,* who suggested that Congress grant two appropriations, one to Reynolds for an Antarctic expedition, and another to Symmes for exploration in the north. They wanted each to be furnished with cannon, so the disgruntled lecturers could fight their duel through the holes in the poles with snowballs for ammunition.

After leaving Philadelphia, according to the *Liberty Hall and Cincinnati Gazette,* John Cleves Symmes delivered his first lecture in Washington on February 18, 1826, and achieved more than moderate success. Since this report probably came from one of Symmes's party, it is more likely he was received only with respect by those who attended his speech. The theorist, unlike Reynolds, never was able to arouse his listeners. The month of March was spent campaigning for recognition in the nation's capital and in many of the nearby Maryland towns.

Symmes lectured before a New York audience which included Dr. Samuel L. Mitchell and some of his associates from the Lyceum of Natural History on April 10. Although his listeners were numerous, much of his success was contingent on the scientists' presence. New Yorkers, like other citizens, thought he was a "very interesting looking old gentleman," possessed of a "dark countenance, a face rather thin, a sharp nose, and as fine a high, philosophical forehead as a phrenologist could wish." His language was "far from being correct," but his modesty, simplicity, and earnestness of manner were "irresistibly pleasing." While lecturing, he was as "familiar as a kind hearted father might be supposed to be to his children." [6] In all, deference rather than approval was the keynote of their attitude. After leaving the city, Symmes headed northward, where he spoke in most of the large New England towns and presented a series of lectures at Union College in Schenectady.

When the disgusted Symmes had departed from Philadelphia, Reynolds had gone directly to New York, where he received praise from the noted Yale scientist, Benjamin Silliman. Silliman credited him with being "pure in his diction, systematic in the argument of his matter, [and] judicious in the selection of his facts. . . ." In short, "Mr. Reynolds . . . handled his subject like an accomplished scholar." [7] The professor's panegyrics were shared by other members of the intelligentsia who urged Reynolds to present his arguments in Washington immediately in

------

[6] *Liberty Hall and Cincinnati Gazette,* April 25, 1826, 3.

[7] Silliman's statements are in the *New England Palladium & Commercial Advertiser,* Boston, June 16, 1826, 1.

order to capitalize on his popularity. Soon notices appeared announcing his intention of speaking there early in August. The lectures were advertised as dealing with an expedition whose object was "discoveries in the polar cosmogony, the interests of science, and of industrious pursuit, of which the whale and seal fisheries, . . . constitute a part." [8] These pronouncements marked the beginning of Reynolds's almost singlehanded propaganda movement for an Antarctic exploring expedition divorced from Symmes's hypothesis.

After speaking in Washington a third time, on August 10, the aspiring Reynolds laid the foundation for a campaign to obtain memorials supporting an Antarctic expedition by more thoroughly introducing himself to the public through the medium of the press. A message was sent to eastern newspapers presenting an outline of his arguments. Reynolds outspokenly opposed northern exploration, because all efforts to solve the mysteries of the globe had been made to improve the northern whale fishery or discover a northwest passage. Nineteenth-century explorers had literally overrun the Arctic, and consequently had overlooked the Antarctic. He was convinced a crew of Nantucket seamen could discover important territories there, even though Captain James Weddell had penetrated the ice pack to the 74th parallel of south latitude. Was it beyond comprehension to believe that islands of great size or even a continent existed near the South Pole? Indeed it was not! Above all, Reynolds exhorted, "the renewal of inquiry, at this time, and by the citizens of this country, with the view to determine the figure of the earth, collect interesting facts in natural history, open channels for commercial enterprise, . . . would be followed by the most important results, tending to the immediate honor and advantage of our common country, and to the world at large." [9]

From the middle of August, 1826, to February, 1827, Reynolds spoke before civic groups and state legislatures in almost every eastern state from Massachusetts to South Carolina, and he showed himself an adept propagandist. He was articulate. His lectures were the product of a mature intellect and were adjusted

----

[8] *National Intelligencer*, Aug. 3, 1826, 3.

[9] *National Intelligencer*, Aug. 17, 1826, 4. See also the *Liberty Hall and Cincinnati Gazette*, Sept. 1, 1826, 2.

to the temper of the times. The propagandist's most persuasive arguments were patriotic presentments in which he attempted to make the exploring expedition a national duty.

Jeremiah Reynolds was not an incurable nationalist, but he was an insatiable opportunist. The United States, he held, had become a powerful nation "capable of defending on the land or at sea, the blessings won by the war for independence," with ships in every foreign port. Americans were masters of everything that "relates to commerce and navigation and the useful, or more immediately necessary arts," but they had never directed their attention "to profound and laborious research into the figure of the earth." Reynolds claimed it was a national responsibility to "return light for light" to those nations of Europe whose powerful exertions for the attainment of scientific and geographical knowledge had brought themselves honor and profits while conferring innumerable benefits on the "human family." Since enlightenment gives power and superiority to nations, the United States could not be "consistent with her true character, [and] remain an idle and indifferent spectator, while other nations are successfully extending the bounds of human knowledge." Reynolds implored his listeners to appeal to Congress for an expedition to further science, and "add something to the common stock of general improvement" by exploring that "interesting and extensive field of enterprise, in the southern hemisphere." [10]

At all times and in all places, Reynolds attuned his ideas to the interests of his audiences. For instance, after discussing the business of an expedition for the men, he often appealed specifically to the women, concluding his addresses with allusions to the patroness of Columbus: "To the ladies who have honoured us with their attendance our acknowledgements are doubly due. . . . This country with all its boasted privileges and high destinies, owes its discovery to the patronage of a single female, Isabella, queen of Spain; who, to the imperishable honour of her sex, even pledged her jewels to sustain the

----

[10] See the memorial from the citizens of Washington County, Maryland, to Congress, Nov., 1826, in the Records of the Department of the Navy, Naval Records and Library Collection, R.G. 45, Subject File—OC Cruises and Voyages (Special), National Archives. The same file includes memorials from Virginia, Pennsylvania, Ohio, and Delaware. Hereafter cited as RDN.

expense of an adventure, which gave to Leon a new world, and to us the happy land in which we live." [11]

These impassioned pleas for patriotism aroused the citizenry of the cities he visited. One lady from Charleston, South Carolina, envisioning herself a nineteenth-century Isabella, donated $50.00 toward equipping the expedition, while two others presented the lecturer with a specially made American flag they said reflected the national glory. Reynolds made the most of these public displays by presenting printed memorials to his listeners for their signatures, and these were forwarded to Congress as visible evidence of the wants of the public.

As the number of Reynolds's supporters grew, newspaper editors fell into line by approving his plans. The editor of the New York *National Advocate* declared that the expedition was no Utopian enterprise, while the editorial pages of Philadelphia's *Franklin Repository* carried the opinion that few individuals could "resist the reasoning in favor of extending scientific research to the South Seas," for it was founded on "*liberal* ground." In their estimation, the United States must embark on a course which could make it deserving of the "thanks of the human race." [12]

With memorials and newspaper editorials as depositions of the expedition's approval, Reynolds next turned to the legislatures of the states he visited for resolutions favoring his plan. Delaware, Maryland, North and South Carolina, New York, Pennsylvania, and others responded. A select committee of the Pennsylvania legislature reflected opinions of other legislative bodies when it described the expedition as one of which no extravagant feelings or expectations were entertained. Although it might not record "*deeds* of wonder," its backers were certain it would "be the means of acquiring much useful information in the hydrography and geography of the Antarctic regions; as well as many important observations, on the atmospherical, magnetical, and electrical phenomena. . . ." [13]

----

[11] *New-York Mirror, and Ladies Literary Gazette*, VI (Oct. 11, 1828), 111.

[12] The extract from this newspaper is quoted in J. N. Reynolds, *Remarks on a Review of Symmes' Theory, which Appeared in the American Quarterly Review* (Washington, 1827), p. 56.

[13] *Ibid.*, p. 69. See also *Niles' Weekly Register*, XXXI (Nov. 25, 1826), 202; and the *National Intelligencer*, June 16, 1827, 3, and Dec. 29, 1827, 3.

A confident Jeremiah N. Reynolds appeared in Baltimore during September, 1827. He was no longer merely a propagandist pleading for national exploration, for the lionizing crowds had contributed funds for a private expedition. With his goal thus close at hand, he became an ambitious planner who had come to Baltimore to woo more of her citizens to his scheme by playing off their particularistic sentiments against those of the people of New York.

On September 23, Reynolds published a letter to the citizens of Baltimore in *Niles' Weekly Register* announcing his intention of contracting with one of their shipbuilders, James Beacham, for the construction of an exploring vessel, provided they contributed more money in support of a cruise than the people of New York. This bit of arrogance was an obvious attempt to gain money and support from merchant classes, but it got Reynolds absolutely nothing. He had given up the idea by the time he reached Washington late in 1827.

The propagandist punctuated his arrival in the nation's capital by answering a review of James McBride's synthesis of Symmes's theory, published in the March number of the *American Quarterly Review*. This essay, his first published, was more than an effort to remove Antarctic exploration irrevocably from any association with the hollow earth concept. It was a declaration of personal success, embodying an outline of his popular lecture tour, a presentation of editorial tributes to his plan, and a description of the type of expedition he favored.

Reynolds said he had learned while lecturing that many citizens, legislators, and editors were more than willing to support an expedition devoted to increasing the bounds of human enlightenment, but not to prove a theory. In every city, town, and hamlet he visited, his proposal for exploration was welcomed as a liberal scheme for the expansion of geographical knowledge.

To convince the economy-minded, Reynolds had argued that Congress should appropriate funds only for a modest expedition. A costly one, in fact, would serve as a detriment to the satisfaction of objectives. It was absolutely unnecessary to fashion a squadron on British models with vessels of 350 to 450 tons, furnished with luxuries such as a press to print articles on London styles. "Plain Republicans" could well afford to do without such superfluities. Two well-braced ships of only 200 tons provisioned for two years could make the discoveries demanded. Chances for success were limitless. The enthusiastic publicist even was willing to declare the expedition worthwhile if its members succeeded "in throwing a *harpoon, catching a seal, or chasing a whale* nearer the South Pole than any other Nation or People had done. . . ." It should be sent out "without making any more *parade* than old Nantucket's sons do, when they go a sealing." [14]

These views also had been reiterated to gain the attention of congressmen. The ubiquitous President John Quincy Adams testified to the adequacy of his means of communication when he said Reynolds's "lectures . . . have been well attended, and much approved as exhibitions of genius and science." [15] He hoped he might accelerate the approach of the expedition, but he was sure it would have no backing in Congress even though many memorials showed its powerful public support.

This Reynolds was determined to avert. On January 22, 1828, he sent a letter containing demands from citizens of Albany, New York; Charleston, South Carolina; Raleigh, North Carolina; and Maryland to Andrew Stevenson, Speaker of the House of Representatives. Later, it was referred to the Committee on Naval Affairs together with memorials from some friends of exploration in Ohio and the Massachusetts whaling centers, Nantucket and New Bedford. The chairman, Michael Hoffman (New York), then called upon Reynolds to submit a discussion of the advantages exploration would provide for overseas trade.

Hoffman's request was timed perfectly, for Reynolds had recently returned from a trip to some of the New England whaling centers, where he had collected information from logbooks and from "frequent conversations with intelligent men long acquainted with . . . trade." These talks had even more convinced him of the attractiveness of Antarctic exploration and the capriciousness of Symmes's theory. In New England, Reynolds was like a young man beginning his higher education. Broad vistas

[14] Reynolds, *Remarks*, p. 72. The review of McBride's book was published in the *American Quarterly Review*, I (March, 1827), 235–53.

[15] *Memoirs of John Quincy Adams, Comprising Portions of His Diary from 1795 to 1848* (12 vols., ed. by Charles Francis Adams, Philadelphia, 1874–77), VII, 168.

were opened to him. Among other things, he apparently learned for the first time that the maritime enterprises of the American people were not confined to the Antarctic or to Europe, but were burgeoning in the Pacific as well. The fleet from New England ports in the Pacific numbered 232 vessels employing 2,352 seamen, an important nursery for the seamen of the United States Navy. Interests there were enormous, so the Pacific had to be included in the surveys of the expedition.

Citizens of the coast cities were forthright in declaring the need for improvement in the fur seal trade and in whaling, but they emphasized that the establishment of new markets was of greater importance. Fisheries in high latitudes might be made more profitable. The mackerel fishery, for example, which had been expanding in importance, could be made even more lucrative if markets for this fish were opened in South America. An expedition could be the instrument for inducing Latin Americans to change their diet on fast days from vegetables to fish, and for acquainting Pacific islanders with manufactured articles from the United States. It was for "our interest and for our *honor* to be well acquainted with the *capacities* of the globe; to see what resources can be drawn from that *common* of nations—the ocean." [16]

Exploration in the southern hemisphere still was uppermost in Reynolds's mind, however. There, he reasoned, a United States expedition could make signal contributions to the knowledge of the world. "There are more than a million and a half square miles entirely unknown, and a coast of more than three hundred degrees of longitude, in which the antarctic circle has never been approached; there are immense regions within the comparatively temperate latitudes but partially known, and which deserve further attention; and, for aught we know, countries corresponding to Lapland, Norway, part of Sweden, and the northern parts of Siberia, in Asia, may still exist in the Southern hemisphere." [17]

After considering Reynolds's statements, Chairman Hoffman invited Samuel Southard to present his opinions respecting ex-

----

[16] 20 Cong., 1 Sess., *House Report* 209, 10.

[17] *Ibid.*, 11.

ploration. The Secretary of the Navy was almost as enthusiastic as the propagandist. He thought an expedition was more than expedient and offered arguments closely paralleling those of Reynolds to support this conclusion. Southard also cautioned the committee not to send out a large or expensive outfit. Other nations had erred on this point. In his estimation, the memorialists wished Congress to afford aid, not furnish the entire expense, and he asked the House to appropriate about $50,000. The committee reported favorably on Southard's proposals, but the House stipulated that the money for the expedition should be paid from funds allotted to the Navy Department.

The resolution which passed the House on May 21, 1828, called upon the Navy Department to send out one of its smaller vessels to conduct an examination of the coasts, islands, harbors, shoals, and reefs in the Pacific Ocean and the South Sea to ascertain their true situation and description. Secretary Southard immediately initiated preparations. The sloop-of-war *Peacock*, then in Brooklyn undergoing repairs, was commissioned as the exploring vessel, negotiations were initiated for the purchase of a second smaller ship, and Captain Thomas Ap Catesby Jones was given command. In Nantucket and New Bedford, seamen were enlisted, while Lieutenant Charles Wilkes, Jr., was commissioned to purchase the necessary nautical and astronomical instruments. Not the least of the Secretary's actions was the appointment of Jeremiah N. Reynolds as an agent to procure accurate information respecting Pacific islands, shoals, and reefs from maritime citizens in New England.

The agent received his instructions from Southard in June, but did not immediately depart for New England. In New York he had made the acquaintance of Edmund Fanning, *"Father of all sealers,"* who recommended the veteran Antarctic mariner, Benjamin Pendleton, for the position of pilot on the expedition. Reynolds forwarded this recommendation to Southard, describing Pendleton as being "as well acquainted with the South Seas, as a Baltimore pilot with his Native [Chesapeake] Bay." [18] Adding to his qualifications was his ownership of a sealing brig which could be used by the government if he were made a

---

[18] J. N. Reynolds to Samuel L. Southard, [New York], July 30, 1828, RDN, Miscellaneous Letters for 1828, VII, 115.

member of the expedition. The Secretary of the Navy hoped to send another vessel with the *Peacock*, but he did not act immediately, and Reynolds left New York for the northeast.

In August, Reynolds told Southard he had arrived in the "region of romance" and had begun collecting information. He was greatly impressed after conversing with mariners more than seventy years of age who had just returned from a whaling voyage. After visiting with them a few days he enthusiastically reported to the Secretary of the Navy: "The importance of my visit cannot be told, till you read my report—I have now in my possession more knowledge of the South Seas and Pacific Ocean, by ten times, than the British Expeditions will have when they return." [19] His enthusiasm got the better of him, however, for soon he wanted to hire a seventeen-year-old Hawaiian as an interpreter to be employed on Pacific islands. Needless to say, Southard did not consider this proposition.

The Secretary of the Navy meanwhile was hastening preparations in other quarters. President Adams had earnestly urged that the exploration should be completed during his present term in office, because he was certain he and Southard would not have the opportunity to carry it through in 1829. This forecast made in July proved correct, because the next February, Robert Y. Hayne, the states' rights Jacksonian Senator from South Carolina, and Chairman of the Committee on Naval Affairs of the upper house, scuttled the project.

The expedition had come to the Senate committee's attention, because Secretary Southard was unable to cover its cost in the naval appropriation. The addition of a second ship was expensive, and the Secretary did not have the money to spend. Chairman Hayne called for a complete explanation from the Executive on the authorization, objectives, progress, and expenses. The senators were especially interested in knowing if the expedition was to examine known coasts or search for unknown lands. Was it to be a surveying or a discovery project? Duty demanded such information, the committee explained, since many people believed the expedition had been sanctioned by both houses of

<hr>

[19] J. N. Reynolds to Samuel L. Southard, n.p., Aug. 12, 1828, RDN, Miscellaneous Letters for 1828, VIII, 48. See also the *National Intelligencer*, Aug. 26, 1828, 3; and *Niles' Weekly Register*, XXXV (Sept. 13, 1828), 39.

Congress, whereas it had never been considered, much less approved, by the Senate.

In his reply to the committee's queries, Southard forth-rightly declared that the House resolution was viewed both as a command to be obeyed and as authorization for the expenditure of the appropriation. No monies had been spent except those sanctioned by law. The *Peacock* had been refitted, something required regardless of her service, and the agent, J. N. Reynolds, had been paid $1,116 to collect data indispensable to the expedition. But knowing the hopes of the supporters of explora-tion, Southard was not considering dispatching only the *Peacock*. He wanted to increase the personnel by adding a civilian corps composed of a commercial agent, astronomer, and a naturalist to satisfy the commercial and scientific objectives. To expedite the surveys and ensure safety for the crews, a second vessel was necessary, moreover. With two ships the exploring could be completed in two and a half years.

As to aims, the explorers would examine both known and un-known coasts. Southard emphasized that the Navy's best charts, as well as most geographical studies, of the South Pacific and the Antarctic were inadequate. Reynolds had learned that at least two hundred uncharted islands, reefs, and shoals existed, imperiling every Pacific voyage. The explorers would extend their surveys into high southern latitudes, pushing as far south as safety and expediency would permit. But they had to avoid becoming frozen in during the Antarctic winter, since their sur-veys were to be concentrated on territories in milder latitudes.

After studying the Navy Department's report, Senator Hayne's committee concluded that the preparations were unauthorized and exploration itself was unreasonable. How the Navy Depart-ment could act without the sanction of both houses of Congress when Article I, Section 7, of the Constitution explicitly requires their approval for every resolution to become law was impossible to understand, the committee said. The action was especially precipitate, the committee continued, because the resolution had been adopted as an expedient after an appropriation bill pro-viding for an expedition had not been acted upon by the House.

The committee entered a general protest against overseas ex-ploration, since any discoveries would cause a departure from traditional American foreign policies. Love of adventure and visions of profit would cause Americans to emigrate and plant a colony. No settlement could be placed "under the protection of the United States, without an abandonment of the fundamental principles of our policy, and a departure from those wise and prudent maxims, which have hitherto restrained us from forming unnecessary connexions abroad." [20] Surveying all the islands and reefs in the South Pacific, furthermore, would be expensive. This expedition would lead to another and still another until thousands, even millions, of dollars had been spent. Such expenditures were unwarranted when many square miles of territory in the United States remained unexplored.

Hayne and his committee may have been economy-minded, but the President, who bore the brunt of their attack, thought any truth the chairman's words may have conveyed was "swallowed up by the passions of party" coupled with arrogance, rancor, and a never-dying personal hatred. Reynolds verified these views when he told Adams he had been assured the project would be resumed during the next session of Congress. In 1836, under their own President, the Jacksonians not only provided for exploration, but created an expedition far larger than the one called for in 1828. At any rate, the committee's report put an end to exploring projects for the time being.

Had the exploring expedition been sent to sea during John Quincy Adams's term as President and under Samuel Southard's administration of the Navy Department, it would have been prepared much more efficiently and at less cost than it was under the Democrats later. For one thing, John Quincy was the son of his father, John Adams, the first President to accelerate Navy development. In fact, the second President Adams had declared in his Annual Message of 1826 that "it was the destiny and the duty of these confederated States to become in regular process of time and by no petty advances a great naval power." [21] He hoped, moreover, to impel these advances.

....

[20] 20 Cong., 2 Sess., *Sen. Doc.* 94, 7.

[21] James D. Richardson, comp., *A Compilation of the Messages and Papers of the Presidents, 1789–1910* (11 vols., New York, 1911), II, 361–62. See also Harold and Margaret Sprout, *The Rise of American Naval Power, 1776–1918* (Princeton, N.J., 1939), pp. 102–4.

Adams's very efficient Navy Secretary shared these views. As Charles Oscar Paullin said, the President and the Secretary "were well-mated, and were vigorous and far-sighted naval administrators." [22] Southard understood the needs of the Navy and he enforced discipline with an even hand, something his successor, Mahlon Dickerson, was unable to do.

Although the exponents of the expedition rued the action of the Senate committee, they refused to give up their plans, for a private Antarctic expedition was not beyond their grasp. Reynolds had retained much of the money collected during his lecture tour, and with his friend Edmund Fanning he succeeded in raising enough additional funds to take two 200-ton sealing brigs, the *Seraph* and the *Annawan*, to sea. Their commanders were the Antarctic veterans, Benjamin Pendleton and Nathaniel B. Palmer. Reynolds, a Philadelphian, John F. Watson, and an experienced naturalist from Albany, Dr. James Eights, made up the corps of scientists, provided with $500 for research by the New York Lyceum of Natural History. The crews were of "as fine and promising Yankee bloods as ever walked a ship's deck." [23]

Even with such promising personnel the expedition was almost completely unsuccessful. The explorers were unable to accomplish their principal aims—the reinvestigation of Palmer Land and the discovery of additional Antarctic territories. The only member gaining distinction was James Eights, who published a scientific treatise on the natural history of the South Shetlands.

The *Seraph* met the *Annawan* off Long Island on October 16, 1829, heading southward to the South Shetlands, where they hoped to take some seal pelts before beginning the difficult task of examining Palmer's discovery. For thirty-five days the weather not only kept them from sealing, but also obviated any thoughts they might have had of penetrating the ice pack. As a result, Pendleton and Palmer sailed their ships westward into the Pacific in search of the islands two Nantucket captains, Macy and

....

[22] "Naval Administration Under the Navy Commissioners, 1815–1842," *United States Naval Institute Proceedings*, 33 (June, 1907), 601.

[23] *National Intelligencer*, Oct. 28, 1829, 4. See also *New-York Mirror, and Ladies Literary Gazette*, VII (Oct. 24, 1829), 126; and John M. Clarke, "Reincarnation of James Eights, Antarctic Explorer," *The Scientific Monthly*, II (Feb., 1916), 189–202.

Swain, had reportedly discovered in 1800, but found nothing even suggesting the proximity of land.

The days of inactivity in the abysmally depressing weather of the South Shetlands had brought the crew close to mutiny. Pendleton attributed it partly to "the ill luck in not making any discoveries," but more importantly to their lack of success in sealing. Part of the crew's compensation was to be a share of the cargo they collected. The commanders were forced to turn northward to Valparaiso, where Palmer delivered part of his crew to the United States consul. This brought unplanned delays, forcing the explorers to abandon their new plans of exploring the coasts of Japan, eastern coast of Asia, and the North Pacific.

"In this dilemma and disappointment," Pendleton reported, "a consultation was had with Captain Palmer and the gentlemen composing the scientific corps," and they decided to "proceed forthwith with the vessels to the coast of Araucania. . . ." [24] The leaders of the expedition thought they could ease the ill-feeling of the crew by sealing on the islands off the coast of Chile, while the scientists attempted to communicate with the hostile Araucanian Indians. On July 22, 1830, after Reynolds and Watson went inland near the Río Arauco to meet the principal cacique, the seal hunters sailed to Chiloe and the island of St. Mary to procure a sizable collection of furs.

The Indian agents described their success as being beyond expectations, because they were allowed to pass into the interior where no foreigners had been permitted for one hundred and fifty years. The hostility of the Indians was well known to Reynolds and Watson and they undoubtedly based their conclusions on this condition. They thought the Araucanians promised to trade with Americans.

Pendleton and Palmer had planned to take Reynolds and Watson aboard their vessels in Talcahuano before sailing northward toward the California ports, but when they arrived there the crew became disorderly and mutinous again even though their quest for skins had not been unsuccessful. "So far did this behavior progress, as to become settled into a stern determina-

[24] Fanning, *Voyages*, p. 481.

tion to desert. . . ." Pendleton was forced to adopt the only expedient which remained—"return home, while a sufficient number [of the crew] remained to navigate the vessels. . . ." [25] Reynolds did not return home with the other explorers because he obtained employment as historiographer on the U.S.S. *Potomac*, Commodore John Downes commanding, engaged in a punitive expedition against the inhabitants of Sumatra.

Two years after the expedition's return, James Eights published a "Description of a New Crustaceous Animal Found on the Shores of the South Shetlands, with Remarks on their Natural History," in the *Transactions* of the Albany Institute. This was the first purely scientific treatise on these Antarctic islands published by an American, and Eights gained a considerable reputation from it.

The article was unique in several respects. Besides describing an unknown animal, Eights anticipated Charles Darwin, of the *Beagle* expedition, some six years by showing that glacial boulders in floating icebergs denoted the presence of a considerable land mass to the south. He held: "The hills of floating ice we encountered, could not form elsewhere than on the land. The drifting fuci we daily saw, grow only in the vicinity of rocky shores, and the penguins and terns, that were almost at all times about us, from my observation of their habits, . . . never leave the land at any great distance." [26]

Eights was clearly disappointed at their failure to explore Palmer Land, for he believed it might prove to be the northeastern termination of an extensive chain of islands, "passing near where Capt. Cook's progress was arrested by firm fields of ice in latitude 71° 10′ S." To him the blame lay with the United States government, which had refused to appropriate funds for

[25] Fanning, *Voyages*, p. 486.

[26] See the *Transactions*, II (1833–52), 68. See also Lawrence Martin, "James Eights' Pioneer Observation and Interpretation of Erratics in Antarctic Icebergs," *Bulletin of the Geological Society of America*, 60 (Jan., 1949), 177–82; the abstract of Martin's address before the Eighth American Scientific Congress entitled "Early Exploration and Investigations in Southern South America and Adjacent Waters by Mariners and Scientists from the United States of America," in 76 Cong., 3 Sess., *Cong. Record*, 86, Appendix 3195; and W. T. Calman, "James Eights, A Pioneer Antarctic Naturalist," *Proceedings of the Linnean Society of London*, 149th Session (Nov. 3, 1937), 171–85.

an expedition. He expressed the opinion that a nation with a "population whose daring enterprize has already carried . . . [the] flag into the remotest corners of the globe" would be unduly lax if they did not carry out an Antarctic expedition, "the expense of which would little exceed that of a vessel doubling Cape Horn." [27]

[27] The *Transactions,* II (1833–52), 69.

chapter seven

SUCCESS?

James Eights gained a modicum of eminence in scientific circles from his discoveries in the South Shetlands, but his fellow explorers, and their agent, Edmund Fanning, obtained nothing from the *Seraph* and *Annawan* expedition except a firm conviction that private means could never satisfy the magnificent desires of the supporters of Antarctic and Pacific exploration. Benjamin Pendleton reflected their feelings with some bitterness when he asserted, "I am now convinced, . . . that an exploring expedition, by any private means, can never produce great or important national benefits: it must be clothed with authority from Government, and the officers and men on regular pay as in the navy." [1] Fanning forwarded these views to members of Congress.

His first attempts to impress the representatives of the people with the need for an expedition financed by the federal government almost fell through, because he obscured his purpose by advancing compensation claims for the losses incurred. The members of both houses of Congress thought his memorial of December, 1831, was an application for a government-financed squadron given to his command or agency as part reward for his previous services.

To mend his fences before they were beyond repair, Fanning addressed letters to Representative C. C. Cambreleng and Senator C. E. Dudley, both from New York, in which he renounced any intention of wanting to direct government exploration. He

---

[1] 23 Cong., 1 Sess., *Sen. Doc.* 10, 10.

was requesting an indemnity for his partners in their late mis-
adventure, he said, because it had been of some benefit to the
people of the United States and had received the notice of the
Navy Department before its departure. His real desire was to
convince Congress that federally sponsored overseas exploration
was imperative.

Fanning's assurances had little effect. It appeared as if his
petitions were destined to die in committees of both houses.
Nevertheless, he moved slowly, for he undoubtedly was busy
completing his valedictory to a busy maritime career—*Voyages
Round the World*. Late in 1832, at the beginning of the next
session of Congress, Fanning made an attempt to keep the
crusade moving by presenting the same memorial to the House
and by seeking the sanction of Secretary of the Navy Levi
Woodbury.

Early in 1833 his *Voyages* appeared, immediately gaining
popularity. Fanning not overmodestly testified that he himself
had difficulty procuring copies at one time. His work definitely
is a landmark in the maritime history of the United States, as
well as the most comprehensive contemporary account of the
Stonington sealers' activities in the Antarctic. Fanning never
visited the South Shetlands or Palmer Land, but throughout his
life he maintained a lively interest in the Antarctic regions. He
accepted the open south polar sea theory of James Weddell and
Benjamin Morrell, believing it was possible to sail to the South
Pole, even though he usually referred to Palmer Land as a
continent, and never discounted the possibility of discovering
extensive bodies of land in the Antarctic. To Fanning the south
polar region offered alluring possibilities to the explorer. Reaching the pole was a goal well worth achieving, as was the discovery of new seal beaches. With these aims in mind he continued propagandizing for exploration.

At the first session of the Twenty-third Congress, Edmund
Fanning presented another memorial to the Senate containing a
concrete proposal regarding the size and cost of a squadron. He
estimated that $100,000 would be an adequate appropriation
and, like others, he considered this small compensation to the
maritime population from a Treasury with a surplus, much of
which had been contributed by traders who "prayed" for ex-

ploration. Earlier he had been especially critical of the Navy Department when it contemplated dispatching an exploring fleet of two or three vessels led by the large sloop-of-war *Peacock*. He favored a more modest force composed only of small vessels, since a large ship would meet fatal situations in high southern latitudes because of her lack of maneuverability. Fanning thought, moreover, that the personnel of the expedition should not exceed 90 to 100 persons.[2]

Shortly after these proposals were presented to Congress in 1834, the energetic Jeremiah Reynolds returned from his cruise to the island of Sumatra. He did not join the propaganda movement of his former partner immediately. His first task was the completion of a history of the voyage. When this book appeared, Reynolds gained somewhat of a following as a literary figure, for he attempted to capitalize on it by writing an introduction to a life of George Washington, written in Latin by a former Ohio tutor, Francis Glass. Later, in 1839, he published his version of the story about the great white whale, "Mocha Dick," which might have influenced Herman Melville when he published his tale.[3] Meanwhile, Fanning was seeking friends willing to memorialize Congress for an expedition.

In all, petitions approving Fanning's proposals were sent to the national legislature from a group of Philadelphia citizens and from members of the East India Marine Society of Salem. The Salem society, composed of veteran mariners who had rounded either the Cape of Good Hope or Cape Horn, favored surveys to correct charts of islands, reefs, and shoals, because many vessels had been lost on account of faulty and incomplete information. Petitions were sent to friends in the Senate Committee on Naval Affairs and the House Committee on Commerce.

The chairman of the House committee, Dutee J. Pearce (R.I.),

---

[2] 23 Cong., 1 Sess., *Sen. Doc.* 10, 13. See also Edmund Fanning to Levi Woodbury, New York, Sept. 23, 1833, RDN, Miscellaneous Letters for 1833, 96.

[3] See the *Voyage of the United States Frigate Potomac. Under the Command of Commodore John Downes, During the Circumnavigation of the Globe, in the Years 1831, 1832, 1833, and 1834* (New York, 1835); Francis Glass, *A Life of George Washington, in Latin Prose* (ed. by J. N. Reynolds, New York, 1835); and "Mocha Dick: or the White Whale of the Pacific: A Leaf from a Manuscript Journal," *The Knickerbocker, or New-York Monthly Magazine*, XIII (May, 1839), 377–92.

and one of its members, John Reed (Mass.), both friends of exploration, welcomed the petitions Fanning had procured. When the committee began deliberating, it received further evidence from two Navy officers, Matthew F. Maury and John Downes, long-time members of the Pacific Squadron, who described the extent of commerce and advocated appropriations for hydrographic surveying. Downes, who was probably writing at the suggestion of his friend Reynolds, thought the dangers from uncharted reefs and rocks in the Pacific could not be overestimated. Many sealing, whaling, and merchant vessels had been destroyed. Besides, the fur seal trade would certainly benefit from discoveries in the Antarctic. In general, Downes stated, no area existed on the globe where an expedition could not make substantial accomplishments. To him the whole business was a practical affair.

Since evidence of the public interest in exploration was mounting, Pearce next asked the House to request the report Reynolds had made to Samuel Southard in 1828 from the new Secretary of the Navy, Mahlon Dickerson. This estimate, which Lieutenant Charles Wilkes later declared wholly inadequate, was comprised of an outline of the discoveries of whalers and sealers, as well as a short list of reefs and shoals in the southern hemisphere not appearing on charts. Needless to say, Reynolds was emphatic about the need for surveys in this region. Much could be done to protect Pacific mariners and to invigorate the fast-declining seal trade. Regarding the Antarctic, he had learned it was entirely possible that the South Shetlands extended farther south than anyone had penetrated. American sealers had sailed along a high, rugged coast trending southwestward from 63° to 66° S., in 63° to 75° W. He probably was describing the sealers' voyages of 1820–21, for the positions mentioned are in the vicinity of Palmer Peninsula. Captain Benjamin Pendleton told Reynolds that the quality of the ice and the nature of the currents indicated that many valuable discoveries might be made in the seas southwest of the Shetlands.

This report completed the information desired by the committee, and on February 7, 1835, Pearce presented its report to the House with a resolution for an expedition. In essence, the committee's statement was a review of the evidence Reynolds and

Fanning had procured, but the members of the House remained uninterested until an appropriation for exploration was added to the Navy Appropriation Bill of 1836 by Senator Samuel L. Southard.

Southard, who now headed the Senate Committee on Naval Affairs, directed his group to present a brief similar to the House Committee's. It soon appeared as if it would suffer the same fate, but Southard was determined to avert the disaster which had befallen the expedition during his administration of the Navy Department. When his resolution was not immediately brought up for debate, he added it to the Navy Appropriation Bill, thus forcing consideration of the measure. The appropriation was increased by $150,000 to include the expedition.

Before Congress adjudged this amendment, Jeremiah N. Reynolds was invited to voice his views in the House chamber. Coming as it did on the eve of debate, this invitation undoubtedly represented an effort to utilize the popular propagandist in swaying fence-sitting congressmen. Reynolds's finest hour was at hand. His escape from humble beginnings was complete. In little more than a decade he had risen from the editorship of an obscure Ohio newspaper to the position of an authority who was now called upon to explain the need for overseas exploration to the society of the nation's capital.

Little was new in his eloquent address. Time-tested arguments were reiterated: the enormous Pacific interests of the United States demanded surveys, this country had to prevent national ignominy by contributing to geographical knowledge, and explorations had to be extended to that virgin field of discovery in the Antarctic. Reynolds was inspired with the thought of American explorers "pushing their adventurous barks into the high southern latitudes, to circle the globe within the Antarctic circle, and attain the pole itself;—yea, to cast anchor on that point where all the meridians terminate, where our eagle and star-spangled banner may be unfurled and planted, and left to wave on the axis of the earth itself!" [4]

While Reynolds's premises were not new, his conception of

[4] J. N. Reynolds, *Address on the Subject of a Surveying and Exploring Expedition to the Pacific Ocean and South Seas. Delivered in the Hall of Representatives on the Evening of April 3, 1836* (New York, 1836), p. 99.

the exploring squadron had changed remarkably. No longer was he thinking of a fleet of two small ships sent to sea with no more fanfare than a Nantucket whaling expedition. No longer was he accepting the thinking of Edmund Fanning on the character of the expedition. "If true to our national character, to the spirit of the age we live in, the first expedition sent out by this great republic must not fall short in any department—from a defective organization, or from adopting too closely the efforts of other nations as models for our own." [5] He wanted a veritable flotilla —a frigate and five ships—a brigade of naval officers, and a corps of scientists to study everything from the tiniest insect to aboriginal man. Exploring an immense region required an immense expedition. This was the view of influential Jacksonians and particularly of the man who was to become commander of the expedition, Captain Thomas Ap Catesby Jones.

Not long after Reynolds's speech, the amended appropriation bill was returned to the House for approval. On May 5, Representative Leonard Jarvis (Maine) amended the amendment, giving the President power to decide whether an expedition was necessary. If he rendered an affirmative decision, an additional $150,000 was to be appropriated beyond the sum Southard requested. An ardent exponent of the expedition, Thomas L. Hamer (Ohio), opposed making exploration conditional, stating that since the members of the House represented the people, they should decide. Richard Hawes (Ky.) was outspokenly against the expenditure of public funds to support the "chimerical" notions of Jeremiah N. Reynolds. The only accomplishment of exploration, he estimated, would be the exposure of Americans to the diseases, hurricanes, and mishaps of the Antarctic and the Pacific.

While a number of congressmen supported the expedition, Representatives Hamer and Reed proved to be its stanchest defenders. When it appeared as if the majority of the Middle-Westerners, whose thoughts were voiced by Hawes, would succeed in defeating the measure, Hamer took the floor, deploring their limited thinking. Exploration actually would benefit the west, he emphasized; since the expedition would promote trade, it would enlarge the capacity of the world "to consume the productions of the farming class of the Mississippi valley." The Ohio

----

[5] *Ibid.*, p. 71.

representative also resented Hawes's reflections on Reynolds's integrity. He knew the propagandist as a friend whose devotion to the expedition was "wholly free from any selfish considerations; and in all he had done for the last seven or eight years to promote it, he had been actuated by those feelings of patriotism that should animate every American heart." [6] Reed too urged magnanimity. The congressmen should cast aside selfish, sectional thoughts, which often caused them to overlook the association of interests seemingly remote. Exploration was enlarged national policy and should be viewed as such. National interest and national good dictated the passage of the amendment.

These orations seemingly carried the day. The House accepted the Southard amendment to the Navy Appropriation Bill as changed by Jarvis, in spite of protests by Representative Hawes. The Senate, however, refused to allow the President to decide upon the expedition, and the House finally agreed. The Secretary of the Navy thus was given $300,000 to spend on exploration, together with any additional funds he could afford to spend from the regular appropriation for his department.

Secretary of the Navy Mahlon Dickerson initiated preparations by giving the command to Captain Jones, a former lieutenant of President Andrew Jackson at the Battle of New Orleans, who had been associated with the expedition at different times through the period of its inception. He had testified on the need for Pacific exploration and had helped shape Reynolds's opinions regarding the character of the squadron. Jones, who was never known for timidity, spoke for an expedition with a dual scientific and military character. He favored a large scientific department manned by scientists from the "literary institutions" of the country, rather than navy officers. To impress the "ferocious" natives of the South Sea islands, moreover, a grand military display should be made. The frigate he wanted as flagship of his fleet was the *Macedonian,* then undergoing construction. President Jackson granted this ship, but he refused to order more than one sloop, one schooner, and one provision ship. He did, however, give Jones some latitude, allowing him to replace the sloop with two schooners or two brigs. It was his hope that the expedition would sail by October, 1836, before the end of his second term.

----

[6] 24 Cong., 1 Sess., *Cong. Globe,* III, Appendix 339.

To accompany the *Macedonian,* the commander chose a store-ship of 463 tons, two brigs of 230 tons each, and a schooner of 114 tons, which he later named the *Relief, Pioneer, Consort,* and *Pilot.* Dickerson ordered the chairman of the Navy Board of Commissioners to command the chiefs of the various navy yards where the vessels were docked, to get them ready for sea, and commissioned officers to begin recruiting.

Meanwhile, Lieutenant Charles Wilkes, Superintendent of the Navy's Charts and Instruments Depot, had been requested to list the instruments required for the expedition, and to decide whether they could be purchased in the United States. Wilkes reported it would be necessary to send an agent to Europe to find most of them, and in July he was ordered to England and the Continent on the first packet. Twenty thousand dollars was put at his disposal.

Not the least of Dickerson's attention was directed toward the extremely vocal and well-respected self-styled progenitor of the expedition, Jeremiah N. Reynolds. Many believed the publicist was a well-trained scientist and an expert on commerce, who had singlehandedly interested the public in the expedition. Because of his great knowledge, they decided he should be given an important, if not the commanding, position in the civilian corps. Typical of this view was this statement by a Massachusetts citizen: "Ever since I heard your lecture here on the whale fishery, as connected with the Annawan's expedition, to say nothing of our many long and social conferences, and found that an Ohio boy . . . could teach the descendants of Nantucket something of their own craft, I have had only one opinion, that is, that you ought to hold a prominent place in the enterprise." [7] But not everybody was taken in by Reynolds. Edmund Fanning, for instance, held an opposite opinion. He was fearful the Navy Department might even place him in charge of the construction of the exploring ships, but President Jackson allayed his fears and those of others by making Reynolds corresponding secretary to the commander with an annual salary of $2,000. His principal duty would be to condense reports the scientists would make.

A scientist, Charles Anthon, viewed this appointment as proof

[7] See Benjamin Rodman to J. N. Reynolds, New Bedford, [Mass.], June 11, 1836, in Reynolds, *Address,* p. 118.

of the high favor Reynolds had with the President, but the newly appointed corresponding secretary was not pleased. Dickerson reported that he asked him to do away with the commission by signing a statement that the President determined to give him a "conspicuous station" with the expedition. The Secretary was powerless to act, but it is doubtful if he would have acceded to Reynolds's demands, because he did not approve giving the corresponding secretary the duty of condensing the reports of the scientists. Dickerson thought he was totally unqualified.

With Reynolds thus disposed of, the Secretary of the Navy next turned to the formulation of a corps of scientists. Shortly after Catesby Jones was appointed to the command, Dickerson had informed him the scientists would number eighteen, but this was not a fixed number. He called upon some of the societies devoted to scientific and maritime pursuits to make recommendations regarding the size of the corps, the subjects to be investigated, and noteworthy individuals willing to accompany the expedition. In August and September, 1836, Dickerson invited the American Philosophical Society, United States Naval Lyceum, New York Lyceum of Natural History, Salem East India Marine Society, Philadelphia Academy of Natural Sciences, and the New Haven, Connecticut, Geological Society to make suggestions.

For the most part, the societies appointed committees to deliberate Dickerson's inquiries before making specific recommendations, but individuals associated with them crowded the desk of the Secretary of the Navy with suggestions of scientists to accompany the expedition. Dickerson welcomed these acknowledgments of his inquiries, but he deferred action until he received the reports of the societies themselves. In the end all the organizations reported to the Navy Department except the New Haven Geological Society, but only the reports of the American Philosophical Society, East India Marine Society, and the Naval Lyceum were directed to the attention of the commander of the expedition.

The latter alone showed any interest in the Antarctic. The committee of the Naval Lyceum refused to discount the presence of large bodies of land there, because Charles Lyell, the British geologist, had reported, "'after the most recent voyages, the area of land still unexplored within the Antarctic circle, is far more

than double the area of Europe.'" Captain Cook, moreover, believed that the intensity of cold in the Antarctic was caused by
a vast territory "between the 70th degree of South Latitude and
the pole." Thus, one of the principal duties of the expedition,
according to the Lyceum, should be to confirm or deny this
"conjecture, by proceeding South on a meridian much farther
westward than the one followed by Captain Weddel." Furthermore, Antarctic exploration undoubtedly would contribute interesting information to the "general theory of climate, and a
knowledge of the distribution of heat on the Globe." [8]

Secretary Dickerson accepted the recommendations of the
societies and their members when he appointed Titian R. Peale,
James Eights, Reynell Coates, and John W. Randall, zoologists;
Asa Gray, botanist; James Dwight Dana, geologist; Charles Pickering, naturalist; Horatio Hale, philologist; Joseph P. Couthuoy,
conchologist; Walter R. Johnson, natural philosopher; and E. H.
Darley, Alfred T. Agate, and Joseph Drayton, natural history
draftsmen. Two painters and a taxidermist were added later. The
corps soon was busy purchasing necessary books and equipment,
for Lieutenant Wilkes had bought only astronomical instruments.

The feverish activity of the scientists did not characterize
preparations for the expedition in other quarters. It soon became
evident that President Jackson's October departure date would
not be met. Recruiting was slow, because officers had to compete
with recruiters for the Pacific and Brazil squadrons, and with
merchantmen, who were paying more substantial wages than the
Navy. Merchant seamen were receiving $15 to $18 per month,
while able seamen in the Navy were paid $12, ordinary seamen
$10, and landsmen $8.

The construction and outfitting of the ships also moved haltingly. Commandants of the navy yards were slow to act when
called upon to make decisions in the absence of Jones. This was
particularly repugnant to the commander, who was anxious to
put his fleet to sea. "It is manifest," he told the Navy Board, "that

----

[8] Report of the Committee of the Naval Lyceum in reference to the letter
of the Honorable Secretary of the Navy, upon the Exploring Expedition to
the South Seas, Nov. 29, 1836, Manuscripts Division, Library of Congress.
This report is printed in "The Exploring Expedition to the South Seas," *The
Naval Magazine*, II (Jan., 1837), 64–86.

no human being, not endowed by *omnipresence,* can superintend *in detail* the building and equipping of five vessels at *four different stations,* the extremes of which are *seven hundred miles apart."* [9] But while Jones complained about the commandants of the yards, they had occasion to grumble themselves. For one thing, the requisitions of the commander were "either for articles not comprised in the regulations, or at extravagant or unauthorized prices. . . ." [10] For another, more matériel was purchased than could be stowed in the ships comprising the squadron.

As if these arguments were not enough, Jones also came into contention with the Secretary of the Navy over the appointment of officers. Even though President Jackson had stated that no officer to whom Jones had valid objections should be ordered to the exploring service, Secretary Dickerson refused to abide completely by the Chief Executive's wishes. He insisted on naming two lieutenants, Alexander Slidell and Charles Wilkes, as commanders of two secondary vessels, because they had particular talents he felt made them useful to the expedition. Dickerson considered Slidell a literary figure and wanted him to serve as "historiographer," while Wilkes was to handle the duties of an astronomer or a meteorologist.

Both were objectionable to the commander, Slidell because he had previously censured Jones's actions, and Wilkes because Jones felt that only civilians should comprise the corps of scientists. If Dickerson considered belles-lettres a paramount qualification for a commander, Jones suggested he should call upon James Kirke Paulding, who was both a more distinguished author and a more experienced mariner than Slidell. Wilkes, he felt, should command nothing more than a surveying party; in addition, both Wilkes and Slidell were junior officers who did not deserve appointments when many seniors were better qualified.

This rift between the Secretary and his commander was widened in December when Slidell brought it to public attention by publishing a summary of his views concerning Jones's actions,

[9] Thomas Ap Catesby Jones to the President of the Board of Navy Commissioners, Near Prospect Hill, Va., Aug. 29, 1836, 25 Cong., 1 Sess., *House Doc.* 50, 13.

[10] John Rodgers to Mahlon Dickerson, Navy Commissioners' Office, March 2, 1837, 25 Cong., 2 Sess., *House Ex. Doc.* 147 (Letters), 264.

as well as the official Navy Department correspondence concerning the affair. He accused Jones of appropriating the powers of the Secretary of the Navy when he claimed authority to name the commanders of the smaller vessels and to exclude officers Dickerson wished to appoint. This was regrettable because few officers desired to sail with Jones for "want of confidence in his claim to those seamanlike attainments which can only be acquired by active employment at sea, or a just indignation at the agency attributed to him in the Navy in defeating the bill for its reorganization, introduced into the Senate by Mr. Southard, by means of opinions conceived as was supposed, in the spirit of his own interests. . . ." [11]

The official correspondence turned over by Dickerson was included, Slidell stated, to correct insinuations made by Jones and Reynolds that he was intriguing to supplant the commander, and to show that Jones lacked the broad experience necessary for directing important explorations. Reynolds himself had said that originally the choice for the command was between Jones and two Master Commandants, Matthew C. Perry and F. H. Gregory. A "tacit compromise," and congressional influence had been employed to gain it for Jones. Without influence he never would have been considered, because his service in gunboats "in and about the Mississippi, in which he acquired distinction," did not enable him to acquire seamanship. "It is sufficient that the practised seaman, the thorough officer, the individual possessing in a high degree the confidence of the profession, . . . was made to give place to one whose disconnection with the service has long been proverbial." [12]

Jones first countered these allegations in a short letter to the editors of the Washington *Globe,* official voice of Jackson's party, decrying them as mere machinations designed to do away with the expedition or at least reduce its effectiveness. Later, his version of the authentic record of the proceedings occupied the front page of this newspaper. He argued that he had received his appointment because of merit, not prompting. His long experience in the Pacific and the favor of President Jackson had brought it

[11] *Army and Navy Chronicle,* III (Dec. 1, 1836), 337.

[12] Alexander Slidell to Mahlon Dickerson, New York, Sept. 28, 1836, *Army and Navy Chronicle,* III, 341.

to him. He had been a comrade-in-arms with the President during the late war, and thus the executive knew of the dangerous service he had performed in the Gulf of Mexico. "At all events," he added, "I am not indebted for it [the appointment] to solicitation. None was made by me—none by any others at my instance; and the whole charge of improper influence being brought to bear to vanquish the Secretary's reluctance to my appointment, is sheer fabrication." [13]

These arguments undoubtedly caught Secretary Dickerson in a tempest he had not expected to arise when he allowed Slidell to publish the correspondence concerning the selection of officers. His commander and his friend had made expedition policy the object of public attention, and by so doing were forcing him to clarify his actions. The Secretary undoubtedly was in a quandary, because he was not a forthright individual. In his letter to the *Globe* of January 19 he tried to straddle the fence. On the one hand, he explained that he himself had recommended Jones for the command because of his over-all competence as an officer. On the other, he maintained that the commander's objections to Slidell and Wilkes were not conclusive. Naval officers capable of carrying out the expedition's objectives should be preferred to equally capable civilians. He had willingly relinquished his right to appoint these officers, however, rather than lose the services of his commander.

Dickerson's surrender to Jones brought a reconciliation and for a time early in 1837 it appeared as if the expedition would soon be at sea. The ships had been completed. The Navy appropriation for the new year had passed Congress without lengthy argument. But this abatement of friction, accompanied by the renewal of activity, was short-lived, because new problems soon arose. Within a few months the ships were back in dry dock undergoing repairs. First of all, much to Jones's surprise, the galleys he had ordered, burning anthracite coal, had to be replaced, since that fuel made such an intense heat it scorched the food, melted the pitch in the seams, and caused the ships to leak. Secondly, it soon became apparent that the *Pioneer, Consort,* and *Pilot* were not the type of ships needed

-----

[13] *The Globe,* Washington, D.C., Jan. 16, 1837, 1. See also Dec. 29, 1836, 3.

to explore in the storm-swept seas of the south polar regions, something Edmund Fanning had been saying for months. When he had heard the brigs were being constructed with heavy timbers on their bottoms and with improper rigging, he had predicted they would lack buoyancy, which in turn would impair their sailing, and make them liable to dismasting by the "Woolies."

In January, 1837, the *Pioneer,* under Lieutenant Josiah Tattnall, was employed to deliver General Antonio Lopez de Santa Anna to Mexico after his ill-timed siesta at San Jacinto and visit to the United States. When he returned, Tattnall reported that his craft had behaved fitfully in rough weather. In fact, she was tossed so badly her masts were endangered. Edmund Fanning's augury had been confirmed.

Tattnall's judgment provoked an outburst from Jones, who had taken the entire fleet on an eight-day shakedown cruise into the "troubled waters, variable winds and cross seas" of the Gulf Stream after the *Pioneer's* return, and considered his ships acceptable sailers. An observer reported, "Commodore Jones had a fair opportunity of trying the sailing qualities of his vessels, and especially of testing them in those situations in which it was thought they would be likely to fail, that is to say, *in light winds with short and cross seas* . . . we understand, that in *every* situation the barques acquitted themselves well, proving to be quick and certain working vessels. . . ."[14] The upshot of the whole affair, however, was the resignation of Tattnall and the assignment by Secretary Dickerson of a board of inquiry to decide upon the capability of the ships.

This board, made up of officers from the Navy Commissioners' Office, reported to the Secretary on July 31. They thought the *Pioneer, Consort,* and *Pilot* were sound, well-built ships, but they would not have recommended them for service had they been called upon earlier to make recommendations. Notwithstanding, "after a careful review of all the information communicated, and a reference to their personal examination of the vessels, the board were of the opinion, that, although these vessels do

----

[14] *Army and Navy Chronicle,* IV (May 25, 1837), 331. See also Thomas Ap Catesby Jones to Josiah Tattnall, Near Prospect Hill, Va., May 27, 1837, 25 Cong., 2 Sess., *House Ex. Doc.* 147 (Letters), 304–12.

not, and probably could not be made to combine to the extent which might be desired, a due proportion of the qualities of sailing and working well, great strength, and capacity for stowage, yet, by some alterations, which could be soon completed, they might be made to answer the purposes proposed sufficiently well to justify their employment." [15]

The appointment of this board convinced the frustrated Jeremiah N. Reynolds that Secretary Dickerson was engaged in a nefarious plan to disrupt and do away with the expedition. He publicly vented his bile in a series of letters from a "Citizen" to Dickerson, which the Secretary answered under the pseudonym "Friend of the Navy." Dickerson was accused of holding up recruiting by refusing a bounty to seamen, of overruling the President on officer appointments, and of failing to support his commander, who believed his ships competent. In addition, he charged, the Secretary's "name was frequently used as authority for stating that the nation was about to squander millions upon this *extravagant enterprise, which had nothing to do with the protection of commerce, and was only to explore in high latitudes south!*" [16]

Dickerson replied that recruiting was delayed because of the needs of the Pacific and Brazil squadrons, and because the growing merchant service was taking more seamen. It was difficult to name officers, he said, since many of them thought the expedition was the project of one individual, not of the citizens of the country. The statement that the squadron would explore in the southern hemisphere had been presented to remove the apprehensions of participants that their lives were to be "unnecessarily exposed among the icebergs near the pole for the purpose of testing certain wild theories that had long been before the public." [17] He obviously was referring to the hollow earth theory.

----

[15] I. Chauncey, C. Morris, L. Warrington, Daniel T. Patterson, and Alex'r S. Wadsworth to Mahlon Dickerson, Washington, D.C., July 13, 1837, 25 Cong., 2 Sess., *House Ex. Doc.* 147 (Letters), 375.

[16] "Citizen" to Mahlon Dickerson, New York, July 21, 1837, in J. N. Reynolds, *Pacific and Indian Oceans: or, The South Sea Surveying and Exploring Expedition: Its Inception, Progress, and Objects* (New York, 1841), p. 334.

[17] "Friend of the Navy" to "Citizen," n.p., Aug. 25, 1837, in Reynolds, *Pacific and Indian Oceans,* p. 383.

These recriminations, prolonged over several weeks, did little to create a good feeling between Catesby Jones and the Secretary. Jones sought a replacement for the totally inefficient *Pilot* and got it, but he and his superior soon came into open disagreement again over the appointment of a historian and hydrographer from the Navy Department. Dickerson had decided a historiographer would be absolutely necessary, while Jones was still steadfastly opposed to the inclusion of such an officer. This disagreement never ended, but it was submerged by more important arguments involving the objectives of the expedition and the composition of the fleet.

Objectives had been debated in the press almost from the time Captain Jones had expressed himself in a letter to Reynolds of May 8, 1836: "I conclude that the objects of the enterprise may be classed under two general heads—*scientific* and *military;* that is, military, so far only as may be necessary for self-preservation and defence against the barbarous, and some times ferocious natives of the countless islands which so thickly stud the most extensive, and perhaps the most interesting field for scientific observation and research that will be visited in the course of the voyage: I allude to the great *equatorial sea, stretching from the west coast of America to the Asiatic shores.*" [18] In other words, the commander did not count exploration in the Antarctic as one of the principal purposes.

Jones also was determined to have a conspicuous squadron led by a frigate to execute the military end. A frigate would scare Pacific islanders sufficiently to guarantee their friendship and provide adequate protection for American whalers and merchantmen. But this was only a preliminary thought. In September, 1836, he sent Dickerson a New York *Journal of Commerce* clipping showing that the British were interested in the Bonin and Hawaiian Islands. The commander believed much could be derived from these islands and he suggested that the United States use the exploring expedition to occupy them!

These views were recapitulated by the commander at various times, and Secretary Dickerson gave tacit approval simply by not disagreeing. They were severely criticized by others, how-

---

[18] *Army and Navy Chronicle,* III (Nov. 24, 1836), 322.

ever. Most of the opposition was levied against the size of the squadron, particularly the inclusion of the *Macedonian.* Concerning size, Edmund Fanning believed the fleet should consist of not more than three vessels, while others thought only two should be employed. Those who supported this latter opinion pointed to the small but successful English and French discovery expeditions. The French explorer La Pérouse had explored throughout the world with two ships and 208 men. In fact, they held, "it is a new era in the history of discovery to set out in search for unknown regions, in a time of universal peace, having no military object in view, with a fleet of five vessels and six hundred men." [19] This in their opinion was the real cause of the recruitment problem.

Individuals who believed the fleet was too large also disapproved of the employment of the frigate with a draft of almost 24 feet and a crew of 500 men. They argued that such a large ship would be useless as an exploring vessel and a liability to the expedition should she be badly damaged. The other smaller vessels could not accommodate her crew and the expedition would be "crippled if not brought to a close." A sloop-of-war with a draft of 14 feet and a crew of 180 men would be much more practicable. Why did Jones demand such a mighty ship? His critics believed that he "suffered something like pride of command to operate with him in this matter. A squadron headed by a first rate frigate is a very respectable command, and . . . Capt. Jones had never had the command of a frigate or of a squadron." [20]

Even though Secretary Dickerson had not commented on the aims or the composition of the squadron, he probably had not failed to hear these criticisms. On June 3, 1837, a few days before he called the board of inquiry, he told the President that he thought the number of ships should be reduced. He then directed the board not only to examine the sailing qualities of the vessels, but the proportions of the expedition as well.

Thomas Ap Catesby Jones, angered because the board had

[19] *Army and Navy Chronicle,* IV (Jan. 5, 1837), 6. See also Edmund Fanning to Martin Van Buren, New York, March 13, 1837, 25 Cong., 2 Sess., *House Ex. Doc.* 147 (Letters), 269–70.

[20] *Army and Navy Chronicle,* III (Oct. 6, 1836), 216.

been summoned, demanded his superior settle the major questions of policy. When the Secretary did not immediately fulfill this request, he prepared a lengthy disquisition concerning the "transactions connected with the incipient organization and subsequent preparation" of the expedition, submitting it to the Navy Department. Jones charged that Dickerson himself had said the expedition was not to be charged solely with reaching the South Pole. The Secretary reputedly had emphasized that only a fool like Jeremiah Reynolds would make Antarctic exploration the prime objective. Both President Jackson and Congress had concurred with these views. Jones reiterated emphatically that the objectives of exploration were: "First, surveying; second, treating with the islands visited; third, research in natural history, and the various branches of science, &c.; fourth, protection of commerce; and lastly, exploration in high southern latitudes, so far as it may be extended without too great hazard to the *primary and more important requisitions of the law.*" [21]

The board of inquiry, however, had not been apprised of such ends, because they reported that the four ships Jones demanded were not needed " 'chiefly to explore the ocean and seas of the southern hemisphere, more particularly in high latitudes, and in regions as near the pole as may be approached without danger.' " [22] After seeing this, the commander concluded that he and the board were talking about two entirely different expeditions.

This report caused the Secretary of the Navy finally to make a statement concerning aims. He said they had always been the same: explore in the south, make surveys, advance scientific knowledge, and only incidentally aid commerce. Speedy movements necessary for the protection of commerce were at variance with slow surveying. Operations were to be confined chiefly to the Antarctic. Thus Jones at last learned that his ideas were not the same as those of Mahlon Dickerson.

In spite of these fundamental differences, the commander moved his fleet from the Navy Yard at Norfolk to New York in

---

[21] 25 Cong., 2 Sess., *House Ex. Doc.* 147 (Letters), 344.
[22] *Ibid.,* 375.

October, 1837, hoping to begin exploring the next month. Since the season for Antarctic exploration was rather far advanced, he decided no serious attempt to survey *Terra Incognita* there should be made that year. Instead, the explorers would attempt to penetrate the pack ice at a more favorable time from the Cape of Good Hope.

On November 9, Dickerson sent instructions for sailing. The primary object, he said, was "the promotion of the great interests of commerce and navigation." Advancing science was of "comparatively secondary importance." To accomplish these, the explorers were to examine the "undiscovered islands, rocks, reefs, and shoals," and "to penetrate into as high southern latitudes as may be approached now without danger to the ships and crews. . . ." [23] Was the Secretary agreeing with his commander's plan?

Regardless, Jones regretted that orders were not "issued at the *first* instead of now, at the eleventh hour of . . . [his] connexion with this ill-fated though most noble of enterprises." [24] He was anxious to terminate his association, because tribulations and trials had robbed him of both health and money. Dickerson was appalled at the thought of Jones's retirement, knowing no "captain or commander in the navy would willingly take the command of a squadron, the vessels of which and the officers of which have been selected without his participation; and it would certainly be unreasonable to require such duty under such circumstances." [25] The commander nevertheless persisted. When many members of the crew on shore leave deserted, he retired to his home in Virginia broken in health and in spirit. The Secretary of the Navy had no alternative but to relieve Thomas Ap Catesby Jones of his command.

[23] Instructions from Mahlon Dickerson to Thomas Ap Catesby Jones, Navy Dept., Nov. 9, 1837, 25 Cong., 2 Sess., *House Ex. Doc.* 147 (Letters), 507.

[24] Thomas Ap Catesby Jones to Mahlon Dickerson, New York, Nov. 14, 1837, *ibid.*, 563.

[25] Mahlon Dickerson to Thomas Ap Catesby Jones, Navy Dept., Nov. 27, 1837, *ibid.*, 580.

chapter eight

TO THE SOUTH!

Secretary Dickerson viewed Catesby Jones's overt departure as a cowardly desertion and as a climax to a discreditable term as the leader of an important naval project. Jones had almost dealt a deathblow to exploration by deserting an ill-prepared expedition. But the former commander was not alone responsible for conditions. The Secretary himself was equally if not more liable. He had vacillated in his instructions and had failed to discipline his refractory commander. One critic described Mahlon Dickerson as an individual whose qualities made him a leader in social life, but destroyed his effectiveness as a public official. Now Dickerson was faced with the unenviable and perplexing task of assigning a new commander and saving the expedition.

First he offered the position to Captain William B. Shubrick, who promptly refused it because the *Macedonian* was much too large and the *Pioneer* and *Consort* were almost totally unfit for exploring. This rejection destroyed whatever confidence the harassed Dickerson had in Jones's fleet, and he appointed another board composed of Commodores J. H. Aulick, Isaac Hull, and James Biddle to decide upon the character of the squadron.

These veteran officers confirmed the Secretary's opinion— the expedition should be reduced in size. It should, they said, include four vessels: a sloop-of-war of the second class; two ships or barques of 300 to 350 tons each; and a storeship of 450 tons. These ships should be lightly armed and their officers and crews should not exceed 330 men. In addition, the frames of one or two decked boats of 20 tons each should be taken by the expedition for surveying in shallow waters.

Even though some of the most experienced officers in the navy supported these conclusions, Dickerson continued to be dogged by ill-luck in his selection of a commander. The position was declined by Captain Lawrence Kearney because the *Macedonian* was to be removed and the other ships did not meet his specifications, as well as by Captain Matthew C. Perry, who could not accept because of personal obligations. At this juncture President Martin Van Buren removed the Secretary of the Navy from a thoroughly embarrassing situation by ordering his Secretary of War, the irrepressible Joel Roberts Poinsett, to direct the planning of the expedition. "Citizen" Reynolds was amazed that the Secretary of War would "prostitute the dignity" of his position "by indecently carrying out the imbecile, vindictive, and proscriptive measures of Secretary Dickerson." [1]

Like his predecessor, Joel Poinsett was not immediately successful in his quest for a commander. His first choice, Captain F. H. Gregory, regretfully announced he could not serve because it would bring desolation and ruin to his family. Poinsett was dismayed at the "refusal of so many officers to accept an honorable command, attended to be sure with some danger and difficulty." He concluded: "Whether their reluctance arises from ill health, indisposition to encounter the hazard of failure, or from the situation of their families, the fact of their withholding service which they are bound by every consideration of duty to render cannot fail to affect injuriously the character of the navy." [2] This rejoinder caused Captain Gregory to submit, but the Secretary had already begun other arrangements.

In March, 1838, Poinsett called upon Captain Joseph Smith. This officer agreed to direct the exploration if Lieutenants Charles Wilkes, A. B. Pinkham, and George S. Blake would consent to command the secondary vessels. Wilkes, who had been rebuffed by Jones, refused, because he was disgusted with the organization and the objectives of the expedition, and as a result Smith declined the commission. Next the Secretary of War defied precedent and gave the command to the young junior officer who had just rejected a secondary position, Charles Wilkes.

----

[1] "Citizen" to Joel R. Poinsett, New York, June 10, 1838, in Reynolds, *Pacific and Indian Oceans*, p. 454.

[2] Joel R. Poinsett to [F. H. Gregory], Washington, Feb. 19, 1838, in the Poinsett Papers, Pennsylvania Historical Society, Philadelphia.

Lieutenant Wilkes was born in New York City on April 3, 1798, the son of John and Mary Seton Wilkes. He was a grand-nephew of John Wilkes, the outspoken British reformer of the eighteenth century. He began his maritime career in 1815, against the wishes of his father, when he joined the ship *Hibernia* bound for the port of Le Havre. Like other neophyte seamen, he suffered many indignities from the veteran members of the crew. They went so far as to smear tar on each of the "beauty spots" on his cheeks, but his longing for naval life did not diminish.

After this maiden voyage Wilkes studied mathematics for a time before shipping out again on a coastal voyage to Wilmington, North Carolina, and on overseas voyages to Europe and Brazil. Shortly after his return from these cruises, he entered the United States Navy as a midshipman, and was ordered to the U.S.S. *Independence,* then in winter quarters in Boston Harbor. Following this service he was assigned to the *Guerriere* for a Mediterranean cruise. Wilkes completed his sea duty by later serving on the *Franklin* in the Pacific, and on the *Boston* in the Mediterranean.

During the periods of inactivity between voyages, Midshipman Wilkes spent his time studying languages, the humanities, mathematics, and geodetics, the latter from Ferdinand R. Hassler, director of the Coastal Survey. These studies enabled him to pass the examinations necessary for promotion and in 1826 he was commissioned a lieutenant. The same year he married Jane Renwick, sister of the Columbia College scientist, James Renwick.

After his promotion he served a short time with the Mediterranean fleet before joining Hassler in the survey of Narragansett Bay. From this service he learned that the Navy Department's stock of charts and instruments was deficient, and he expressed his views about the shortage to the Navy Commissioners. It is likely his interest in geodetics and hydrographic surveying, plus his realization of the needs of the Navy in these departments, brought his appointment to the superintendency of the newly established Charts and Instruments Depot in 1833. His principal duties were to collect instruments and to check their accuracy.

Charles Wilkes was placed in charge of the procurement of instruments for the exploring expedition in 1828 and again in

1836, when he was sent to Europe to purchase those which could not be found in the United States. Although the scientific corps criticized his purchases because they were limited to astronomical and meteorological instruments, Wilkes thought he had carried out his orders fully. After all, he had not been told exactly what would be needed, and naturally bought instruments useful at all times to the Navy.

Because of his training and connection with the expedition, Wilkes expected to be put in charge of the astronomical and physical departments, and was disillusioned when Jones objected. After he and Professor Renwick had checked the accuracy of his purchases at Columbia College, he was given the job of directing the survey of Georges Shoal and Bank in the Atlantic east of Cape Cod. The survey was completed in 1838, when Wilkes was given the U.S. brig *Porpoise,* his surveying vessel, and was directed to search for a pirate craft which had been victimizing mariners in the harbors at Charleston and Savannah. While engaged in this activity he was called home to command the United States Exploring Expedition.

Since Wilkes was given command of the expedition following his refusal to serve under Captain Smith, he and Secretary Poinsett were accused of using Smith to pave the way for his own assumption of leadership. These charges, of course, were vigorously denied. Although Poinsett had sounded out James Renwick regarding his brother-in-law's availability, Wilkes said his recall to Washington was a complete surprise. He had refused the commission under Smith because he had become thoroughly disgusted with the organization of the exploring cruise. In fact, he asserted, he had declined to accept the command until the Secretary of War agreed to allow him some voice in its preparation. Surprisingly, few senior officers openly objected to Poinsett's selection, but the appointment of an officer to be second in command created a delicate situation.

Lieutenant William L. Hudson, who enjoyed a higher position on the naval register than Wilkes, was Poinsett's personal choice for the second position, but he refused the station because of his rank. Poinsett did not demur, however, for he thought it of "great importance that the commander should have as his second in command, an officer in whose zeal and efficient co-operation he can rely." He was indeed sorry that a "mere matter of etiquette" would stand in Hudson's way, because the expedition was *purely civil, not military.* Poinsett asserted, "It is the opinion of the President, as well as my own, that an Expedition, undertaken to promote science, and extend the bounds of human knowledge, ought to command the services of all who can contribute to its success, in whatever station it may be thought most advantageous to place them; and I venture to hope, that waiving all claim to superior rank, you will accept the command now tendered you." [3]

Hudson accepted the position and Secretary Dickerson issued an order legalizing and clarifying Poinsett's statements. Since the objectives were "scientific and useful," Dickerson said, the expedition was "considered to be entirely divested of all military character," and would return to the United States even if the nation were involved in war.[4] Wilkes did not approve these orders, for he asked that he and Hudson be given temporary appointments as Commanders, which would give them power to discipline their fellow officers. Furthermore, he added, the appearance of rank would lend dignity to the expedition in foreign ports. His wishes were not granted, but privately James Kirke Paulding, who succeeded Dickerson as Secretary of the Navy, gave Wilkes these orders: "Cabals of discontented officers must be promptly arrested, and their leaders either kept in subjection or detached from the squadron, as it is not to be endured that the purposes you are sent to attain are to be defeated by the *fantastic claims of rank.* . . ." [5] But these were not made public nor were they given to the other officers. As a result, Lieutenant Wilkes was faced with instances of insubordination throughout the voyage and had to submit to a court-martial trial on his return for maintaining discipline!

With the Lieutenant's assignment as commander, preparations were again renewed, but reaction in the House of Representatives against the expenditure of more funds for exploration almost destroyed the expedition. Criticism was centered on the admin-

---

[3] Joel R. Poinsett to Lieutenant Hudson, Washington, June 5, 1838, in Wilkes, *Narrative*, I, 352.

[4] *Army and Navy Chronicle*, VI (June 28, 1838), 416.

[5] *Niles' National Register*, LXII (Aug. 20, 1842), 385.

istration, on Wilkes, and on Jones. Three congressmen from
Jones's home state, Virginia, Charles Mercer, Henry Wise, and
Francis Mallory, who were joined by Isaac Bronson of New
York, generally believed the objectives of the supporters of exploration would not be satisfied, because of the incompetence
of the Navy Department and the new commander, and on
account of widespread opposition to the expedition. Mercer did
not think the President and Cabinet together had sufficient
mental capacity to furnish instructions, while Wise testified that
he had learned Wilkes's appointment was made, not on the
basis of his scientific attainments or fitness, but because he had
agreed to dismiss members of the scientific corps who were dis-
liked by the Department. Even the father of the expedition,
Jeremiah N. Reynolds, who had propagandized for exploration
longer than Columbus, was to be left at home.

Mallory presented a statement prepared by Jones which
emphasized that the Secretary of the Navy should be reproved
for the failure of the squadron to go to sea. Dickerson, it said,
had repeatedly changed the objectives of the expedition and
throughout had displayed a want of confidence in his commander. The Virginia congressman also signalized the thoughts
of many by claiming that the commissioning of a junior officer
was a "violation of rank, and consequently a violation of right."
It was Bronson who called attention to the extensive public
and official opposition to the expedition, and asserted that the
appointment of a junior would only increase dissatisfaction and
lead to dissension during the voyage.

These men, excepting Mercer, wanted to convert the exploring
fleet into an Atlantic coast squadron, or at least discontinue
exploration for the time being. Wise especially wanted to employ
the fleet to protect the ports and to carry out coastal surveys.
He did not think the United States Navy should embark on
foreign adventures when "not a single lieutenant in it . . .
could pilot a man-of-war into one of our own ports." [6]

Among those favoring a continuation of exploration, John
Reed, Isaac E. Crary of Michigan, Ogden Hoffman of New York,
and John Quincy Adams of Massachusetts, stood out. Reed

[6] 25 Cong., 2 Sess., *Cong. Globe*, VI, 274.

maintained that censure should be given Secretary Dickerson and the President. Their mismanagement had produced failure. But this did not mean that exploration should be abandoned and the fleet converted into a coast squadron. In the first place, the exploring ships were not suited to coastal surveying because of their large size, and secondly, much useful knowledge for the seafaring population still could be gained.

Crary could not agree with Reed, for in his estimation Thomas Ap Catesby Jones alone was responsible for conditions. He argued that the grandiose scheme which the expedition had become was attributable to him, not to the Navy Department. Jones had envisioned an expedition which would give him lasting renown, not only among his own countrymen, but with the learned people of the world. After all, it was the former commander who required a "body guard" of scientists, and was more interested in chasing butterflies than exploring unknown coasts. Crary emphasized that the expedition would now be completing its duties if it had been sent out as authorized originally.

Ogden Hoffman and John Quincy Adams were Wilkes's most resolute defenders. The congressman from New York thought the new commander was "pre-eminently qualified," and he affirmed that his appointment did not violate the seniority rule since it applied only in wartime. Adams likewise emphasized that the expedition was now under a competent commander—a scientist who had distinguished himself in many ways, and that consequently, it surely would provide benefits if it went to sea. On the other hand, he went on, the United States would lose face throughout the world if the exploration was suspended now after it had been widely publicized. Why not give the administration another chance to redeem itself from the multitude of errors it had committed.

In the end, debate was brought to a conclusion by William Key Boon of Ohio, who reminded the House that more money than the appropriation for continuing the expedition was being wasted by useless argument. The question was called for on April 11, and the appropriation passed the House by a margin of two votes. A few weeks later it passed the Senate, where the debate paralleled that of the House, but was much less extensive.

Meanwhile, it had become abundantly apparent that the *Consort* and *Active*, which had been purchased to replace the deficient *Pilot*, were almost totally unfit for service in rough seas. They had been given trial runs in February, 1838, and pitched heavily in the turbulent Atlantic. As a result, the leaders decided not to tempt fate by taking any of Jones's ships into the Antarctic, and all but the storeship *Relief* were replaced by supposedly more efficient vessels. The flagship of Wilkes's squadron was the sloop-of-war *Vincennes,* 780 tons, while the secondary vessels were the 650-ton sloop *Peacock,* the gun brig *Porpoise,* 230 tons, and the two tenders, *Sea Gull,* 110 tons, and *Flying Fish,* 97 tons, which were reconstructed New York pilot boats. These ships, which Wilkes thought all that could be desired, were assembled at Norfolk and the inexperienced officers began collecting supplies.

Although Charles Wilkes's lieutenants worried the Commissioners of the Navy with extravagant requisitions, this was the least of the troubles confronting the leaders of the expedition. Poinsett, Dickerson, who was soon to be replaced as head of the Navy Department by James Kirke Paulding, and Wilkes decided that Jeremiah N. Reynolds should not accompany the squadron, and that the corps of scientists should be reduced. Reynolds, who was now trying to obtain the post of commercial agent, was told he would be given no position at all because individual desires had to be subordinated to the successful completion of the objectives.

The unwanted members of the scientific corps were not dismissed with similar forthrightness. On April 30, Titian Ramsay Peale reported that he, Charles Pickering, and Asa Gray, thought some of the members should be removed. Gray thought such a plan had the "advantage of leaving home all the blockheads and taking the best fellows," but he resigned later because the organization of the expedition had been changed. Wilkes, for his part, believed the "blockheads" who should be discharged were the incompetent John W. Randall, Reynell Coates, who was "out of his senses," James Eights, a man with bad habits, Walter Johnson, Horatio Hale, and the painters. He saw no "difficulty now to occur . . . from this ridiculously overgrown corps, if the Department will only suffer their pay to continue until the sailing of the Expedition. . . ." [7] Poinsett adopted this plan and the unwitting scientists, who were to be left at home, continued to make preparations for duty until the expedition sailed. Of the group discharged, only Horatio Hale was spared, for pressure was brought to bear on the Secretary of War for the retention of a philologist.

On July 26, President Van Buren, the new Secretary of the Navy, Paulding, and Poinsett visited the fleet at Norfolk, much to the pleasure of the explorers. Wilkes reported: "On this occasion, . . . a salute was fired, (none of the instruments had then been embarked,) by all the vessels, and the yards were manned. This produced a good effect on all, for it showed us that a watchful eye was kept over us, and that much interest was felt in the undertaking. This visit formed an epoch to which I often heard reference made during the cruise. Few are able to estimate the feelings that such acts occasion to those engaged in undertakings like this." [8] All the instruments and provisions were stowed in less than a month, and by August 14 Wilkes was impatiently awaiting orders from his superiors to take the fleet to sea. Paulding's instructions arrived on August 17 and two days later the United States Exploring Expedition sailed out of Hampton Roads.

Wilkes was ordered to take his fleet southward via Rio de Janeiro to Tierra del Fuego, where the first attempt to penetrate the Antarctic ice was to be made. When this cruise was completed, surveys were to be made of such Pacific islands as the Navigator's Group and the Fijis before the fleet moved to Sydney, Australia, to refit and replenish supplies. A second Antarctic cruise was to be made from Tasmania during the Antarctic summer season of 1840 with Kerguelen Island as the ultimate destination. Then Wilkes was to take his fleet northward via the Hawaiian Islands to the northwest coast of North America and the seas of Japan.

Since the rules and regulations of the naval service required

----

[7] Charles Wilkes to Joel R. Poinsett, New York, May 1, 1838, Poinsett Papers.

[8] Wilkes, *Narrative*, I, xv. See also the Journal of Lieutenant Charles Wilkes Aboard the *Vincennes* and the *Porpoise* (3 vols.), I, July 26, 1838, in the Records of the Hydrographic Office, R.G. 37, Department of the Navy, National Archives Microfilm Publication, M 75. Hereafter cited as NA, M 75.

all officers to keep a journal, Paulding ordered that under no circumstances should Wilkes or any member of his command furnish "any persons not belonging to the Expedition, with copies of any journal, chart, plan, memorandum, specimen, drawing, painting, or information of any kind, which had any reference to the objects or proceedings of the Expedition." [9] The commander added that his officers should keep a "diary, in which will be noticed all that relates to public information, being a record of all objects of interest, however small, which may take place during the cruise, in the scientific or any other department." [10] They could briefly express their opinions if they felt the need.

The voyage southward was performed easily, and on January 26, 1839, the fleet, with the exception of the sluggish *Relief*, anchored in the nearly land-locked Orange Harbor, New Island, Tierra del Fuego. Wilkes immediately began preparations for a cruise into the Antarctic, although the lateness of the season precluded one of any duration. The explorers wanted to get some experience in Antarctic seas, and they hoped the ice masses would be sufficiently detached from Palmer Land to afford a landing.

To make a thorough investigation of Palmer's discovery, Wilkes thought it necessary to divide his fleet. First of all, he did not wish to endanger the larger, less maneuverable ships and he assigned them to perform surveys of Tierra del Fuego. The crew of the *Vincennes* was to conduct investigations in the vicinity of Orange Harbor, while the *Relief* was to be used to examine the Strait of Magellan. Lieutenant Wilkes decided to board the *Porpoise*, commanded by Lieutenant Cadwallader Ringgold, which was to sail in company with the *Sea Gull*, under Lieutenant Robert Johnson. It was his hope to explore the eastern shore of Palmer Land as far southward as possible.

Lieutenant Hudson, on the other hand, was to take the *Peacock* and the *Flying Fish*, Lieutenant William Walker commanding, westward to the *ne plus ultra* of Captain Cook in 105°

....
[9] James Kirke Paulding to Charles Wilkes, Navy Dept., Aug. 11, 1838, in Wilkes, *Narrative*, I, xxx.

[10] "General Order," U.S. Ship Vincennes, Sept. 13, 1838, in Wilkes, *Narrative*, I, 367.

W., before pushing southward and eastward toward the western extremities of Palmer's discovery. In so doing, they were to get "more and more to the southward, and to pass to the southward of the two small islands called Peter I. and Alexander, (the farthest land south discovered by the Russians in 1821,) and then [to] fall in with . . . Palmer's Land." [11] Although Wilkes thought the land Palmer had sighted extended farther south-westward than Bellingshausen's discoveries, he did not discount the possibility of circumnavigating it. Hudson was instructed to pursue such a plan.

By February 25, the Antarctic fleet was prepared for departure and the ships sailed out of Orange Harbor early that morning. The commander was depressed because he visualized the "very many dangers" they would encounter. The next day the *Porpoise* and *Sea Gull* fell in with the whaleship *America*, from New Zealand, bound for New York. The crew was jubilant because their hold was filled with oil, but Wilkes said he had never seen a more ill-kempt group of mariners. He was surprised scurvy had not completely ravaged them. Their captain agreed to carry a packet of mail to New York.

Early on the first of March the explorers were greeted by snow flurries and saw their first ice island, which excited an unusual amount of curiosity. Later that day they made the shores of Ridley Island, one of the smallest members of the main group of the South Shetlands. "It was high, broken, and rugged, with the top covered with snow." The surf was much too heavy to permit a landing and the two ships bore on to Bransfield's King George Island, which Wilkes said was well placed on the charts. He thought it was about 1,000 feet high and of volcanic origin. Both the highlands and the valleys were completely covered with snow.

Wilkes and Johnson headed their ships eastward the next day and sighted O'Brien and Aspland Islands before doubling back to the southwest toward Bridgeman Island in Bransfield Strait between Palmer Land and the central group of the South Shetlands. Because the explorers could distinctly see smoke rising, Wilkes determined to land, but before a boat could be

---

[11] Charles Wilkes to Wm. L. Hudson, U.S. Ship Vincennes, Orange Harbour, Terra [sic] del Fuego, Feb. 22, 1839, in Wilkes, *Narrative*, I, 394.

lowered, the mist they had encountered previously became a thick fog and the attempt was thus halted. After waiting for a break, the ships were steered southward under short sail.

The next morning the fog cleared and the *Porpoise* and *Sea Gull* were given full canvas and steered toward Palmer Land. Cape pigeons, petrels, and penguins "seemed astonished at encountering so unusual an object as a vessel in these frozen seas," Wilkes testified. The explorers soon "made land" which they believed was Mount Hope or Hope Island, "the eastern extremity of Palmer's Land," and they pushed toward the shore through drift ice and icebergs. Wilkes declared, "I have rarely seen a finer sight. The sea was literally studded with these beautiful masses, some of pure white, others showing all the shades of opal, others emerald green, and occasionally here and there some of deep black, forming a strong contrast to the pure white." [12] Within this aura of dreadful brilliance the explorers discovered three very large rocks they named the Adventure Islets.

Wilkes soon decided it would be impossible to make a landing on the coast of Palmer's discovery which trended southeastward 25 to 30 miles, because the difficulties were insurmountable. The decks of the ships were covered with ice, while the men were suffering "not only from want of sufficient room to accommodate the numbers in the vessel, but from the inadequacy of the clothing with which they had been supplied." Since this clothing had been purchased at a great expense, Wilkes was disheartened to find it was "entirely unworthy the service, and inferior in every way to the samples exhibited." [13]

On March 5, the danger from the constant fog and mist, the huge ice islands, and the sunken, deceptive masses of floe ice was augmented by a fierce gale, which further reduced the maneuverability of the ice-encased vessels. Because the lateness of the summer precluded any favorable change in the weather, Wilkes ordered Johnson to take his little schooner to Deception Island and eventually to Orange Harbor, while he sailed the *Porpoise* back toward the South Shetlands in order to further

----

[12] Wilkes, *Narrative*, I, 136. See also the Journal of Lieutenant Charles Wilkes, I, March 3, 1839.

[13] Wilkes, *Narrative*, I, 137.

examine them. Actually the commander hoped to search for the legendary Aurora Islands, but the weakness of his crew from constant exposure and the threat of the dreaded scurvy changed his plans. Instead, he decided to make a hurried investigation of Elephant and Cornwallis Islands while proceeding to Orange Harbor.

The northward voyage of the *Porpoise* was accomplished without accident, although Wilkes and his men had many anxious moments. The wind blew light and fresh, while the ship was constantly enveloped by fog and surrounded by treacherous ice. These conditions almost caused the explorers to run their ship aground on Elephant Island, which they reached on March 7. Again the sea was too high to permit a landing, so Wilkes sailed through the channel separating Elephant and Cornwallis Islands past the Seal Rocks and westward to his port of embarkation.

Meanwhile, the little *Sea Gull*, whose commander had not been "particularly grieved" when Wilkes changed his plans, was undergoing similar problems. The same day Wilkes was avoiding the rocks of Elephant Island the schooner was tacking westward from King George Island toward Deception, where Lieutenant Johnson hoped to find a thermometer which the English Captain William Foster had left in 1829. The explorers were unable to locate the instrument, but they did discover a boiling spring which they thought was an unusual phenomenon in the land of ice. On March 17, after examining this breached crater, Johnson planted a staff over two bottles containing information on their voyage to and the exploration of Deception, and made sail for Orange Harbor.

The commanders of the *Peacock* and the 96-ton *Flying Fish* were not nearly so successful in the performance of their duties. On February 26, the day after they had slipped out of Orange Harbor, Lieutenants Hudson and Walker encountered a fierce gale and were separated even though they observed all the precautions such as firing guns and burning blue lights. After fourteen hours of waiting, Hudson steered his sloop-of-war toward their first point of rendezvous, hoping to intercept the *Flying Fish* there. The boisterous weather kept him from reaching it, however, and he steered the *Peacock* southward in the face of severe southwest gales in an effort to fulfill Wilkes's instructions.

During this voyage a veteran seaman, William Stewart, "captain of the main-top," lost his footing while climbing the yardarm and fell into the wind-swept ocean. The injuries he sustained were fatal and on March 11 his body "was committed to the deep." The moroseness felt by all members of the crew at Stewart's funeral gave way momentarily to the excitement of sighting ice islands in 63° 30′ S., 80° W., but these harbingers of the Antarctic became constant and decidedly troublesome companions throughout the duration of this cruise southward.

The explorers encountered every difficulty associated with early Antarctic exploring. When strong gales did not raise the heavy seas over the side of the vessel, thick fogs encompassed it, completely destroying visibility. The officers were convinced their situation would not become better. The ice was constantly "making on every part of the ship outside & also upon the Gundeck which . . . [was] open at the fore & main hatches. . . ." [14] To combat the bitter cold, Hudson gave each member of the crew an extra serving of coffee daily because they were not receiving rations of whiskey.

When the *Peacock* was in 68° 08′ S., longitude 95° 44′ W., on March 25, the spirits of the explorers lifted suddenly when the *Flying Fish* appeared. In a short time Lieutenant Walker was aboard the sloop-of-war and he told Hudson he had made each place of rendezvous, but had lost his boats and most of his rigging and sails while doing so. Still he had continued southward, hoping to pass Captain James Cook's farthest point. During the week between March 19 and 26 Walker had guided his little craft through the ice floes and islands along a barrier of ice between 68° and 70° south, and 105° and 95° west, while attempting to find a passage through it. The explorers reached

[14] Journal of Lt. George F. Emmons, on Board the U.S. Sloop of War Peacock, in the United States Exploring Expedition, March 17, 1839, in the William Robertson Coe Collection, Yale University Library, New Haven, Conn. See also Wm. L. Hudson to Charles Wilkes, U.S. Ship Peacock, At Sea, lat. 60° S., long. 84° W., April 1, 1839, in Wilkes, *Narrative*, I, 406; and the Journal of J. Frederick Sickels, Assistant Surgeon, Aboard the *Peacock* and *Relief*, March 4, 1839, NA, M 75. Hereafter cited as Sickels, Journal.

the 70th parallel of south latitude on March 22, where they found a clear passage, but when they entered this avenue to the south, thick weather and intense cold greeted them. The commander, who had grown accustomed to such adversities, was not unduly alarmed, and he stepped below to stick his toes into the stove. He was soon rudely interrupted by a call from the lookout—the *Flying Fish* was completely encircled by ice! Walker "jumped on deck" and found his ship in "narrow fields of ice, with narrow passages of water between." He said, "I did not know at first how I should proceed; but, after a careful look round, I ran over to the . . . shore of the pond, and stood along it in search of a passage, that I could not find; but, observing at intervals 'sutures' in the ice, where it did not appear firmly formed, I resolved to take advantage of this, and, if possible, force a passage, feeling it necessary at all hazards, to extricate ourselves as soon as possible." [15] At this juncture the wind favored Walker's daring plan by blowing free and he gave his little craft the main-sheet and "got about six knots . . . on her." When the proper distance from one of the sutures was reached, the young commander brought his vessel around and headed for it. With contact the ice cracked ominously, the ship heaved, but remained intact, and in a short time the explorers were in a "tolerably clear sea." Walker said, "I believe all must have returned thanks to Heaven for their deliverance." It took another similar episode, however, to make the explorers turn toward Orange Harbor. On this voyage they met the *Peacock*.

Lieutenant Walker's news destroyed any inclinations Lieutenant Hudson might have had to continue the search for the southwestern extremities of Palmer Land, and he decided to take the *Peacock* and her consort to Tierra del Fuego. This decision required a great deal of "moral courage" because at the moment there was less ice in the neighborhood than previously and Hudson was inclined to continue the search. He concluded, however, "had I followed my own inclinations merely, and allowed the promptings of ambition, or love of praise, to have governed my decisions, regardless of the future operations of the Expedition, the lives of my officers and men, and the trust

---

[15] William M. Walker to William L. Hudson, U.S. Schooner Flying-Fish, At Sea, March 26, 1839, in Wilkes, *Narrative*, I, 412.

reposed in me by the government, I should indeed have been unworthy of the trust I hold, and ever felt a consciousness, that whatever more might have been achieved, by any further attempt south, at that late season, would have been acquired only by recklessly hazarding, . . . the lives intrusted to my care." [16]

The explorers turned their ships northward with little to show for their strenuous efforts except some observations on the climate, currents, and the aurora borealis. Titian Ramsay Peale, the lone scientist accompanying them, made a collection of Antarctic birds.

---

[16] Wm. L. Hudson to Charles Wilkes, U.S. Ship Peacock, At Sea, 60° S., long. 84° W., April 1, 1839, Wilkes, *Narrative*, I, 407.

chapter nine

AN ANTARCTIC CONTINENT

Following their brief but strenuous excursion into the Antarctic, only the *Porpoise, Flying Fish,* and *Sea Gull* assembled at Orange Harbor. Lieutenant Hudson left the *Flying Fish* off Cape Horn, taking the *Peacock* to Valparaiso, Chile, where he was joined by Lieutenant Andrew K. Long in the dilatory *Relief.* The commander of the storeship, with most of the scientists in his charge, had been completely unsuccessful in his attempt to enter the western entrance of Magellan's Strait. He had tacked too far south from the rugged coast of Tierra del Fuego to get back in the face of strong southwest winds. For twenty days Long had maneuvered his cumbersome craft toward a small island the explorers called Noir Island, hoping to find haven in a harbor there. Getting in was a feat, but an unrewarding one. The harbor was totally unprotected and the *Relief's* anchors were lost when she was moored. Her captain then had decided to head northward toward Valparaiso rather than brave the boisterous waters between Noir Island and Orange Harbor.

Since Lieutenant Wilkes believed the *Relief* would return to Tierra del Fuego, he ordered the commanders of the *Sea Gull* and *Flying Fish* to wait and provide the scientists with more rapid transit to Valparaiso. The tenders tarried for ten days before beginning their circuit of Cape Horn. At midnight on April 26, the little ships separated. Midshipman Samuel R. Knox, commanding the *Flying Fish,* had seen his consort for the last time, because "shortly afterwards, it began to blow in strong squalls, and rapidly increased to a gale." By morning the wind was blowing furiously, forcing Knox back to Orange Harbor.

Two days went by before the gale reduced sufficiently to permit another attempt at the Horn. On this voyage the explorers fell in with a whaler, "who seemed not a little surprised to find a New York pilot-boat off the Cape, and to have an interrogatory put to him, to know if he wanted a Cape Pilot." [1]

When the *Flying Fish* alone was anchored with the rest of the fleet in Valparaiso Harbor on May 19, Lieutenant Wilkes felt some uneasiness about the *Sea Gull*, but no great alarm, and he left Lieutenant Thomas T. Craven, second in command of the *Vincennes*, in the Chilean port to take charge of the tender when she arrived. After remaining several months Craven boarded the schooner *Boxer* of the Pacific squadron and conducted an unsuccessful search for the *Sea Gull* in all places she could have met disaster. It was concluded that the converted pilot boat had gone down in the perilous waters off the Horn. Still Wilkes refused to believe the little tender had not reached safety, such was his confidence in her officers. The loss of these men, Midshipmen James W. E. Reid and Frederick A. Bacon, and of their ship was "a great disadvantage to the Expedition, which was felt . . . during the remainder of the cruise, these vessels being well calculated for the southern seas, particularly in the low latitudes, though much exposed in boisterous weather." [2] The trouble the *Flying Fish* later experienced does not bear this out, however.

From Valparaiso, the *Vincennes, Peacock, Porpoise,* and *Flying Fish* followed the coast of South America to Callao, Peru, where they took different tracks into the Pacific to survey the Tuamotu Archipelago, Society Islands, Samoa, the Fijis, New Hebrides, and New Caledonia. Lieutenant Long was ordered to return with the storeship to the United States after landing provisions at Hawaii and Sydney, Australia, where the fleet was to rendezvous before making a second and last attempt to discover an Antarctic land mass.

After dark on November 29, 1839, the *Vincennes* and *Peacock* edged into the narrow Port Jackson at Sydney, where they were joined later by the *Porpoise* and the *Flying Fish.* "When the good people of Sydney looked abroad in the morning they were

[1] Wilkes, *Narrative,* I, 206.
[2] *Ibid.*

much astonished to see two men-of-war lying among their shipping, which had entered their harbour in spite of the difficulties
of the channel, without being reported, and unknown to pilots." [3]
One officer reported that several newspapers described the fleet's
arrival as being remarkable. They jokingly declared it was an
American trick to save the cost of a pilot.

The streets of the city were "speedily alive" with the officers and
men of the expedition, who were delighted to be in a civilized
country where the English language was spoken. The sailors saw
many strange practices, but none elicited as many exclamations of
surprise as the mixed marriages between Negroes and whites. One
member of the small corps of marines accompanying the explorers
asserted that he had heard of this custom, but had never seen such
an unusual sight. To him something in the marriage seemed "*so
unnatural*."

While the members of the crew were becoming acquainted with
the capital of New South Wales, Lieutenants Wilkes and Hudson
were busy exchanging official greetings with the United States
consul, J. W. Williams, and the Governor, Sir George Gipps. Their
reception by the Governor was most generous. Besides giving the
first of a round of lavish parties for the Americans, he allowed
Wilkes to set up an observatory in Fort Macquarie, Sydney Harbor, and offered every facility for conducting experiments.

Shortly all members of the expedition were occupied. Wilkes
was busy with his astronomical studies, the scientists had begun
inland journeys in search of specimens, while the other officers and
seamen performed routine repairs on the ships and stowed provisions. By December 18 Wilkes had completed his observatory
duties, and the preparation of the ships for their forthcoming Antarctic employment was begun in earnest. The commander had
been nonplused at the attitude of many visitors to the squadron.
They compared it with what they had learned about the British
expedition under Captain James Clark Ross and concluded it was
decidedly ill-prepared. Wilkes said, "They inquired, whether we
had compartments in our ships to prevent us from sinking? How we

---

[3] Wilkes, *Narrative*, II, 160. See also the Letters Relating to the Wilkes
Exploring Expedition (2 vols.), I, Charles Wilkes to James Kirke Paulding,
U.S. Flag Ship Vincennes, Sydney Cove, Dec. 1, 1839, NA, M 75. Here-
after cited as Exploring Expedition Letters (At Sea).

intended to keep ourselves warm? What kind of antiscorbutic [preventative for scurvy] we were to use? and where were our great ice-saws?" His answer to each of these queries was negative, and he decided that "this want of preparation certainly did not add to the character for wisdom of our government, with this community; but they saw us all cheerful, young and healthy, and gave us the character, that . . . our countrymen generally bear, of recklessness of life and limb." [4] The Australians were certain the carefree Americans were "doomed to be frozen to death."

Charles Wilkes certainly did not look forward to such a fate, but he was not completely convinced they could survive if forced to winter in the Antarctic. The ships were not spacious enough to accommodate provisions for more than twelve months, while their fuel was inadequate for more than seven months. The commander's anxiety over these limitations was amplified by the condition of his second largest ship, the *Peacock*. When she had arrived in Sydney the carpenter had reported that her "upperworks" were rotted, and a thorough examination revealed her state to be much worse than represented. Wilkes and Hudson held long consultations before deciding it would be impossible to make repairs without giving up the Antarctic cruise. "We made up our minds," Wilkes explained, "that it was absolutely necessary for the credit of the Expedition and the country for her to perform it; for we were well satisfied that improper imputations and motives, would be ascribed to us, if she did not, and was detained undergoing repairs, in a state of inactivity, during the season for operations in the high southern latitudes. The necessity I felt of subjecting so many lives in so unworthy a ship, caused me great anxiety during the whole cruise." [5] Thus the *Peacock* remained in her deplorable state, but the artisans of Sydney, whose wages Wilkes thought were exorbitant, fulfilled the minor needs of the rest of the ships.

As the day for departure neared, every member of the expedi-

---

[4] Wilkes, *Narrative*, II, 275.

[5] *Ibid.* See also Jonas Dibble to William L. Hudson, U.S. Ship Peacock, Sydney Cove, New South Wales, Dec. 21, 1839, in Wilkes, *Narrative*, II, 449; Wm. L. Hudson to Charles Wilkes, U.S. Ship Peacock, Sydney, New South Wales, Dec. 22, 1839, in Wilkes, *Narrative*, II, 449; and Charles Wilkes to James Kirke Paulding, U.S. Ship Vincennes, Sydney Cove, Dec. 22, 1839, in Exploring Expedition Letters (At Sea), I.

tion felt and expressed regret at being compelled to leave their friends in the capital of New South Wales. These people had taken the explorers into their homes, making the long days away from their families pleasant ones. Wilkes summarized the feelings of his men by declaring that Sydney was a "glorious colony"—a colony that should be accorded much more attention by the home government. After expressing appreciation for everything done for them, the Americans boarded their ships on Christmas Day and soon began their transit out of Port Jackson.

Lieutenant Wilkes's instructions to his commanders, Lieutenants Hudson, Cadwallader Ringgold of the *Porpoise,* and R. F. Pinkney of the *Flying Fish,* were explicit but not detailed. The objectives of this cruise were to reach as high a southern latitude as could be attained without hazarding the ships, and to make astronomical, magnetic, and hydrographic observations in the seas of the Antarctic. At all times the officers were to give their most careful attention to both the health and comfort of their men and the "most economical care and expenditure" of their stores and provisions. Since Wilkes knew the lives of the seamen would be jeopardized under ordinary south polar conditions, he urged his lieutenants to prevent the separation of the ships, because their greatest protection was in keeping together.

If a separation occurred during their voyage southward, they were to rendezvous first at Macquarie Island, and then at Emerald Isle. From the latter any lost ship was to proceed to the first impenetrable barrier of ice and sail westward along it between 160° and 105° E. until March 1. The return voyage was to take them to the Bay of Islands, New Zealand, and thence to the Friendly or Tonga Group. Wilkes believed any separated members would be able to join the remainder of the fleet at either of these places.

In spite of the commander's most earnest desires and strenuous efforts, the ships were unable to sail together. First, the schooner *Flying Fish* was lost on January 1, a day Wilkes termed a "weatherbreeder." The sea was smooth and placid, but in a short time the temperature dropped sharply while the breeze increased in force. Before long the ships were sailing briskly, with the larger ones quickly outdistancing the tender even though they shortened sail. When a dense fog forced them to halt temporarily the next day, Wilkes ordered the commanders of the *Peacock* and *Porpoise* to sail east and west in search of the schooner. Later the three stood over to Macquarie Island, but the *Flying Fish* was not seen again until they returned from their cruise. "The officers and crew were not slow in assigning to the Flying Fish a similar fate with her unfortunate mate, the Sea Gull."

Next, on the third, it was the *Peacock* that disappeared temporarily. Horns, bells, drums, and guns sounded on the *Vincennes* and *Porpoise* brought no response and Hudson's vessel was not sighted before the fleet had reached the area of pack ice and bergs. Wilkes and Ringgold were able to keep their ships together, however, until they reached the ice shelf attached to the Antarctic Continent. They stood in for their first place of rendezvous on January 7, but the strong current kept them away. Emerald Isle was not located in 57° S., 162° E., where it was placed on their charts and undoubtedly was another legendary territory.

When the ships reached latitude 61° 08′ S., longitude 162° 32′ E. on January 10, the explorers saw their first icebergs, "much worn by the sea into cavities, [and] exhibiting fissures as though they were ready to be rent asunder." Soon these grim reminders of what was to come became so numerous that Wilkes and Ringgold had to alter their course constantly to avoid them. In the vicinity of the 64th parallel their progress was halted by an immense barrier consisting of closely packed ice masses. "One and all felt disappointed," Wilkes testified, "for we had flattered ourselves that the way was open to further progress to the southward, and had imbibed the impression (from the extraordinary weather we had had at Sydney, and the reports of icebergs having been seen farther to the northward than usual, by all the vessels arriving) that the season would be an open one." [6] The belief in the possibility of an open south polar sea was a persistent one.

The explorers' disappointment at having their progress blocked was nothing, however, when compared to their discomfort from the intense cold and constant dampness. Some of the men had "to turn in their hammocks with damp clothes," because the small stoves on the *Vincennes* afforded almost no means of drying them. Wilkes immediately began taking precautions against exposure, requiring all hands to muster thrice daily to have their clothing

[6] Wilkes, *Narrative*, II, 286–87.

examined. "Every man was examined seperately [sic] to see if he had flannel on, and the result reported to the Capt." An extra pint of steaming coffee was furnished to them at midday. One seaman, unstinting in his praise for Wilkes, said he thought the commander was using every care "to mitigate as far as possible the hardships and suffering incident to such a hazardous cruise." [7]

By virtually hugging the barrier, Wilkes and Ringgold were able to advance to 65° S., where the color of the water changed from inky blue indicating depth to the soft olive green of shallow areas. The explorers thought this and the appearance of numerous birds and whales meant land was nearby. But their soundings in 100 fathoms found no bottom. Only their "credulity magnified Ice Islands into terra firma." They continued their course until they spoke the *Peacock* on January 15 and took separate tracks westward.

Although he had been unable to obtain positive soundings, Wilkes was confident they were on the brink of a discovery. As they pushed southwestward, the color of the sea did not change and the whales, seals, albatrosses, and petrels were their constant companions. When the *Vincennes* reached a position in 66° S., 158° 56′ E. on January 16, the seamen aloft noticed snow-covered elevations beyond the barrier which they described as the "loom of land." Wilkes too was convinced a discovery had been made until he dropped a lead 250 fathoms without finding bottom. He was perplexed at the depth of the water, but he sketched the "loom of land" in his journal. The commander did not realize that the immense ice masses attached to Antarctica had worn away the shelf, making it impossible in most places to find the ocean floor at the normal 50- to 200-fathom depth.

Three days later the ice-covered elevations beyond the barrier were seen again. They must be hills, Wilkes concluded. But the *Vincennes* ran into fog and he was unable to perceive them dis-

---

[7] [Joseph G. Clark], Journal of a Cruise in the U.S. Ship Vincennes, Charles Wilkes, Commander in Chief, in the Years 1838, 1839, 1840, 1841, 1842, Jan. 10, 1840, Manuscripts Division, Library of Congress. This is believed to be Clark's journal because many passages in it are similar to ones in his book *Lights and Shadows of Sailor Life, as Exemplified in Fifteen Years' Experience, Including the More Thrilling Events of the U.S. Expedition* . . . (Boston, 1847). Hereafter cited as [Clark], Journal.

tinctly. Some of the "most experienced seamen" verified his beliefs, but the officers almost to a man did not. The commander disgustedly decided they were doing everything in their power to make his "exertions go for nothing." [8]

The explorers skirted the wall of ice for several miles before "a large open space showed itself to the southward." Wilkes hoped this would be their avenue to the "land," but the shelf again halted their progress in latitude 67° 04′ S., longitude 147° 30′ E. Wilkes rather forlornly named this opening Disappointment Bay and steered his ship out again. Forty miles were put between the *Vincennes* and the opening when it was discovered Lieutenant Joseph A. Underwood had noted on the log-slate that there had been an opening to the south. Why Underwood did this is not evident, but Wilkes turned back to Disappointment Bay to put the "matter to rest." On January 25 the *Vincennes* again reached its termination and found no passage.

At this stage, the weather, which had been thick and dangerous, cleared, but a violent gale made the movements of the ships constantly perilous. Large ice islands and submerged drift ice blocked their path, but the explorers pushed onward until they were compelled to leave the immediate vicinity of the shelf. "During the whole of this bad weather Capt Wilkes . . . [was] almost constantly upon Deck, sometimes not going down to his meals but have it brot. [sic] upon Deck to him." [9] The commander undoubtedly felt his presence near the wheel was necessary to safeguard the lives of his seamen, but this was not the only consideration causing him to forsake rest and to expose himself to the rigors of the climate. Each day Wilkes and his men thought they were able to see the ridges of Antarctica to the south and east.

On January 28, the *Vincennes* again was enveloped in fog, making the position of the explorers critical. The wind grew stronger, forcing them to retrace their track to find better weather. But this maneuver did not ease their plight. The *Vincennes* suddenly was embayed by large bodies of ice, and it quickly became obvious she

---

[8] Journal of Lieutenant Charles Wilkes, I, Jan. 16 and 19, 1840. See also the Journal of William Briskee, Armorer, Aboard the *Vincennes*, Jan. 18, 1840, NA, M 75. Hereafter cited as Briskee, Journal. See in addition Clark, *Lights and Shadows*, pp. 103–4.

[9] Briskee, Journal, Jan. 25, 1840.

could not regain her course. Nothing could be done "but . . . keep a good look-out, and the ship under sufficient way to steer well." In the face of a violent snowstorm the explorers cautiously made their way through perilously heavy seas, narrowly missing masses of ice, until they found an open passage to tolerably clear water. As Wilkes put it, they "had escaped an awful death."

After this harrying experience, transit along the shelf was facilitated by clear weather until January 30, when the explorers entered a small indentation in the barrier where they had observed black rocks protruding through the snow on an elevated area seemingly about a mile and a half from the ship. Wilkes was exultant. He heralded the discovery by labelling his journal entry for that day "Antarctic Land discovered beyond cavil." In his printed *Narrative* he declared he "gave the land the name of the Antarctic Continent." [10]

These highlands, about 3,000 feet high and stretching east and west approximately 60 miles, were in 66° 45′ S., 140° 02′ E. Some of the crew members thought they "observed some columns bearing south, which had the appearance of volcanic smoke," but Wilkes decided they were nothing but snow squalls. Their joy at this undeniable discovery was short-lived, however, because the constantly moving ice had placed the *Vincennes* in a precarious position again, while the boisterous weather made extrication problematical. "To run the gauntlet again among the icebergs was out of the question," Wilkes decided, "for a large quantity of field-ice would have to be passed through, which must have done us considerable damage, if it did not entirely disable us." [11] Fortunately, a channel soon appeared and the explorers escaped without injury.

Although Lieutenant Wilkes had successfully avoided injury to his vessel during the rough weather, the exposure to wind, rain, sleet, and snow had taken its toll of the crew. The day following

----

[10] Journal of Lieutenant Charles Wilkes, I, Jan. 30, 1840; and his *Narrative*, II, 316. Although he does not mention the name "Antarctic Continent" in his journal for that day, it must have been voiced among the officers, because R. R. Waldron used it when he wrote to Wilkes on January 31. See *Narrative*, II, 462. See also Charles Wilkes to James Kirke Paulding, U.S. Ship Vincennes, New South Wales, March 11, 1840, Exploring Expedition Letters (At Sea), II.

[11] Wilkes, *Narrative*, II, 317.

their positive discovery of the Antarctic mountain range the assistant surgeons on the *Vincennes* reported that fifteen seamen were ill and recommended that the ship be turned northward. If the seamen suffered further exposure their number would be so reduced by sickness that the safety of all on board would be hazarded. Wilkes, now possessed by a fierce desire to make further discoveries, ordered his officers to present their opinions on the matter, even restoring the suspended chief surgeon, Dr. Edward Gilchrist, to duty to make investigations. All these men verified the assistant surgeons' opinions and advised the commander to give up the cruise. Their thoughts were shared by Purser R. R. Waldron, who said they should return to Sydney forthwith, because the advantages to be gained from landing on the "Antarctic Continent" would not be commensurate with the dangers it would necessarily incur. Notwithstanding, Wilkes was "satisfied that there was [not] sufficient cause to change . . . [his] original determination" of sailing westward to 105° E. In fact, after giving full consideration to the problem he concluded that it was his duty to proceed regardless of the peril to his ship and crew. He explained: "In bringing myself to this decision, I believe that I viewed the case on all sides with fairness, and allowed my duty to my country, my care for those whom it had committed to my charge, and my responsibility to the world, each to have its due weight." [12] Luckily, the weather moderated and the sick list did not become much larger.

As the *Vincennes* pushed westward along the barrier, the explorers saw "appearances of land" almost every day. On February 8, Wilkes decided that the high land which trended southwestward almost parallel with their track was not of ordinary size. The ice islands were larger and older. They could have formed only on an immense land mass. Four days later these conclusions were confirmed by the discovery of a lofty, snow-covered mountain range in latitude 65° 20′ S., longitude 112° E. Even Wilkes climbed the mainmast to observe it. "The . . . land," he declared, "clearly

[12] Wilkes, *Narrative*, II, 320. See also J. L. Fox and J. S. Whittle to Charles Wilkes, U.S. Ship Vincennes, At Sea, Jan. 31, 1840, *ibid.*, 318–19; and Overton Carr, A. Ludlow Case, Joseph A. Underwood, Edmund H. De Haven, and Samuel R. Knox to Charles Wilkes, U. S. Ship Vincennes, At Sea, Jan. 31, 1840, *ibid.*, 461.

determines or settles the question of our having discovered, the *Antarctic Continent.*" [13] After all, during most of the past month they had followed its coast more than 800 miles.

Soon several ice islands carrying embedded boulders and large pieces of rock were seen. Here was further verification of the commander's conclusions regarding their formation. A boat was immediately lowered and a landing was made. Wilkes was amused "to see the avidity with which the men possessed themselves of a piece of the newly discovered *Antarctic Continent.*" [14] The *Vincennes* was kept on her course along the shelf until February 21, when the decision to return to Sydney was made, not because of the crew's condition, but because they had water enough for only twenty-five days.

After the *Peacock* was separated from the *Vincennes* and the *Porpoise* on January 3, Lieutenant Hudson set sail for Macquarie Island hoping to rendezvous with his comrades there, but the other ships were not seen. The explorers on the *Peacock* had more success approaching its coasts than Wilkes and Ringgold, and Midshipman Henry Eld led a party ashore to investigate the rookeries of penguins and other water fowl. On January 12, the *Peacock* passed within a degree of the position of Emerald Isle and proceeded southward because no signs of land were apparent.

When the shelf was reached, Hudson steered his sloop-of-war westward until he spoke the *Porpoise* and sighted the *Vincennes* on January 15 in 66° 01' S., 165° E. There the ships parted again, continuing their transit along the barrier on slightly different tracks. Two days later Midshipmen Eld and William Reynolds sighted what they believed was a high mountain beyond the ice, but they could not be certain of their discovery. No bare earth was

---

[13] Journal of Lieutenant Charles Wilkes, II, Feb. 12, 1840. See also the Journal of Passed Midshipman Joseph Perry Sanford, Aboard the *Vincennes*, Feb. 12, 1840, NA, M 75. Hereafter cited as Sanford, Journal.

[14] Journal of Lieutenant Charles Wilkes, II, Feb. 14, 1840. See also the Journals of Jared Leigh Elliott, Kept while Serving as Chaplain on the United States Exploring Expedition (2 vols.), I, Feb. 14, 1840, Manuscripts Division, Library of Congress; Anonymous Journal Kept Aboard the *Vincennes*, Feb. 14, 1840, NA, M 75; Briskee, Journal, Feb. 14, 1840; Sanford, Journal, Feb. 14, 1840; and Charles Wilkes to James Kirke Paulding, U.S. Ship Vincennes, Sydney, New South Wales, March 11, 1840, Exploring Expedition Letters (At Sea), II.

visible. The green color of the water, as well as numerous whales and birds, convinced Hudson of the proximity of territory and he continued his course, searching for an opening to the south.

Their investigation was rewarded on January 19, when they discovered a large passage where the sea was quite smooth. "About this period something was seen in the distance peering over the compact ice at the head of the bay very much resembling high craggy land covered with snow." As Lieutenant George Emmons reported, "*Discovery stock* ran high—Spy Glasses were in great requisition—& many officers confirmed their opinions by a survey from the mast heads." [15] They pushed forward through the drift and small bergs until midnight, when the appearance of the shelf again forced them to stop many miles from their discovery. Lieutenant Hudson was particularly disheartened because he was not convinced the snow-covered elevations were land.

Again, on January 23, the explorers "made, . . . high land [to the south], at least so far as terra firma can be distinguished where every thing is covered with snow." They worked their way into another bay which the *Porpoise* was leaving for a nearer and more exact examination. There the water "changed to a dark dull green, and gave every indication that . . . [they] were on soundings, and not far from land." [16] Other finds soon confirmed their suspicions. They located a bottom of "slate-coloured mud" in 320 fathoms, and captured a large king penguin carrying 32 pebbles of various sizes in its craw. To the heretofore conservative Lieutenant Emmons this was substantial proof that they were on land. Henry Eld and Clerk Frederic Stuart decided these discoveries confirmed the presence of their snow-covered mountains seen on January 17.

While steering up the bay, the *Peacock* "came into contact with a large piece of ice, which carried away one of the wheel ropes, wrenched the neck of the rudder, and [thus] rendered it useless."

----

[15] Journal of Lt. George F. Emmons, Jan. 19, 1840. See also the Journal of Frederic D. Stuart, Captain's Clerk, Aboard the *Peacock*, Jan. 19, 1840, NA, M 75.

[16] Wm. L. Hudson to James Kirke Paulding, U.S. Ship Peacock, Sydney, New South Wales, March 3, 1840, Exploring Expedition Letters (At Sea), II. See also Henry Eld to his Family, U.S. Ship Peacock, Sydney, New South Wales, March 10, 1840, in the Henry Eld Papers, Manuscripts Division, Library of Congress; and the Journal of Lt. George F. Emmons, Jan. 23, 1840.

Hudson and his men "immediately commenced working [the] ship with sails and ice-anchors into a more open sea," while the carpenter frantically tried to repair the damaged steering apparatus.[17] Progress by these expedients was fleeting, for the wind increased in velocity. When it suddenly changed direction, the ship was "completely beset" by the ice again, her rudder completely destroyed.

The *Peacock* was drifting toward a huge ice island "full 6 miles square with perpendicular sides, from 100 to 150 feet above the surface of the sea," in spite of all exertions to guide her. "In this situation," Hudson reported, "we pulled all but the fore-and-aft sails, and hung by our ice anchors." A large piece of floe ice lay between the *Peacock* and the ice island and "it was thought . . . that it would serve as a fender to keep . . . [the ship] from coming in contact with the latter" while repairs were being expedited on the wheel ropes and rudder.[18] These hopes soon were dashed when a dead swell and current removed the "fender" from their path.

The *Peacock* did not capsize when she crashed against the perpendicular sides of the ice island, but her stern davits, stern boat, and spanker boom were destroyed. Providentially, the explorers soon noticed a narrow channel to open water and Hudson determined to force the sloop-of-war through it, "or grind and thump the ship to pieces in the attempt." He was taking no undue chance, because there was no other alternative. The ship was solidly embayed on all sides. His daring plan was "aided by a kind Providence," allowing them to reach open sea on the morning of January 25. They were soon able to restore the rudder. Since it was impossible to completely determine the extent of the damage on the *Peacock*'s hull, Hudson decided to hasten to Sydney, carry out repairs of the ship, and be ready to cooperate with the rest of the squadron as soon as possible.

While pursuing an individual course toward 105° E. on January 16, Lieutenant Cadwallader Ringgold on the *Porpoise* "saw over the field of ice, an object, large, dark, and rounding, resembling a

[17] Wm. L. Hudson to James Kirke Paulding, U.S. Ship Peacock, New South Wales, March 3, 1840, Exploring Expedition Letters (At Sea), II.
[18] *Ibid.* See also the Journal of Lt. George F. Emmons, Jan. 24, 1840.

mountain in the distance." But he became convinced his discovery was bona fide only after he "watched for an hour to see if the sun in his decline would change the colour of the object by a difference of rays: it remained the same, with a white cloud above, similar to those generally hovering over high land. . . ." [19] This might be an island surrounded by ice. As he proceeded westward, the green water and many birds substantiated this conclusion.

The *Porpoise* reached her farthest position south a week later when she sailed to the "southern extreme of an extensive gulf, studded with islands of ice," in 66° 49′ S., 151° 24′ E. As Ringgold retraced his track he exchanged colors with his compatriots on the *Peacock* then entering the bay. Had they remained together, the crew of the *Porpoise* might have aided their fellows, but it is more likely they would have experienced the same difficulties that befell the *Peacock*. At the time of her collision the ice islands were being driven to the southern section of the bay by the wind and current.

During the week following this meeting, Ringgold and his crew were much too busy dodging ice masses to pursue their search for land. On January 27, they spoke the *Vincennes* and compared chronometers before heading into a fierce snowstorm and a dense fog which remained constant until January 30, when two sails were seen in the distance. Supposing they were the *Vincennes* and *Peacock*, Ringgold stood to the north to communicate with them. As the *Porpoise* approached, he discovered they were not his consorts. He hoisted his colors immediately, knowing that an English expedition under Captain James Clark Ross was to explore in these seas. The Americans "stood ready to cheer the discoverer of the North Magnetic Pole," but when the strangers were within hailing distance they saw a French pennant and knew they were members of the expedition under Captain Jules Sébastien César Dumont d'Urville.

This expedition, composed of the ships *Astrolabe* and *Zélée*, had been sent by the French government to make explorations in the Pacific, and, at the insistence of the Citizen-King Louis Philippe, the Antarctic. This additional burden of exploring the south polar regions was not particularly palatable to the commander, an eth-

....
[19] See the extract from Ringgold's journal in Cadwallader Ringgold to Charles Wilkes, U.S. Brig Porpoise, Bay of Islands, New Zealand, March 31, 1840, in Wilkes, *Narrative*, II, 470.

nologist who knew he would be hard-pressed to practice his voca-
tion there. He suffered from gout, furthermore, resulting no doubt
from consumption of the very Bordeaux wine he later employed
to toast his discovery of land south of Australia.

D'Urville's fleet proceeded southward from Toulon toward
Magellan's Strait in September, 1837, where surveys were performed before pushing into the seas beyond Tierra del Fuego early
in January. It was the Frenchman's intention to at least duplicate
the voyage of James Weddell. This was the principal objective of
the Antarctic cruise envisioned by the French king. For almost two
months the explorers skirted the shelf ice, returning several times
to the South Orkneys, without finding an opening which would
have allowed them to reach the farthest point of the British sealer.
They did sight the peninsula seen earlier by Bransfield and the
American sealers. Supposing this was a discovery, d'Urville named
it Louis Philippe Land.

Before leaving the southern hemisphere, d'Urville resolved to
make an attempt to reach the magnetic pole, thus contributing
substantially to knowledge of terrestrial magnetism. This plan was
in excess of his instructions, but he could not avoid responding to
competition from the expeditions of James Clark Ross and Wilkes.
Preparations for this cruise were completed by New Year's Day,
1840, and the Frenchmen departed from Hobart, Tasmania, taking
a course more to the southwest than the American expedition.
After crossing the 60th parallel they saw their first ice islands,
which they believed were too massive to have been formed in the
open sea. Nevertheless, they remained confident of passing 70° S.

By the time d'Urville reached 66°, he too had noticed the change
in the color of the water and the numerous birds and whales. On
the twentieth, a high land completely covered with ice and snow
stretched from east to west. Although the explorers saw no bare
peak or even a black spot, none doubted the existence of terra
firma. It was named Adélie Land. These mountains, moreover,
continued to be clearly visible. D'Urville described them as gently
rolling, much like sand dunes. As they proceeded westward, the
man on watch discovered several rocky islets. A landing was made
on the most westerly and loftiest one, where the Frenchmen
planted the tricolor, taking possession. On January 29, while hunting for a passage through the barrier, the *Porpoise* was sighted.

The discrepancy in dates—Ringgold said they met on January 30 —occurred because the French commander had neglected to change his log when he crossed the International Date Line.[20]

When Lieutenant Ringgold decided the ships were the French fleet he "closed with them, designing to pass within hail under the flag-ship's stern," but to his surprise the Frenchmen made sail. The astonished Americans hauled down their colors immediately and continued their course. D'Urville explained his maneuver by saying he had opened his sails to the wind to keep up with the *Porpoise*, which was closing in at a much faster rate than the *Astrolabe* and would have passed her. He later shortened sail, proceeding slowly along his course to speak the Americans if they returned. The Frenchmen thought they saw land again the next day and named the ice cliffs they were skirting Clarie Coast. Ringgold, who was sailing in the vicinity, made no such discovery.

During the first days of February the Americans were occupied with the exigencies of self-preservation and consequently made no further discoveries until the weather moderated on the twelfth, when "many strong indications of land presented themselves." They had reached 64° 54' S., 105° E. There the barrier exhibited "numerous stratified veins of earth and rocks, . . . with lofty and conical peaks." [21] Ringgold, anxious to get nearer the barrier, took the *Porpoise* into a narrow and dangerous inlet where his ship quickly became embayed. Fortunately a strong southeast wind began to blow and the *Porpoise* safely cleared her icy enclosure.

After procuring specimens of rock from the barrier on February 12, the explorers turned about and stood to the northeast for Auckland Island. They anchored there in a harbor called Sarah's Bosom on March 17, taking on a supply of wood and water before sailing on to the Bay of Islands, North Island, New Zealand.

When the schooner *Flying Fish* departed from Sydney on Christmas Day, her acting master, George T. Sinclair, asserted that "no vessel ever sailed under the U.S. Pennant with such a miser-

---

[20] This discrepancy is pointed out by Rear-Admiral John E. Pillsbury, U.S.N., "Wilkes's and D'Urville's Discoveries in Wilkes Land," *United States Naval Institute Proceedings*, 36 (June, 1910), 465-68.

[21] Cadwallader Ringgold to Charles Wilkes, U.S. Brig Porpoise, Bay of Islands, New Zealand, March 31, 1840, Wilkes, *Narrative*, II, 471.

able crew." She had no cook and only seven seamen, who were for the most part miserably incapable. Lieutenant R. F. Pinkney, the commander, was ill, and there was little prospect of his regaining health because no medical officer had been assigned to the tender. Their situation was partially alleviated on December 28, however, when a cook was transferred from the *Vincennes*.

The boisterous breezes greeting the explorers on the first day of 1840 tore away part of the schooner's sails, preventing her from keeping up with the larger ships. Her officers were amazed to see Wilkes, Hudson, and Ringgold continue their course without giving assistance. Many members of the crew expressed an inability ever to forgive their commander for this act of disregard. They pushed southward, however, sighting Macquarie Island on January 9, where they noticed the *Peacock* lying at anchor. No contact was made unfortunately, because the sloop-of-war departed during a heavy fog. The despairing Sinclair led a party ashore to leave a communication for Wilkes and letters to relatives and friends explaining their plight.

Like the other members of the fleet, the explorers on the schooner were unable to find Emerald Isle as they threaded their way southward through icebergs and floes toward the shelf. Sinclair marvelled at this wall of Antarctica, describing it as "masses of ice of different sizes, so closely packed and wedged together that it would be utterly impossible to penetrate it." He thought he would rather "run a vessel on to the broad side of America," than try to penetrate the shelf, because a ship would be ground to pieces.[22] Their westward passage along it after January 21 was barren of discovery, but not devoid of interest.

As the *Flying Fish* sailed westward, her crew noticed the usual indications of land but they were too occupied avoiding masses of ice to give any serious consideration to the snow-covered highlands beyond the barrier. Like the *Porpoise*, the tender encountered violent storms and heavy seas during February. At no time was the entire crew available for duty, and those who were able to work received very little rest. One poor fellow stood bare-footed at the helm for three or four days, because his feet were too swollen for him to wear shoes.

[22] Journal of George T. Sinclair, Acting Master, Aboard the *Flying Fish*, Jan. 21, 1840, NA, M 75.

By February 5, Sinclair had become convinced the *Flying Fish* would founder if the wind did not abate within twenty-four hours, but only then did the miserable seamen ask to turn northward because of their condition. Four were sick, one of whom had the open ulcers of the dreaded scurvy on his hands and legs, and the incapacitated Lieutenant Pinkney wisely gave up the exploration. They stood into the Bay of Islands on March 9 and mustered the "Ghostly crew in their best bib & tucker." Sinclair testified that he had never seen such wretched human beings. "Fallstaffs troop would have been left in the background by comparison." [23] He believed only the "Divine will" had spared them from a watery grave.

[23] *Ibid.*, March 9, 1840.

chapter ten

WILKES VERSUS ROSS

Shortly after the *Vincennes* anchored in Port Jackson on March 11, 1840, Lieutenant Charles Wilkes dispatched a report to his superior, Secretary of the Navy James Kirke Paulding, in which he self-confidently announced: "From our discoveries of the land through forty degrees of long. and the observations made during this interesting cruise, with the similarity of formation and position of the ice during our close examination of it, I consider that there can scarcely be a doubt of the existence of the Antarctic continent, extending the whole distance of seventy degrees from East to West." [1]

The Sydney *Herald* of March 13 relayed this news to the local population, who generously feted the explorers at several celebrations. The Americans were particularly impressed by the hospitality of the people of the Saint Patrick Society. Their dance and party was held in the courthouse and was attended by Sir George Gipps and many other dignitaries. Music was provided by two military bands, and "quadrilles and country dances followed in rapid succession." The climax came toward the close of the evening, when the guests were treated to an elegant and delectable dinner.

In the midst of this gaiety, news arrived in the United States from Hobart, Tasmania, that d'Urville's French fleet had discovered land on January 19, the same day the Americans had seen it several degrees to the eastward. Although the Frenchmen did not pretend to have discovered a continental land mass, this informa-

-----

[1] Charles Wilkes to James Kirke Paulding, U.S. Flag Ship Vincennes, Sydney, New South Wales, March 11, 1840, Exploring Expedition Letters (At Sea), II.

tion cast doubt on Wilkes's right of prior discovery and proved to be the first of many onslaughts on the validity of the American's Antarctic landfalls.

After leaving the capital of New South Wales for the Bay of Islands in New Zealand, the exuberant commander of the United States Exploring Expedition sent a letter describing his cruise, together with a chart showing his discoveries, to the British explorer, Captain James Clark Ross, who was expected there momentarily. By doing this, Wilkes was openly disregarding Secretary of the Navy Paulding's instructions which specifically had prohibited any member of the expedition from providing information to outsiders. In justification he told the Secretary he wished "in some small degree [to] repay the obligations this Expedition is under to all those who are deeply interested in that which Captain Ross now commands, who had himself afforded me all the assistance in his power while I was engaged in procuring the instruments for this expedition." [2]

This English expedition was sent to the Antarctic as a result of propaganda by members of the British Association for the Advancement of Science, who recognized the deficiency of their knowledge of terrestrial magnetism. These zealous scientists gained the support of members of the Royal Society, as well as the renowned German scholar, Alexander von Humboldt, and petitioned their government to send an exploring fleet to high southern latitudes between Australia and Cape Horn to make magnetic observations. The Cabinet complied, and on April 8, 1839, Ross was given command of an expedition with orders to equip it "upon the most liberal scale." The bomb-vessel *Erebus* of 370 tons was to be the flagship, and she was later joined by the ship *Terror*, built in 1836 to withstand Arctic ice.

By all accounts the expedition of James Clark Ross was the best prepared of its time. The decks of the ships were made of two thicknesses and filled with waterproof cloth to afford the provisions in the hold and the sleeping quarters of the seamen a maximum dryness and comfort, while the vulnerable sections of their hulls were buttressed by a doubly coppered, outer lay of planking. The provisions, preserved by the most up-to-date methods, in-

[2] Charles Wilkes to James Kirke Paulding, U.S. Ship Vincennes, New Zealand, April 6, 1840, Exploring Expedition Letters (At Sea), II.

cluded an unusual amount of canned meats and soups, and enormous quantities of fresh and pickled vegetables to forestall scurvy. About five tons of carrots and over four tons of pickled cucumbers, cabbage, and onions were stowed. Warm clothing of the very best quality also was issued to the officers and men. It is not difficult to see why the interested citizens of Sydney thought Wilkes and his men would perish when they compared the United States Exploring Expedition with advance notices they had received of this one.

Ross's objectives were to make magnetic observations and to locate the position of the magnetic South Pole. Permanent observatories were to be erected on the island of St. Helena, the Cape of Good Hope, and Tasmania, while experiments were to be conducted at the island of Madeira, Kerguelen Island, New Zealand, and the Falklands or South Shetlands. If the explorers were able to complete their observations at Kerguelen Island by February, 1840, they were to proceed directly to the southward to verify prior discoveries. But they were to give every consideration to avoid being "beset in the ice," because nothing should be allowed to interfere with the magnetical observations to be conducted next in Tasmania.

Hobart was to serve as a base for Ross's cruise to the magnetic pole during the Antarctic summer of 1840. Again he was advised to take every precaution to keep from wintering in the Antarctic, because the completion of his observations was the paramount consideration. During the succeeding summer he was to resume exploration of the ice zone. If he discovered land of any great extent he was to "lay down the prominent parts of its coast line; and . . . endeavor not only to correct the positions of Graham [Palmer] Land and Enderby Land, and other places which had been seen only at a distance, but to obtain some knowledge of the nature of yet unvisited tracts of geographical research. . . ." [3] The explorers were to return to England via Cape Horn and the Falklands or South Shetlands to make their final scientific studies.

Lieutenant Wilkes hoped to facilitate the Antarctic voyage of this celebrated Arctic mariner by describing weather conditions,

....

[3] Captain Sir James Clark Ross, R.N., *A Voyage of Discovery and Research in the Southern and Antarctic Regions, During the Years 1839–43* (2 vols., London, 1847), I, xxv.

discussing his magnetic observations, and by charting his discoveries of territory. During his cruise along the barrier he had found no perceptible current, although fierce gales often caused him to believe one existed. Thus the wind, not the water, was responsible for moving the ice masses, which never melted and changed very slightly owing to the continental land mass in East Antarctica south of Australia. In that area Ross's only prospect of reaching land was through forty miles of ice-filled ocean. On the other hand, Wilkes advised the Englishman to attempt to duplicate Weddell's feat, because no large territories, except Palmer Land, existed in West Antarctica to create such stable ice conditions. It is manifest that he believed Palmer Peninsula was not part of the Antarctic Continent.

The Americans assumed, moreover, that they had passed very near the magnetic pole in latitude 67° 04′ S., 147° 30′ E., although "it was difficult to get a good observation, on account of the sluggishness of . . . [their] compasses." They estimated that the pole must lie near 70° W., 140° E. The chart Wilkes forwarded, showing the tracks of his ships and the condition of the ice, was constructed from "carefully-kept diagrams by the officer of the deck during his watch." [4]

Since the Americans had kept their movements along the continent "profoundly secret" when they reached Sydney, Ross said he felt all the more indebted to Charles Wilkes, whose documents would have been of "infinite value" had the Englishmen explored between the meridians the American expedition had surveyed. These statements undoubtedly were a mask for Ross's real feelings, because later he petulantly condemned both Wilkes and d'Urville for interfering with his plans by penetrating the Antarctic in the very area his expedition was to explore. "I should have expected their national pride would have caused them rather to have chosen any other path in the wide field before them, than one thus pointed out, if no higher consideration had power to prevent such interference." [5] Ross obviously was overlooking the fact that Wilkes had received his instructions almost a year before the members of

----

[4] Charles Wilkes to Capt. J. C. Ross, U.S. Flag Ship Vincennes, Bay of Islands, N. Zealand, April 4, 1840, Exploring Expedition Letters (At Sea), II.

[5] Ross, *Voyage*, I, 116–17.

the British Association for the Advancement of Science had even considered an expedition to increase their knowledge of terrestrial magnetism.

Since Ross professed to be infected with the British national feeling that their nation had always led the advance of discovery into both the north and south, pride did not allow him to follow the tracks of other expeditions. He chose to penetrate the Antarctic following the 170th meridian. On November 13, 1840, the *Erebus* and *Terror* were pushed southward from New Zealand to the Auckland Islands, where the Englishmen found a paper enclosed in a bottle deposited by Lieutenant Ringgold when he had stopped there on his northward voyage. They "were all much surprised that no mention was made of the 'Antarctic Continent' discovered by Lieutenant Wilkes, but supposed that secrecy had been enforced upon him, as to any discoveries he might make. . . ." [6] Some magnetic observations were made there before the explorers continued their course, which took them across the Antarctic Circle on January 1, and into the area of pack ice near 66° 32′ S., 169° 45′ E. From this position Ross threaded his way through icebergs and floes until January 11, when a range of mountains was discovered bearing S.S.W. to S.E. by E. almost a hundred miles. The land was named Victoria Land, the mountain range Admiralty Range, and the highest peak, about 10,000 feet high, was called Mount Sabine. While skirting the barrier on the same day they reached 71° 15′ S., in about 171° E., a latitudinal point corresponding to Captain Cook's farthest southern position.

Ross followed the mountain range almost directly southward from Mount Sabine, making discoveries nearly every day. From January 11 to February 28, the explorers sighted several peaks they considered higher than Mount Sabine, as well as a chain of small, ice-encased islands, the largest of which they named Coulman, Possession, and Franklin. Their most interesting find was a "mountain twelve thousand four hundred feet of elevation above the level of the sea, emitting flame and smoke in great profusion. . . ." [7] This Mount Erebus, in 76° S., 168° E., is one of several active volcanoes in Antarctica. It marked the termination of Ross's

---

[6] Ross, *Voyage*, I, 134.

[7] *Ibid.*, p. 216.

land discoveries, because his progress southward was halted by an immense barrier of ice trending to the south and west. While skirting it, the Englishmen reached their highest southern point in latitude 78° S., longitude 187° W., before standing to the northwestward in order to locate the South Magnetic Pole.

During this voyage Ross and his men sighted two small islands in 67° 28′ S., 165° 30′ E., on March 1, which undoubtedly had been discovered by the British whaler John Balleny in 1839. The track they followed westward took them to the area of Wilkes's landfalls. Four days later the British ships reached a position in latitude 65° 34′ S., 167° 40′ E., "as nearly as possible in the latitude and between forty and fifty miles distant from the N.E. extreme of Lieutenant Wilkes land." The disappointment of the Englishmen was distinct when they failed to see the American's discovery. Ross stated that they began to "suspect that from having had but little experience of the delusive appearances in these icy regions, he had mistaken for land some of the dense well-defined clouds which so continually hang over extensive packs of ice,—a mistake which we had ourselves, on many occasions, to guard against, when appearances were so strong, for several days in succession, that few in either ship could be persuaded that it was not really land until we actually sailed over the spot." [8]

At daybreak on January 16 the sky was perfectly clear, providing an extensive view in every direction, and an appearance of land was reported. Ross was "quite unable to distinguish any thing but a dark misty appearance," but the "appearance" was inserted in the log as bearing S.S.W. to S.W. by W. in "the exact direction of Balleny Islands" which they had passed almost twelve days earlier. At noon on the same day, their observations told them they were in 64° 51′ S., 164° 45′ E., and "therefore very nearly in the centre of the mountainous patch of land laid down in Lieutenant Wilkes's chart as forming a part of the 'antarctic continent.'" [9] Ross later reported to his countrymen that he was "obliged to confess that this position, at least, of the pseudo-antarctic continent, and the nearly 200 miles of barrier represented to extend from it, have no real existence!!" [10]

....

[8] Ross, *Voyage*, I, 278–79.
[9] *Ibid.*, 280.
[10] *The Times* (London), Sept. 11, 1843, 6.

When the ships of the United States Exploring Expedition were moored in New York Harbor on June 11, 1842, Lieutenant Wilkes, who had heard of Ross's disclosures in Honolulu, was greeted with the news again. The commander also was informed that he would soon be forced to stand trial before a court-martial on charges advanced by a disgruntled assistant surgeon, and on information presented by Lieutenant R. F. Pinkney. Among other things, his accusers declared that he had uttered a "deliberate and wilful falsehood" when he claimed the discovery of land on January 19, 1840. Charles Wilkes complained bitterly to John Quincy Adams that "all the . . . officers and men, . . . had naturally expected to be welcomed with some cheering smile and some kind word from the government of their country. They had found, instead of this, a cold insulting silence." [11]

The first official rejoinder to Ross's charges came from the commander of the expedition himself during a speech before the newly formed National Institute on June 20, 1842. Wilkes protested that the Englishman had badly misinterpreted his chart. All the landfalls east of 160° longitude, Wilkes asserted, were discoveries of the Englishman Balleny of which he had been apprised when his expedition returned to Sydney from the Antarctic. He was "not a little surprised that so intelligent a navigator as Capt. Ross, on finding that he had run over this position, should not have closely inquired into statements relative to . . . [the American] discoveries that had been published in the Sydney and Hobart Town papers." [12] He was disgusted, moreover, that a United States naval officer, Captain J. H. Aulick, would confirm the Englishman's statements without reservation and would publicize them in Honolulu.

These arguments excited little attention. No government officials publicly sided with Wilkes. No substantial groups of citizens

[11] *The Diary of John Quincy Adams, 1794–1845; American Diplomacy, and Political, Social, and Intellectual Life, from Washington to Polk* (ed. by Allan Nevins, New York, 1951), June 15, 1842.

[12] Charles Wilkes, *Synopsis of the Cruise of the U.S. Exploring Expedition. Delivered Before the National Institute, June 20, 1842* (Washington, 1842), 18. The rejoinders which appeared in the newspapers prior to June 20 were essentially the same. See *The Globe*, June 13, 1842, 3; *National Intelligencer*, June 14, 1842, 2; *New York Tribune*, June 13, 1842, 2; and the *Boston Daily Advertiser*, June 17, 1842, 2.

rallied to the support of the American's position. Joel R. Poinsett grumbled: "This narrative of an achievement so honorable to the navy, so useful to the commerce and navigation of the country, so creditable to its projectors, and so beneficial to science, has excited less of public attention in the United States than any of the hundred tales of misery and crime which daily occupy the columns of our papers in all their disgusting details." [13] He could not understand why the beneficial exertions of the explorers were not repaid by acclamation.

When Wilkes's speech was published in November, 1842, Captain Aulick addressed a letter to the editors of the Washington *Spectator,* answering the charges of the commander of the expedition. He declared that Wilkes had made both him and Ross appear very shortsighted and "dull of comprehension," but in so doing he had omitted one salient fact. "Namely, that in laying down the *land of Bellamy* [Balleny] on the chart he sent Captain Ross, *he neglected to affix thereto the name of its discoverer,* or to distinguish it in any way from his own land there traced out and almost connected with it." [14] Because of this, the English explorer inadvertently made the error.

Concerning the matter of Ross's checking the Sydney and Hobart Town newspapers, Aulick believed he could not have been expected to examine them since he had Wilkes's letter and chart at hand. With these documents in his possession what further evidence of the American discoveries was needed? Aulick stated:

On my visit to Captain Ross, on board the Erebus, he spread . . . [Wilkes's] chart before me in the presence of Captain Crozier and two of my own officers. It was distinctly drawn out on tracing paper— the whole appearing, so far as I observed, one connected operation, representing nothing but the result of his own (Wilkes's) explorations. Ross believing it to be such, had transcribed it at length on his chart, which he also placed before us, and pointed out the tracks of his vessels, marked on it in red ink, *and passing directly over the spot assigned to the land,* which we all considered as laid down by Lieutenant Wilkes, to represent the Northeastern limit of his supposed Antarctic Continent, and where he (Ross) said they had a clear sea as far as the eye could reach. Such was the evidence on which my belief in his report was founded. To my mind it was conclusive.[15]

....

[13] [Joel R. Poinsett], *North American Review,* LVI (April, 1843), 257.
[14] Nov. 12, 1842, 3.
[15] *Ibid.*

Wilkes wasted little time answering Aulick's contentions. One week after the letter appeared, the editors of the *Spectator* published one from the commander of the expedition. He stated that he eschewed the allusion that he had claimed more territory than the expedition actually had discovered. If he was a deceiver, would he have sent his letter and chart to Captain Ross? This act alone should convince the public that he did not fear an experienced rival, whose objective was to follow his track in order to verify his landfalls.

It was unfortunate, he continued, that in trying to advance the English expedition, he might have misled Ross by sending a chart which was not an exact tracing of his own, showing "the English discovery . . . detached and separate." But whether or not the English discovery was labelled was unessential. Ross, after all, was acquainted with Balleny's islands and should have identified them at once on the American chart since they were located accurately. Wilkes was convinced "that the only erroneous conclusion Captain Ross could have been led into by it, was that I had verified Bellamy's [sic] discovery." [16]

While the Lieutenant was defending his exploration against the judgments of Aulick, the court-martial board was listening to testimony regarding his alleged deliberate falsehood of January 19, 1840. John Williamson, a gunner on the *Vincennes,* and Midshipmen Alonzo B. Davis and Henry Eld of the *Peacock,* professed to have definitely seen land on that day, while Lieutenant James Alden of the *Vincennes,* who admitted calling Wilkes's attention to the landfall, refused to confirm it. The commanders of the *Peacock* and the *Porpoise,* Lieutenants Hudson and Ringgold, did not think the discovery was definite until they had heard Wilkes's report in Sydney. Hudson, who had requested Midshipman Davis to label his discovery as a large iceberg, even altered his log to substantiate Wilkes's land, but not at his commander's insistence. He said favorable soundings and later discoveries caused him to alter his views. For a time it appeared as if the commander of the *Peacock,* rather than Wilkes, was undergoing prosecution, because he was questioned intensively about his refusal to confirm the discoveries of two of his midshipmen, Eld and William Reynolds,

---

[16] Nov. 19, 1842, 2.

who forcefully maintained they had seen land on January 16. The
members of the court halted this comic opera, wisely concluding
Wilkes had not been proved guilty.

The decision of the court-martial board did nothing to settle the
controversy over the American landfalls, and after the commander
of the expedition published his five-volume *Narrative* of the expedition in 1845, it was continued by reviewers. The widely read and
influential *North American Review* and the *Southern Quarterly
Review* supported Wilkes's claim to the discovery of a continental
land mass in the Antarctic. Concerning the land, the reviewer in
the *North American* said, "Although it was not actually seen as a
continuous line of shore, Captain Wilkes, for reasons which seem
to be good and fairly stated, gives it the name of a continent." [17]
But other reviewing media were not so approving as these two.
The *Southern Literary Messenger* expressed the opinion that the
discovery was of little consequence and that Wilkes exhibited
"great puerility about the discovery of land," while Eliakim Littell's eclectic *Living Age* published a British review which concluded that the "frequent and necessary use of the words 'may be'
show that the whole matter was doubtful." [18]

This reviewer's criticism was not illustrative of all intelligent
opinion in Britain, because the Royal Geographical Society
honored Wilkes with its Founder's Medal in 1847, the same year
James Clark Ross answered the American's animadversions in the
published journal of his cruise. The English captain maintained
that "the land . . . we sailed over is laid down upon the chart at
least seventy miles from . . . [Balleny Islands], and is exactly in
the position of the mountains said [by Wilkes in his printed *Narrative*] to have been seen by Lieutenant Ringgold [on January 13,
1840]." [19] He knew furthermore that the colonial secretary in
Sydney had given authentic information regarding the position
of Balleny's discovery to Wilkes, who exclaimed at the time that
his labor in the Antarctic had been in vain. To show the ludicrous-
ness of the American commander's statements, Ross published a
copy of the chart he had been given, on which he placed Balleny

----

[17] *North American Review*, LXI (July, 1845), 70.

[18] *Littell's Living Age*, V (April 12, 1845), 65. See also *The Southern
Literary Messenger*, XI (May, 1845), 313.

[19] Ross, *Voyage*, I, 293–94.

Islands in their correct position, many miles south of Wilkes's highlands and barrier ice.

In a letter to the editor of the Washington *Union,* Wilkes countered these charges by claiming that there was not the slightest resemblance between his chart and the one published by Ross. For one thing, the mountainous land placed on his map was 27 miles long, while the Englishman's was over 80 miles. For another, "Ross knew that Bellany [sic] had sailed over the position that this 'mountainous land' occupied on the chart. Why then did he not say so, instead of vaunting that he had sailed over . . . [the American] discoveries." [20] Wilkes also claimed that he had heard of Balleny's discovery from another English whaler, Captain John Biscoe, who did not know if his compatriot's find was land or a group of islands, and placed it in 65° 50′ S., 164° 27′ E., approximately fifty miles from its true position. This rejoinder ended the arguments between Wilkes and Ross, but the American's landfalls continued to be censured by later explorers in East Antarctica.

The first was an English whaler named Tapsell, who sailed westward from the Auckland Islands in 1850, sighted Balleny's Islands, and pursued a course westward to 143° E. in a higher latitude than the Americans had followed without seeing any land. In 1874, Captain George Nares challenged the validity of Wilkes's farthest western landfall, Termination Land, when he sailed within fifteen miles of it without seeing any mountains. A hazy atmosphere, the presence of pack ice, and a large number of icebergs, however, convinced him land was nearby. The German explorer, Erich von Drygalski, proved conclusively in 1902 that Termination Land did not exist by failing to find bottom in 1,730 fathoms near its charted position.

Two years after von Drygalski repudiated Wilkes's claims between 97° and 95° E., Captain Robert F. Scott, on an expedition in the ship *Discovery,* which was sponsored by the Royal Geographical Society, Royal Society, and others, not only verified Ross's statements, but disproved the existence of Wilkes's important discovery of January 19, 1840, in 154° E., named Hudson Land. After sailing close to the shelf in the same longitude as these landfalls, Scott declared that "there is no case for any land east-

[20] See the extracts from the letter in *The American Journal of Science and Arts,* V (March, 1848), 288.

ward of [d'Urville's] Adelie Land," and unjustly concluded that "once and for all . . . [he had] definitely disposed of Wilkes Land." [21] In 1909, Ernest Shackleton added to the evidence against the existence of the disputed American discoveries east of the 160th meridian.

Captain John King Davis, commander of the ship *Aurora* in the Australasian Antarctic Expedition of 1911–14 headed by Sir Douglas Mawson, pursued a course similar to that of the *Vincennes* from 160° to 95° E., and added Wilkes's Cape Carr, discovered January 6, 1840, in 64° 23′ S., 135° E., and Totten's High Land, latitude 65° 27′ S., longitude 122° 35′ E., which had been indistinctly seen but placed on Wilkes's chart, to the list of questionable landfalls. This Australian, however, appreciated the extremely difficult conditions which had confronted the inexperienced Americans, and was highly commendatory of the manner in which their commander "managed to lay down the ice barrier attached to Antarctica, from Adelie Land westward. . . ." Moreover, "small errors in judging distances, or in observations for longitude, under the adverse circumstances of his voyage, must be allowed for in a generous spirit. In any case, [he concluded] some of the positions he gave have not been *disproved*." [22]

Wilkes and his fellow explorers did make distinct landfalls during their voyage along the shelf, as Douglas Mawson proved in his sterling defense of the American commander, published after his expedition to the same area during the years 1929 to 1931. He was well aware that Wilkes had frequently made incorrect observations, but he credited these to his unfamiliarity with Antarctic conditions. In "seas, especially in the zone marginal to the continent, there are constantly being sighted floating or grounded icebergs which, seen at a distance, in themselves or distorted by mirage, have every appearance of ice-covered islands." [23] Likewise, rocky islands are often found in the area of pack ice, which might be confused as hummocky land, while the "miraged sil-

....
[21] Captain Robert F. Scott, *The Voyage of the "Discovery"* (2 vols., New York, 1905), II, 392–93.

[22] John King Davis, *With the "Aurora" in the Antarctic, 1911–1914* (London, 1919), p. 164.

[23] Douglas Mawson, "Wilkes's Antarctic Landfalls," *Proceedings of the Royal Geographical Society of Australasia, South Australian Branch*, XXXIV (1932–33), 81.

houette" of ice masses over 100 miles in length viewed across the stretches of pack may simulate it also. These features, accompanied by shallow soundings, have often caused Antarctic explorers to make mistakes.

Furthermore, Mawson held, low-hanging clouds look like high lands. Captain J. R. Stenhouse in the ship *Aurora* of Shackleton's last expedition, 1911–17, testified to this when he was off Wilkes's Cape Hudson in 1915. On a foggy day the Cape appeared " 'through the mists in the form of a high, bold headland, with low undulating land stretching away to the south-south-east and to the westward of it,' " but the following clear day no vestige of land was observed. He decided that Wilkes's discovery was really "Cape Flyaway," and declared, " 'no wonder Wilkes reported land.' " [24]

One of the paradoxes of Antarctic research is that clear weather, like fog and low clouds, frequently causes inaccurate observations to be made, because of the "comparative absence of dust-motes and water vapour." This phenomenon of looming often brings land into view which is far below the horizon and thus makes it appear much closer than it really is. Douglas Mawson also contended, "where an extended region is to be traversed in a single season, there may be no opportunity for checking observations. The weather is fickle, and during much of the time all is obscured by fog or falling snow. Problems concerning the diagnosis of features simulating land may arise in short, clear intervals before the shroud of obscurity descends and prohibits further checking of the phenomena." [25]

Mawson attributed many of Wilkes's errors to a lack of knowledge of these conditions. His discovery of January 16, 1840, in 157° E., which Lieutenant Ringgold and Midshipmen Eld and Reynolds verified, was undoubtedly an ice-covered island or a large, well-worn berg, judging from his sketch of it, while Cape Carr was badly misplaced due to looming. The much criticized Cape Hudson was beyond doubt a mirage. On the other hand, the overly ambitious American commander left himself open to censure by charting all elevations seen only indistinctly. Of such dubious ori-

----

[24] Shackleton, *South*, p. 332.

[25] Mawson, "Wilkes's Antarctic Landfalls," *Proceedings of the Royal Geographical Society of Australasia*, XXXIV, 82.

gin were Lieutenant Ringgold's appearances of land in 163° E., Totten's High Land, and Termination Land. The last two were not inserted in Wilkes's journal and were nonexistent until they appeared on his chart and in his printed version of his cruise. But to say the American drew on his imagination is untenable, for he definitely *thought* he saw a land mass.

Several significant, never-failing signs of land were witnessed by Lieutenant Charles Wilkes and his explorers. During their transit along the shelf, petrels, albatrosses, penguins, seals, and whales were their constant companions, while on frequent occasions when the weather permitted, favorable soundings on the continental shelf were made. Moreover, Wilkes correctly accounted for the presence of immense masses of ice, which he held were formed on a continental land mass and later dislodged from it. That a high, hummocky plateau does exist between 160° and 95° E. has been proved, and it is entirely plausible that Wilkes's credulity magnified its elevations into mountains. Thus, his statement that his explorers discovered a vast Antarctic Continent, "not a range of detached islands," cannot be denied.

As Edwin Swift Balch stated, "The cruise of Wilkes [in the Antarctic] will remain among the remarkable voyages of all time." [26] In ill-equipped and ill-constructed ships he and his explorers discovered what they thought were elevations beyond the barrier of shelf ice and coasted it 1,500 miles—far enough for Wilkes to declare it was of continental proportions. The discovery represented a triumph for pluck and fortitude. It was a conspicuous achievement for an expedition founded in good faith, but contrived by supernumeraries whose good intentions brought improper preparation and consequently adversity. But as Joel Roberts Poinsett contended: "Notwithstanding the singular efforts, that have been made to deprive our navy and country of the honor of this discovery, we have no doubt, that, when all the facts, . . . come to be spread before the public, every impartial observer will accord the priority of this discovery to our squadron." [27] *Finis coronat opus.*

At the beginning of the nineteenth century when Americans became interested in the sealing trade, and subsequently in the pos-

---

[26] *Antarctica*, p. 161.

[27] *North American Review,* LVI (April, 1843), 265.

sibility of finding seal-populated lands in the South Atlantic and South Pacific, the geographical conception of the Antarctic as presented by Captain James Cook was that sizable terra firma probably did not exist there. Yet within half a century after Cook's voyage this conception was changed. Not only were islands discovered and the coasts of a peninsula explored by American sealers and others, but the Wilkes Expedition traced the coastline of a great continent.

Edmund Fanning, Nathaniel Brown Palmer, John Davis, Christopher Burdick, Benjamin Pendleton, and Benjamin Morrell did not discover seal rookeries which revived the formerly lucrative sealing trade, but their penetration of the seafaring frontier in the Antarctic set the stage for the work done by Jeremiah Reynolds and ultimately by Lieutenant Charles Wilkes. Reynolds's perseverance in his movement to gain the expenditure of federal funds for overseas exploration brought results. When the United States Exploring Expedition put to sea, a precedent for the use of federal funds to explore throughout the world was established, while Charles Wilkes and his explorers wrote an important chapter in the annals of exploration. A seventh continent was added to geographical knowledge. Thus, American beginnings in the Antarctic were conspicuous ones.

ESSAY ON SOURCES

I. HISTORIES OF ANTARCTIC EXPLORATION

United States exploration in the Antarctic must be studied as part of a developing interest in that area, not as a detached and separate subject. As emphasized in this study, the contributions of the American sealers and the Wilkes Expedition were but links in the evolving chain of geographical knowledge regarding that remote section of the world, a chain beginning with conjectures by the ancients and continuing to the explorations of the recent International Geophysical Year.

Among recent histories dealing with exploration in the Antarctic, Walter Sullivan, *Quest for a Continent,* McGraw-Hill Book Co., Inc., New York, 1957, stands out. Sullivan, a *New York Times* correspondent, accompanied most of the recent United States expeditions to Antarctica. Of interest also because of the author's first-hand experience is Admiral Lord Mountevans, *The Antarctic Challenged,* John de Graff, Inc., New York, 1955. Admiral Mountevans is the only living survivor of Captain Robert Falcon Scott's ill-fated dash to the South Pole. The most substantial older works are: Hugh Robert Mill, *The Siege of the South Pole: The Story of Antarctic Exploration,* Alston Rivers, Ltd., London, 1905; James Gordon Hayes, *Conquest of the South Pole: Antarctic Exploration, 1906–31,* T. Butterworth, Ltd., London, 1932; and Edwin Swift Balch, *Antarctica,* Allen, Lane & Scott, Philadelphia, 1902. See also Walter B. Hayward, *Last Continent of Adventure: A Narrative of Gallant Men & Bold Exploits in Antarctica,* Dodd, Mead & Co., New York, 1930; James Gordon Hayes, *Antarctica: A Treatise on the Southern Continent,* The Richards Press, London, 1928; Russell Owen, *The Antarctic Ocean,* McGraw-Hill Book Co., New York, 1941; and William H. Hobbs, *Explorers of the Antarctic,* House of Field, Inc., New York, 1941.

For the conjectures of ancient geographers concerning a land mass in the southern frigid regions, see the excellent study of Lloyd A. Brown, *Story of Maps*, Little, Brown and Co., Boston, 1949; E. H. Bunbury's encyclopedic *History of Ancient Geography Among the Greeks and Romans from the Earliest Ages till the Fall of the Roman Empire*, 2 vols., John Murray, London, 1883; H. F. Tozer, *A History of Ancient Geography*, University Press, London, 1935; and J. Oliver Thomson, *History of Ancient Geography*, Harvard University Press, Cambridge, Mass., 1948.

The status of geographical knowledge during the Middle Ages is summed up in three comprehensive works: C. Raymond Beazley, *The Dawn of Modern Geography*, 3 vols., The Clarendon Press, Oxford, 1901–6; George H. T. Kimble, *Geography in the Middle Ages*, Methuen & Co., London, 1938; and John Kirtland Wright, *The Geographical Lore of the Time of the Crusades: A Study of the History of Medieval Science and Tradition in Western Europe*, American Geographical Society, *Research Series*, no. 15, ed. by W. L. G. Joerg, New York, 1925.

Fact and theory regarding the Antarctic from the Age of Discovery to the eighteenth-century explorations of Captain James Cook are detailed in James Burney, *A Chronological History of the Discoveries in the South Sea or Pacific Ocean*, 5 vols., Luke Hansard, London, 1803–17; R. H. Major, ed., *Early Voyages to Terra Australis, now called Australia: A Collection of Documents, and Extracts from Early Maps, Illustrative of the History of Discovery on the Coasts of that Vast Island, from the Beginning of the Sixteenth Century to the Time of Captain Cook*, The Hakluyt Society, First Series, vol. 25, London, 1859; and John Callander, ed., *Terra Australis Cognita: or Voyages to the Terra Australis, or Southern Hemisphere during the Sixteenth, Seventeenth, and Eighteenth Centuries*, 3 vols., A. Donaldson, Edinburgh, 1766–68. See also two substantial monographs: Edward Heawood, *A History of Geographical Discovery in the Seventeenth and Eighteenth Centuries*, University Press, Cambridge, 1912; and J. S. Beaglehole, *The Exploration of the Pacific*, A. & C. Black, Ltd., London, 1934.

Alexander Dalrymple's propaganda to prove that a habitable *terra australis incognita* was located in the South Pacific is in his *Historical Collection of the Several Voyages and Discoveries in the South Pacific Ocean*, 2 vols., Printed by the Author, London, 1770–71; while Captain Cook's voyages are described in Andrew Kippis, *Captain Cook's Voyages, with an Account of his Life During the Previous and Intervening Periods*, Alfred A. Knopf, New York, 1925. Cook's own journal has appeared in several editions.

II. BIBLIOGRAPHICAL AIDS FOR UNITED STATES ANTARCTIC EXPLORATION

Students of United States exploration in the Antarctic are indebted to Daniel C. Haskell, formerly of the New York Public Library staff, for his indispensable bibliographical study of the Wilkes Expedition,

"The United States Exploring Expedition, 1838–1842, and Its Publications, 1844–1874: A Bibliography," *Bulletin of the New York Public Library*, 45 (Jan., 1941), 69–89; (July, 1941), 507–32; (Oct., 1941), 821–58; 46 (Jan., 1942), 103–51. This is a monograph concerning the problems associated with the publication of the expedition reports by the United States government, but Haskell has also provided a comprehensive list of manuscripts and printed sources relating to the expedition's preparation and exploration.

Also valuable, especially for twentieth-century research, is the *Antarctic Bibliography*, Bureau of Aeronautics, Department of the Navy, Washington, D.C., 1951. A brief list of sources, emphasizing the Wilkes Expedition's contributions to natural history, is in Max Meisel, *A Bibliography of American Natural History: The Pioneer Century, 1769–1865*, 3 vols., The Premier Publishing Co., Brooklyn, N.Y., 1924–29.

III. MANUSCRIPTS

Little manuscript evidence exists regarding the activities of American sealers in the exploration of the Antarctic, but the significant logs of the cruises to the continent undertaken by Captains Nathaniel Brown Palmer, John Davis, and Christopher Burdick have been preserved. The logbook of the *Hero*, describing Palmer's voyage in November, 1820, to the peninsula bearing his name, is among the Papers of Nathaniel B. and Alexander S. Palmer, Manuscripts Division, Library of Congress. The other items in this collection are letters, copies of letters, and memoranda dealing with the Palmers' several sealing voyages, but they contain little of value concerning exploration in latitudes south of the South Shetlands.

Mr. Alexander O. Vietor, Curator of Maps, Yale University Library, and Director of the Cartography Laboratory at Yale, discovered the log of the *Huron*, containing the record of Captain Davis's voyage to the continent in the *Cecilia*, and the sealers' landing on the shores of Hughes Bay. He has placed it in the Sterling Library at Yale.

Captain Christopher Burdick's log of the *Huntress* was resurrected by Mr. Edouard A. Stackpole, Curator of the Marine Historical Association, Mystic, Connecticut, from beneath pictures pasted on its pages. This document had been used as a scrapbook, but Stackpole now has it in his possession. His thoughtful monograph, *The Voyage of the Huron and the Huntress*, in which pertinent sections of the logs of these vessels have been reproduced, was employed in the preparation of this study, rather than the MS logs themselves.

A small and insignificant collection of the papers of Edmund Fanning is in the Library of the American Geographical Society, New York City. These manuscripts deal with the Stonington sealing expedition of 1821–22, the publication of Fanning's autobiographical *Voyages Round the World*, and with his failure to gain what he believed was proper recognition for his efforts to achieve government-sponsored overseas exploration. After the United States Exploring Expedition was approved by Congress, Fanning became bitterly disappointed because most of the public and official acclaim for promoting it went to Jeremiah N. Reynolds.

In addition, a memorial and a letter briefly reviewing the exploits of Benjamin Morrell are among the Miscellaneous Letters for 1831 in the Records of the Department of the Navy, Naval Records and Library Collection, R.G. 45, National Archives. James Byers's letters to General Daniel Parker requesting the employment of a United States Navy ship to facilitate the occupation of the South Shetlands by American sealers in 1820 are among the Records of the Department of State, R.G. 59, Miscellaneous Letters for 1820, National Archives; while John Quincy Adams's MS Diary, showing his interest in this project, is in the Adams Papers, Massachusetts Historical Society, Boston. Finally, Nathaniel Palmer's voyage to the South Shetlands in 1821 on the *James Monroe* is charted in the Journal of the Schooner *Alabama Packet*, Library of the Marine Historical Association, Mystic.

No reliable assessment of the role of American sealers in the discovery and exploration of Palmer Peninsula can be made without reference to Edward Bransfield's manuscript chart marked Ael S92 among the Original Documents, Hydrographic Office, Admiralty, Cornwall House, London; the Chart of New South Britain, Discovered by Captain 'Smith, in the Brig Williams, Feb. 19, 1819, Drawn by Wm. Henry Goddard, Press Mark Ael S91, *ibid.;* and the Memorial of William Smith, Discoverer of the South Shetlands, to the Lords Commissioners of the Admiralty, Public Records Office, Admiralty, Secretary, Letters 5029, for 1821, London.

Letters, notes, essays, memoranda, and draft newspaper articles of John Cleves Symmes, Jr., the theorist, which illuminate his theory of concentric spheres, as well as his efforts to gain acceptance of his ideas, are in the papers of his uncle, John Cleves Symmes, the Miami purchaser, among the Draper Manuscripts, Wisconsin Historical Society, Madison. Unfortunately, no substantial collection of Jeremiah N. Reynolds's papers has been preserved, but some of his letters, as well as those of Edmund Fanning, to the Navy Department and members of Congress can be found in the Records of the Department of the Navy, Miscellaneous Letters for 1827, 1828, 1831, 1832, and 1833, National Archives.

In contrast to the sources for the sealers, the manuscript evidence concerning the preparation of the Wilkes Expedition, and its exploration, is voluminous. The bulk of these records are in the National Archives, and have been microfilmed as *National Archives Microfilm Publication, M 75*. The work of Captain Thomas Ap Catesby Jones, Secretary of the Navy Mahlon Dickerson, and others, is spelled out in the four volumes of Letters Relating to Preparations for the Wilkes Exploring Expedition, while the final outfitting under the new commander and the explorations of the squadron are detailed in the two

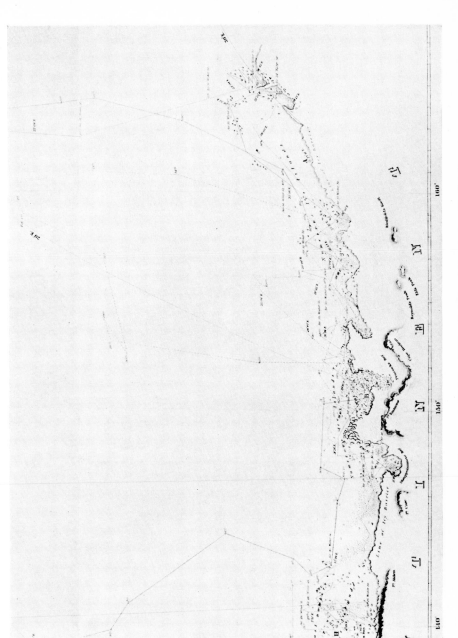

Section of Lieutenant Charles Wilkes's map of the Antarctic Continent

volumes of Letters Relating to the Wilkes Exploring Expedition. Besides these materials, the collection includes many of the personal journals kept during the cruise by officers and crew members. The most important of these, bearing on the two treks into the Antarctic, the first from Tierra del Fuego, and the other from Australia, is the three-volume Journal of Lieutenant Charles Wilkes Aboard the *Vincennes* and the *Porpoise*. This manuscript, together with the pertinent chapters in volume II of the commander's printed *Narrative*, present the most complete record of the explorer's discoveries in East Antarctica. The journals of Wilkes's principal lieutenants, William L. Hudson and Cadwallader Ringgold, apparently do not exist.

Supplementing Wilkes's record of the explorations south of Tierra del Fuego are the Journal Kept Aboard the *Porpoise* and *Relief* by Lieutenant Henry J. Hartstene; and the Journal of Lieutenant Robert Johnson Aboard the *Sea Gull;* while the cruise of the *Peacock* in the same seas is related in the Journal of J. Frederick Sickels, Assistant Surgeon, Aboard the *Peacock* and *Relief;* and the Journal of Frederic D. Stuart, Captain's Clerk, Aboard the *Peacock*.

For the tracks of the ships and the discoveries of the explorers south of Australia, see, in addition to the journals listed above, the Anonymous Journal Kept Aboard the *Vincennes;* Journal of Passed Midshipman Joseph Perry Sanford Aboard the *Vincennes;* Journal of Edward Gilchrist, Assistant Surgeon, Aboard the *Vincennes;* Journal of William Briskee, Armorer, Aboard the *Vincennes;* the Log Kept Aboard the *Vincennes* and the *Porpoise* by Acting Midshipman Samuel B. Elliott; and the Journal of George T. Sinclair, Acting Master, Aboard the *Flying Fish*. This collection also includes the record of Charles Wilkes's court-martial trial.

The Charles Wilkes Papers, Manuscripts Division, Library of Congress, shed light on his career as an explorer. Especially important is his 10-volume MS "Autobiography," but it should be used only with caution, for it was prepared during the last years of Wilkes's life after his forced retirement from the Navy owing to the *Trent* affair, and is thoroughly vitriolic and vindictive. The ambitious Wilkes never achieved the goals he set for himself, and his autobiography is devoted to blaming his failure on others.

The Manuscripts Division also contains the Henry Eld Papers, including his important letter of March 10, 1840, to his family, in which the voyage of the *Peacock* along the coast of Antarctica is delineated; Journal of a Cruise in the U.S. Ship *Vincennes,* Charles Wilkes, Commander in Chief, in the Years 1838, 1839, 1840, 1841, 1842, presumed to have been kept by Joseph G. Clark, because of its similarity to his *Lights and Shadows of Sailor Life;* Journals of Jared Leigh Elliott, Kept while Serving as Chaplain on the United States Exploring Expedition (2 vols.); and the reports of committees of the American Philosophical Society and the United States Naval Lyceum to Secretary of the Navy Dickerson, detailing the scientific subjects to be studied by the expedition. The Naval Lyceum report has been printed, along with letters from various scientists, in *The Naval Magazine,* II (Jan., 1837), 64–86.

The principal manuscript record of the *Peacock's* voyage along Antarctica is the Journal of Lieutenant George Foster Emmons, Kept while Attached to the South Sea Surveying and Exploring Expedition, U.S. Sloop-of-War *Peacock,* in the William Robertson Coe Collection, Yale University Library. Joel Roberts Poinsett's part in finally getting the United States Exploring Expedition to sea is portrayed in letters in the Poinsett Papers, Pennsylvania Historical Society, Philadelphia. The MS of Titian Ramsay Peale's article, "The South Sea Surveying and Exploring Expedition. Origin, Organization, Equipment, Purposes, Results, and Termination," which deals briefly with the explorations south of 63° S., is in the Archives of the United States National Museum. It was published in *The American Historical Record,* III (June and July, 1874), 244–51, 305–11.

IV. PRINTED JOURNALS AND REPORTS OF VOYAGES AND TRAVELS

The most comprehensive document covering the activities and accomplishments of American sealers in the Pacific, at the South Shetland Islands, and in the Antarctic is Edmund Fanning's *Voyages Round the World; with Selected Sketches of Voyages to the South Seas, North and South Pacific Oceans, China, etc., Performed Under the Command and Agency of the Author* . . . , Collins & Hannay, New York, 1833. Parts of this narrative are untrustworthy, however. In the first place, the author's description of the voyage of the *Hersilia* in 1819, when Captain James Sheffield located the South Shetlands, undoubtedly is spurious. Secondly, he helped to perpetuate the fallacious story of Nathaniel Palmer's conversation with the Russian Captain, Fabian von Bellingshausen, during his supposed voyage to the Antarctic Continent in January, 1821. (See chapters 2 and 3 of this study.) An abridged edition of this book was published in 1924 under the title *Voyages & Discoveries in the South Seas, 1792–1832,* as Publication no. 6 of the Marine Research Society of Salem, Massachusetts. This compendium contains the first thirteen chapters of the 1833 edition. Later, Fanning attempted to draw attention to his part in the movement for a national exploring expedition, and to increase his stature as a sealing and whaling agent, by publishing a small volume containing some of his memorials and letters urging overseas exploration, as well as the narratives of several voyages he sponsored. See his *Voyages to the South Seas, Indian and Pacific Oceans, China Sea, North-West Coast, Feejee Islands, South Shetlands* . . . , 2nd ed., William H. Vermilye, New York, 1838.

Edward Bransfield's discovery of the Antarctic Continent is outlined in "New Shetland," *Literary Gazette, and Journal of Belles Lettres, Arts, Science, &c.,* X (Nov. 3, 1821), 691–92; (Nov. 10, 1821), 712–

13; and (Nov. 24, 1821), 746–47. See also the "Notice of the Voyage of Edward Barnsfield [sic], Master of His Majesty's Ship Andromache, to New South Shetland," *Edinburgh Philosophical Journal*, IV (April, 1821), 345–48; and the *Imperial Magazine; or Compendium of Religious, Moral & Philosophical Knowledge*, II (Sept., 1820), col. 755.

Nathaniel Palmer's meeting with Captain Bellingshausen at the South Shetlands, as well as the Russian Antarctic discoveries during 1820–21, are described in *The Voyage of Captain Bellingshausen to the Antarctic Seas, 1819–21*, 2 vols., trans. from the Russian, ed. by Frank Debenham, The Hakluyt Society, ser. 2, vols. 91–92, London, 1945; while George Powell delineates his cooperative voyage with the Stonington sealer when the South Orkney Islands were discovered in *Notes on South-Shetland, &c. Printed to Accompany the Chart of these Newly Discovered Lands, which has been Constructed from the Explorations of the sloop Dove*, R. H. Laurie, London, 1822. Palmer Land is shown on Powell's chart. Important observations on both Palmer's and Benjamin Morrell's discoveries are made by Henryk Arctowski in "The Antarctic Voyage of the 'Belgica' During the Years, 1897, 1898, and 1899," *Geographical Journal*, XVIII (Oct., 1901), 353–94; and Lieut. M. F. Maury, *Explanations and Sailing Directions to Accompany the Wind and Current Charts . . . ,* C. Alexander, Washington, 1851.

The Antarctic discoveries of Benjamin Morrell are sketched in his hyperbolical *Narrative of Four Voyages, to the South Sea, North and South Pacific Ocean, Chinese Sea, Ethiopic and Southern Atlantic Ocean, Indian and Antarctic Ocean, from the Year 1822 to 1831 . . . ,* J. & J. Harper, New York, 1832. The validity of the supposed landfalls reported by Morrell should be checked in the journals of modern explorers. See Dr. N. Otto G. Nordenskjöld and Dr. Joh. Gunnar Andersson, *Antarctica, or Two Years Amongst the Ice of the South Pole*, Hurst and Blackett, Ltd., London, 1905; and Sir Ernest Shackleton, *South: The Story of Shackleton's Last Expedition, 1914–1917*, The Macmillan Co., New York, 1920. The Frenchman Dumont d'Urville's account of his Antarctic cruise should be examined not only for his report that New South Greenland did not exist, but for his discovery of Adélie Land and Clarie Coast at the time Wilkes and his men were exploring in the same seas. See the *Voyage au Pôle Sud et dans l'Océanie sur les corvettes l'Astrolabe et la Zélée Executé par ordre du Roi pendant 1837, 1838, 1839, et 1840*, 23 vols., Gide, Paris, 1841–45, especially II and VIII. In relation to Morrell see also R. N. Rudmose Brown, R. C. Mossman, and J. H. Harvey Pirie, *The Voyage of the "Scotia," Being the Record of a Voyage of Exploration in Antarctic Seas*, William Blackwood and Sons, Edinburgh, 1906; James Weddell, *A Voyage Towards the South Pole, Performed in the Years 1822–'24 . . . ,* 2nd ed., Longman, Hurst, Rees, Orme, Brown, and Green, London, 1825; and J. M. Wordie, "Shackleton Antarctic Expedition, 1914–1917: The Natural History of Pack-Ice as Observed in the Weddell Sea," *Transactions of the Royal Society of Edinburgh,* LII (1920–21), 795–831.

Amasa Delano, *Narrative of Voyages and Travels, in the Northern and Southern Hemispheres* . . . , E. G. House for the Author, Boston, 1817, provides first-hand descriptions of sealing and some early voyages to the South Atlantic and Pacific; while the first sealing voyage from the United States in the Boston ship, *The States,* is discussed laconically in "The Diary of Mr. Ebenezer Townsend, Jr., the Supercargo of the Sealing Ship 'Neptune,' on her Voyage to the South Pacific and Canton," *Papers of the New Haven Colony Historical Society,* IV (1888), 1–115. The interest of Chinese merchants in furs is shown in Captain James Cook and Captain James King, *A Voyage to the Pacific Ocean. Undertaken, by the Command of his Majesty for making Discoveries in the Northern Hemisphere* . . . , 3 vols., H. Hughs, London, 1785, III; and [John Ledyard], *Journal of Captain Cook's Last Voyage to the Pacific Ocean, and in Quest of a North-West Passage* . . . , Nathaniel Patton, Hartford, Conn., 1783.

Charles Wilkes, *Narrative of the United States Exploring Expedition, During the Years 1838, 1839, 1840, 1841, 1842,* 5 vols., Lea & Blanchard, Philadelphia, 1845, contains the commander's considered version of the explorations. For the Antarctic phases see vols. I and II, and their appendices, which contain letters from the commanders of the secondary vessels. A one-volume edition of the *Narrative* appeared under the title *Voyage Round the World* . . . , G. Putnam, Boston, 1851. Three other printed journals bear on Wilkes's cruise in the *Vincennes:* Lieut. Geo. M. Colvocorresses, *Four Years in the Government Exploring Expedition; Commanded by Captain Charles Wilkes* . . . , 2nd ed., R. T. Young, New York, 1853; Joseph G. Clark, *Lights and Shadows of Sailor Life, as Exemplified in Fifteen Years' Experience, Including the More Thrilling Events of the U.S. Expedition* . . . , John Putnam, Boston, 1847; and Charles Erskine, *Twenty Years Before the Mast, with the More Thrilling Scenes and Incidents while Circumnavigating the Globe under the Command of the Late Admiral Charles Wilkes, 1838–1842,* Published by the Author, Boston, 1890.

The controversy over the authenticity of Wilkes's landfalls took form in Captain Sir James Clark Ross, *A Voyage of Discovery and Research in the Southern and Antarctic Regions, During the Years 1839–43,* 2 vols., John Murray, London, 1847; Charles Wilkes, *Synopsis of the Cruise of the U.S. Exploring Expedition. Delivered Before the National Institute, June 20, 1842,* P. Force, Washington, 1842; Charles Enderby, "Note on Sabrina Land, &c.," *Proceedings of the Royal Geographical Society,* II (Jan. 25, 1858), 172; John Murray, *A Summary of the Scientific Results Obtained at the Soundings, Dredging, and Trawling Stations of H.M.S. Challenger,* 2 vols. in 1, Neill and Co., Edinburgh, 1895; C. E. Borchgrevink, *First on the Antarctic Continent: Being an Account of the British Antarctic Expedi-*

tion, 1899–1900, George Newnes, Ltd., London, 1901; Erich von Drygalski, "The German Antarctic Expedition," *Geographical Journal,* XXIV (Aug., 1904), 130–48; Captain Robert F. Scott, *The Voyage of the "Discovery,"* 2 vols., Charles Scribner's Sons, New York, 1905; E. H. Shackleton, *The Heart of the Antarctic; Being the Story of the British Antarctic Expedition, 1907–1909,* 2 vols., J. B. Lippincott Co., Philadelphia, 1909; John King Davis, *With the "Aurora" in the Antarctic, 1911–1914,* Andrew Melrose, Ltd., London, 1919; and Sir Douglas Mawson, *The Home of the Blizzard: Being the Story of the Australasian Antarctic Expedition, 1911–1914,* 2 vols., William Heinemann, London, 1914.

V. GOVERNMENT DOCUMENTS

See 20 Cong., 2 Sess., *Register of Debates in Congress,* V; 24 Cong., 1 Sess., *Cong. Globe,* III; and 25 Cong., 2 Sess., *Cong. Globe,* VI, for the debates inspired by Senator Robert Y. Hayne on the authorization of the expedition of 1828, the discussions regarding the bill creating the United States Exploring Expedition, and the arguments for converting the expedition into an Atlantic coast squadron after Jones's resignation and Wilkes's assumption of command. The latter are elaborated in the debates printed in the *National Intelligencer,* March 31, 1828, 2–3; April 7, 1838, 1; April 12, 1838, 1; and April 14, 1838, 1.

Some of Jeremiah N. Reynolds's propaganda for exploration after his break with John Cleves Symmes is shown in his letter to the Speaker of the House of Representatives, 1828, in 20 Cong., 1 Sess., *House Doc.* 88; the petition of New Bedford citizens, 20 Cong., 1 Sess., *House Doc.* 201; and in the Report of the House Committee on Naval Affairs to which many memorials and petitions had been submitted, 20 Cong., 1 Sess., *House Report* 209. These petitions helped to inspire the House Resolution calling for an expedition, but preparations of the ships only were begun before it was scuttled by Robert Y. Hayne's Senate Committee on Naval Affairs. See 20 Cong., 2 Sess., *Sen. Doc.* 77, for Secretary of the Navy Samuel L. Southard's report on the expenditures and objectives of the expedition; and 20 Cong., 2 Sess., *Sen. Doc.* 94, for the judgments of the Hayne Committee. Information concerning the Pacific, which was collected by Reynolds in New England, is printed in 23 Cong., 1 Sess., *House Doc.* 105.

Following the failure of the voyage in the *Seraph* and the *Annawan,* 1829–30, Edmund Fanning began the movement for a government-sponsored expedition again; 22 Cong., 1 Sess., *House Doc.* 61; and 23 Cong., 1 Sess., *Sen. Doc.* 10, contain his memorials. The tempo of this activity increased after Reynolds's return to the United States following service as historiographer on the punitive expedition to Sumatra. See 23 Cong., 2 Sess., *House Doc.* 48; 23 Cong., 2 Sess., *Sen. Doc.* 25; and the important memorial of the East India Marine Society of Salem in 23 Cong., 2 Sess., *Sen. Doc.* 75. These and other petitions brought the reports favoring exploration in 23 Cong., 2 Sess., *House Report* 94; and 24 Cong., 1 Sess., *Sen. Doc.* 262.

When the preparation of the expedition moved haltingly under Captain Jones, the House called for explanations from the Executive at various times, usually when additional appropriations were requested. See 24 Cong., 2 Sess., *House Doc.* 138; 25 Cong., 1 Sess., *House Doc.* 50; 25 Cong., 2 Sess., *House Doc.* 255; and 25 Cong., 2 Sess., *House Ex. Doc.* 147, which contains several hundred letters bearing on almost every problem faced by the Navy Department and by the commander before his departure. This document supplements the four volumes of MS Letters Relating to the Preparation of the Wilkes Expedition in the National Archives.

Edmund Fanning was convinced that the ships of the United States Exploring Expedition could not withstand Antarctic conditions and called for another fleet made up of vessels built according to his specifications in 26 Cong., 1 Sess., *House Doc.* 57.

VI. LETTERS

The letters of Secretary of State Adams and President Monroe on the sealers' occupation of the South Shetlands in 1820 have been published under the title, "The First American Discoveries in the Antarctic, 1819," *American Historical Review*, XVI (July, 1911), 794–98. *Letters of Asa Gray*, 2 vols., ed. by Jane Loring Gray, Houghton Mifflin Co., Boston, 1894, I, contains the botanist's observations on his colleagues in the scientific corps, as well as statements concerning the scientific objectives of the Wilkes Expedition. Charles Wilkes's letter to the editor of the Washington *Union* answering James Clark Ross's criticisms of his discoveries was published under "Antarctic Exploration," *American Journal of Science and Arts*, V (March, 1848), 287–89. It was printed as a pamphlet also. See *Antarctic Exploration. Letter of Captain Wilkes to the Editor of the Union* [Washington], [1847].

VII. DIARIES AND MEMOIRS

See the *Diary of John Quincy Adams, 1794–1845; American Diplomacy, and Political, Social, and Intellectual Life, from Washington to Polk*, ed. by Allan Nevins, Charles Scribner's Sons, New York, 1951; and *Memoirs of John Quincy Adams, Comprising Portions of His Diary from 1795–1848*, 12 vols., ed. by Charles Francis Adams, J. B. Lippincott Co., Philadelphia, 1874–77, VII, VIII, for comments concerning overseas exploration. Wilkes published his defense against the court-martial charges: *Defence: The Following Defence of Lieutenant Charles Wilkes to the Charges on which He has been Tried*, [Washington], [1842].

VIII. SPEECHES

The most significant single declaration of the supporters of overseas exploration was Jeremiah N. Reynolds's memorable speech in the

House Chamber, *Address on the Subject of a Surveying and Exploring Expedition to the Pacific Ocean and South Seas Delivered in the Hall of Representatives on the Evening of April 3, 1836,* Harper and Brothers, New York, 1836. Representative Thomas L. Hamer's influential address favoring Reynolds's and Fanning's project was published in pamphlet form as the *Speech of Mr. Thomas L. Hamer, of Ohio, on the Bill Authorizing Appropriations for a Survey and Exploring Expedition to the South Seas,* P. Force, Washington, 1836; while Joel Roberts Poinsett tried to draw attention to Wilkes's discoveries in his *Discourse on the Objects and Importance of the National Institution for the Promotion of Science,* P. Force, Washington, 1841.

IX. NEWSPAPERS

The *National Intelligencer,* Washington, D.C., Jan., 1818–July, 1842; and *Niles' Weekly Register,* Baltimore, Jan., 1820–Oct., 1842, are the most substantial files, covering the sealers, the movement for national exploration, and the Wilkes Expedition.

Symmes's and Reynolds's tracks as lecturers, as well as the development of the theory of concentric spheres, can be traced in *The Western Spy, and Cincinnati General Advertiser,* Feb. 20, 1819–Dec. 18, 1819; and the *Liberty Hall and Cincinnati Gazette,* Dec., 1818–Jan., 1827. See also the significant articles in *The Western Spy,* Cincinnati, Oct. 3 and 17, 1818; and the *Cincinnati Advertiser,* May 4, 1819–Nov. 2, 1819.

See *The Globe,* Washington, D.C., April, 1836–July, 1842, for the controversy over the appointment of officers involving Lieutenant Alexander Slidell, Captain Thomas Ap Catesby Jones, and Secretary Mahlon Dickerson, and for the opinion of the Democratic administrations regarding the expedition. The exchange of statements regarding the discoveries of the United States Exploring Expedition in East Antarctica between Captain J. H. Aulick and Lieutenant Wilkes is in *The Spectator,* Washington, D.C., Nov. 12 and 19, 1842.

X. MONOGRAPHS AND BIOGRAPHIES

The most penetrating and comprehensive study of the sealers' explorations of 1820–21 is Edouard Stackpole's *The Voyage of the Huron and the Huntress: The American Sealers and the Discovery of the Continent of Antarctica,* Connecticut Printers, Inc., Hartford, Conn., 1955. See also his *Sea-Hunters: New England Whalemen During Two Centuries, 1635–1835,* J. B. Lippincott Co., Philadelphia, 1953. The value of William Herbert Hobbs's *Discoveries of Antarctica within the American Sector, as Revealed by Maps and Documents, Transactions of the American Philosophical Society,* n.s., vol. XXXI, pt. 1, Jan., 1939, Philadelphia, 1939, is obscured by his prejudiced efforts to prove that Palmer, not Bransfield, discovered the Antarctic Continent.

John R. Spears, *Captain Nathaniel Brown Palmer, an Old-Time Sailor of the Sea,* Macmillan Co., New York, 1922, is of little use for

Palmer's Antarctic explorations, because the author misinterprets the MS Logbook of the *Hero*. Other biographical data on Palmer and the Stonington sealers is in Richard Anson Wheeler, *History of the Town of Stonington, County of New London, Connecticut, from its First Settlement in 1649 to 1900 . . .* , Press of the Day Publishing Co., New London, Conn., 1900; D. Hamilton Hurd, comp., *History of New London County, Connecticut, with Biographical Sketches of Many of its Pioneers and Prominent Men,* J. W. Lewis & Co., Philadelphia, 1882; Spears, *The Story of New England Whalers,* Macmillan Co., New York, 1908; Jacques and Helen La Grange, *Clipper Ships of America and Great Britain, 1833–1869,* G. P. Putnam's Sons, New York, 1936; Helen Augur, *Tall Ships to Cathay,* Doubleday & Co., Inc., Garden City, N.Y., 1951; and Alexander Laing, *Clipper Ship Men,* Duell, Sloan and Pearce, New York, 1944.

Dr. Karl Fricker believed Benjamin Morrell was a fabricator. See his *Antarctic Regions,* trans. by A. Sonnenschein, Swan Sonnenschein & Co., Ltd., London, 1900.

The Symmes theory is clarified and explained in [James McBride], *Symmes's Theory of Concentric Spheres; Demonstrating that the Earth is Hollow, Habitable Within, and Widely Open About the Poles.* By a Citizen of the United States, Morgan, Lodge and Fisher, Cincinnati, 1826; and Americus Symmes, comp., *The Symmes Theory of Concentric Spheres, Demonstrating that the Earth is Hollow, Habitable Within, and Widely Open About the Poles,* Bradley & Gilbert, Louisville, Ky., 1878. See Henry Howe, *Historical Collections of Ohio,* 3 vols., Henry Howe & Son, Columbus, 1891, I; and James McBride, *Pioneer Biography, Sketches of the Lives of Some of the Early Settlers of Butler County, Ohio,* 2 vols., Robert Clarke & Co., Cincinnati, 1871, II, for biographical information on the theorist. His theory is satirized in Captain Adam Seaborn, *Symzonia: Voyage of Discovery,* J. Seymour, New York, 1820.

Interest in Symmes's theory and similar ones persisted long after it had become obvious the earth was not hollow or widely open at the poles. See Edna Kenton's historical and analytical *Book of Earths,* William Morrow & Co., New York, 1928; and J. W. Buel's popular, *World's Wonders, as Seen by the Great Tropical and Polar Explorers . . . ,* Historical Publishing Co., St. Louis, 1884. See also Frederick Culmer, *The Inner World: A New Theory, Based on Scientific and Theological Facts, Showing that the Earth is a Sphere Containing an Internal and Inhabited Region,* n.p., Salt Lake City, 1886; John Merrill, *Cosmogony; or, Thoughts on Philosophy,* Published for the Author, n.p., 1871; William Reed, *The Phantom of the Poles,* Walter S. Rockey Co., New York, 1906; and William F. Warren, *Paradise Found, the Cradle of the Human Race at the North Pole: A Study of the Prehistoric World,* Sampson Low, Marston, Searle & Rivington, London, 1885.

J. N. Reynolds, *Pacific and Indian Oceans: or, The South Sea Sur-*

veying and Exploring Expedition: Its Inception, Progress, and Objects, Harper & Brothers, New York, 1841, is largely an attack on Mahlon Dickerson, important for the series of letters written by Reynolds ("Citizen") and Dickerson ("Friend of the Navy") concerning exploration policy, published originally in the *New York Times* and New York *Courier and Enquirer.* For biographical and personal material on the propagandist see *The History of Clinton County, Ohio, Containing a History of the County; Its Townships, Cities, Towns, Schools, Churches* . . . , W. H. Beers & Co., Chicago, 1882; and Howe, *Historical Collections of Ohio,* I.

Daniel Henderson's *Hidden Coasts,* William Sloane Associates, New York, 1953, the only biography of Wilkes, is eulogistic and thinly based. Descriptions of the Wilkes explorations are in J. E. Nourse, *American Explorations in the Ice Zones* . . . , D. Lothrop and Co., Boston, 1884; Anna E. Carrell, *The Star of the West,* Miller, Orton & Mulligan, New York, 1857; John Stilwell Jenkins, *Voyage of the U.S. Exploring Squadron, Commanded by Captain Charles Wilkes* . . . , James M. Alden, Auburn, N.Y., 1850; Jenkins, *Explorations and Adventures In and Around the Pacific and Antarctic Oceans* . . . , Hurst & Co., New York, 1882; and Henry Howe, *Travels and Adventures of Celebrated Travelers in the Principal Countries of the World,* Henry Howe, Cincinnati, 1856.

Joel Poinsett's association with the expedition is described briefly in J. Fred Rippy, *Joel R. Poinsett, Versatile American,* Duke University Press, Durham, N.C., 1935.

XI. ARTICLES AND REVIEWS

Colonel Lawrence Martin's "Antarctica Discovered by a Connecticut Yankee, Captain Nathaniel Brown Palmer," *Geographical Review,* XXX (Oct., 1940), 529–52, is the definitive interpretation of Nathaniel Palmer's cruise to Antarctica. He adds details in "Palmer's Instrumental Observations in Connection with the Discovery of Antarctica," *Science,* 87 (May 20, 1938), 465–66; and "The Log of Palmer's Discovery of Antarctica," *Science,* 87 (Feb. 18, 1938), 165–66. Edwin Swift Balch has printed most of the Palmer Papers, Library of Congress, in "Stonington Antarctic Explorers," *Bulletin of the American Geographical Society,* XLI (Aug., 1909), 473–92; while Hugh Robert Mill, "Bellingshausen's Antarctic Voyage," *Geographical Journal,* XXI (Feb., 1903), 150–59; Major General A. W. Greely, "American Discoveries of the Antarctic Continent," *National Geographic Magazine,* XXIII (March, 1912), 298–312; "The Whale Fishery," *North American Review,* XXXVIII (Jan., 1834), 84–115; " 'Nat' Palmer and the Antarctic," *The Outing Magazine,* LXII (April, 1913), 48, also treat the Stonington sealer's explorations. See, in addition, Hugh Robert Mill's review of Edwin Swift Balch's *Antarctica* in the *Geographical Journal,* XXXI (May, 1903), 525–29, and the author's reply in *Science,* XVIII (July 10, 1903), 55–56.

Edward H. Raymond, "The Fur-Seal Fishery and Salem," *Essex Institute Historical Collections*, LXXII (July, 1936), 181–207, covers the birth of the sealing industry; and Edouard Stackpole argues that Christopher Burdick's Log of the *Huntress* contains the first recognition of Antarctica as a continent in "The First Recognition of Antarctica," *Boston Public Library Quarterly*, IV (Jan., 1952), 3–19, but this interpretation has been superseded in his *Voyages of the Huron and the Huntress*.

Early nineteenth-century English explorations in the Antarctic, including Edward Bransfield's discovery of the continent, are set forth in Lieutenant-Commander R. T. Gould, "The First Sighting of the Antarctic Continent," *Geographical Journal*, LXV (March, 1925), 220–25; Gould, "The Charting of the South Shetlands, 1819–1828," *Mariner's Mirror, The Journal of the Society of Nautical Research*, XXVII (July, 1941), 206–43; and Ida Lee, "The Voyages of Captain William Smith and Others to the South Shetlands," *Geographical Journal*, XLII (Oct., 1913), 365–70.

William H. Hobbs's contentions in his *Discoveries of Antarctica* that English claims of Bransfield's discovery of the Continent are not based on substantial evidence brought rebuttals in reviews across the Atlantic. See R. N. Rudmose Brown, "Antarctic History: A Reply to Professor W. H. Hobbs," *Scottish Geographical Magazine*, LXV (May, 1939), 170–73; A[rthur] R. H[inks]., "On Some Misrepresentations of Antarctic History," *Geographical Journal*, XCIV (Oct., 1939), 309–30; and Gould, "Charting of the South Shetlands." Edwin Swift Balch endorses the Bransfield evidence in "The First Sighting of West Antarctica," *Geographical Review*, XV (Oct., 1925), 650–53.

Benjamin Morrell's supposed discoveries have inspired some controversy as to his reliability. For opinions that he is the "Baron Munchausen of the Antarctic" see William H. Hobbs, "The Pack-Ice of the Weddell Sea," *Annals of the Association of American Geographers*, XXIX (June, 1939), 150–61; and J. E. Davis's remarks in Captain R. V. Hamilton's "On Morrell's Antarctic Voyage in the Year 1823, with Remarks on the Advantages Steam will Confer on Future Antarctic Explorers," *Proceedings of the Royal Geographical Society*, XIV (March 14, 1870), 145–56. The author of this article defends the American sealer. See also Dr. William S. Bruce, "The Weddell Sea: An Historical Retrospect," *Scottish Geographical Magazine*, XXXIII (June, 1917), 245–52; O. Schück, "Entwicklung unserer Kenntnis der Länder im Süden von Amerika," *Zeitschrift für Wissenschaftliche Geographie unter Mitberücksichtigung des Höheren Geographischen Unterrichts*, VI (1888), 244–64; and Angelo Heilprin, "Our Present Knowledge of the Antarctic Regions," *Popular Science Monthly*, 50 (Jan., 1897), 323–36. Other estimates of Morrell are in "Sir Ernest Shackleton's Antarctic Expedition," *Nature, A Weekly Illustrated Journal of Science*, XCVII (June 8, 1916), 301–3; A. Petermann, "Neue Karte der Süd-Polar-Regionen," *Mittheilungen aus Justus*

Perthes' Geographischer Anstalt über Wichtige Neue Erförschungen auf dem Gesammtgebiete der Geographie, IX (1863), 407–28; John Murray, "The Exploration of the Antarctic Regions," *Scottish Geographical Magazine,* II (Sept., 1886), 527–43; and the review of his *Four Voyages* in the *American Quarterly Review,* XXVI (June, 1833), 314–36.

Symmes's theory is sketched in Elmore Symmes, "John Cleves Symmes, the Theorist," *Southern Bivouac: A Monthly Literary and Historical Magazine,* V, n.s. II (Feb., 1887), 555–66; (March, 1887), 621–31; (April, 1887), 682–93; P. Clark, "The Symmes Theory of the Earth," *Atlantic Monthly,* XXXI (April, 1873), 471–80; John Wells Peck, "Symmes Theory," *Ohio Archaeological and Historical Publications,* XVIII (1909), 29–42; and William Marion Miller, "The Theory of Concentric Spheres," *Isis: An International Review Devoted to the History of Science and Civilization,* XXXIII (1941), 507–14. See also the reviews of Adam Seaborn's *Symzonia* and *Symmes's Theory. . . . By a Citizen of the United States* in the *North American Review,* XIII (July, 1821), 134–43; and the *American Quarterly Review,* I (March, 1827), 235–53, respectively.

Jeremiah N. Reynolds announced his successful lecture tour and presented his plan for exploration in *Remarks on a Review of Symmes' Theory, which Appeared in the American Quarterly Review,* Gales & Seaton, Washington, 1827. The *New-York Mirror, and Ladies' Literary Gazette,* V (April 26, 1828), 334–35; VI (Oct. 11, 1828), 111; VII (Sept. 26, 1829), 95; and (Oct. 24, 1829), 126, contain articles on Reynolds's propaganda and the *Seraph* and *Annawan* expedition. Robert F. Almy shows the propagandist's relationship with Edgar Allan Poe in "J. N. Reynolds: A Brief Biography with Particular Reference to Poe and Symmes," *The Colophon,* II (Winter, 1937), 227–45. Reynolds's writings concerning the Antarctic and Symmes's theory apparently influenced Poe's writing of the novel, *The Narrative of Arthur Gordon Pym.*

James Eights, the naturalist, was the only participant in the fruitless voyage of the *Seraph* and *Annawan* to contribute to knowledge of the Antarctic regions. See his perceptive papers "Description of a Crustaceous Animal Found on the Shores of the South Shetland Islands, with Remarks on their Natural History," *Transactions of the Albany Institute,* II (1833–52), 53–69; "Description of a New Animal Belonging to the Crustacean, Discovered in the Antarctic Seas," *Transactions of the Albany Institute,* II (1833–52), 331–34; and "Description of an Isopod Crustacean from the Antarctic Seas, with Observations on the New South Shetlands," *American Journal of Science and Arts,* XXII (Nov., 1856), 391–97. Biographical data and interpretations of Eights's scientific papers are supplied by Lawrence Martin, "James Eights' Pioneer Observation and Interpretation of Erratics in Antarctic Icebergs," *Bulletin of the Geological Society of America,* 60 (Jan., 1949), 177–82; Martin, "Early Explorations and Investigations in

Southern South America and Adjacent Waters by Mariners and Scientists from the United States of America," Abstract of an Address before the Eighth American Scientific Congress, 76 Cong., 3 Sess., *Cong. Record,* 86, Appendix 3195; W. T. Calman, "James Eights, A Pioneer Antarctic Naturalist," *Proceedings of the Linnean Society of London,* 149th Session (Nov. 3, 1937), 171–85; and John M. Clarke, "Reincarnation of James Eights, Antarctic Explorer," *The Scientific Monthly,* II (Feb., 1916), 189–202.

A number of contemporary journals contain salient material on the outfitting and exploration of the Wilkes Expedition. The progress of the preparations under Captain Jones's leadership, as well as Navy policy and politics during Mahlon Dickerson's service as Secretary, are detailed in the *Army and Navy Chronicle.* See especially III (July 21, 1836), 44; (Aug. 4, 1836), 72; (Oct. 6, 1836), 215–16; (Oct. 27, 1836), 267; (Nov. 3, 1836), 283–84; (Nov. 10, 1836), 299; (Nov. 24, 1836), 322–23, 333; (Dec. 1, 1836), 337–42; IV (Jan. 5, 1837), 6; (Jan. 19, 1837), 35–43; (Jan. 26, 1837), 49–51; (Feb. 9, 1837), 91–92; (May 11, 1837), 299–300; (May 25, 1837), 331; VI (Jan. 25, 1838), 57; (Feb. 8, 1838), 85–86, 86–87, 89, 91; (Feb. 22, 1838), 113–17; (April 12, 1838), 228–29; (April 19, 1838), 248–50; (May 10, 1838), 297–300; (May 31, 1838), 346–47; (June 28, 1838), 416; VII (Aug. 9, 1838), 91; (Aug. 23, 1838), 117, 120; (Aug. 30, 1838), 139, 140, 141, 142; (Sept. 6, 1838), 158; (Sept. 20, 1838), 189; and (Dec. 6, 1838), 355–57.

Important observations also appear in the *Southern Literary Messenger,* II (Aug., 1836), 587–89; III (Jan., 1837), 68–72; (Nov., 1837), 698–700; IV (Sept., 1838), 566–69; VI (April, 1840), 233–40; (May, 1840), 305–20; (Dec., 1840), 785–800; VII (Jan., 1841), 2–25; (May and June, 1841), 345–79; and the critical review of Wilkes's *Narrative* in XI (May, 1845), 305–22.

The *North American Review* helped to promote exploration and to create an informed opinion favorable to Wilkes's work. See the review of Reynolds's *Address,* XLV (Oct., 1837), 361–90; Joel Poinsett's significant estimate of Wilkes's *Synopsis,* LVI (April, 1843), 257–70; and Charles Davis's appreciation of the commander's *Narrative,* LXI (July, 1845), 54–107.

In addition, "United States Exploring Expedition," *American Journal of Science and Arts,* XLIV (April, 1843), 393–408, is an exposition of the expedition's accomplishments; Wilkes's letter to Secretary Paulding, March 10, 1840, announcing his discovery of an Antarctic Continent, is in *ibid.,* XL (April, 1841), 394–99; and "The Antarctic Circle," *Hunt's Merchants Magazine and Commercial Review,* III (Sept., 1840), 250, presents a chart and a list of Wilkes's landfalls.

Favorable reviews of Wilkes's *Narrative* are in the *Southern Quarterly Review,* VIII (July, 1845), 1–69; *The Merchants' Magazine,* XII (May, 1845), 444–51; and *The Edinburgh Review,* LXXXIII (April, 1846), 431–52; while critical ones can be found in *Littell's*

Living Age, IV (March 8, 1845), 579–86; (March 22, 1845), 692–97; V (April 12, 1845), 59–66; and *The Westminster Review,* XLIV (1845), 469–96.

Among more recent articles, Douglas Mawson's "Wilkes's Antarctic Landfalls," *Proceedings of the Royal Geographical Society of Australasia, South Australian Branch,* XXXIV (1932–33), 70–113, is indispensable to an understanding of the difficulties faced by Wilkes and other inexperienced early explorers. A perceptive discussion of the work of the American and French expeditions is Rear-Admiral John E. Pillsbury, "Wilkes's and D'Urville's Discoveries in Wilkes Land," *United States Naval Institute Proceedings,* 36 (June, 1910), 465–68. Charles O. Paullin, "Naval Administration Under the Navy Commissioners, 1815–1842," *United States Naval Institute Proceedings,* 33 (June, 1907), 597–641, is a pioneer study of Naval administration, which illuminates Samuel Southard's and Mahlon Dickerson's methods and policies as Secretary of the Navy. A major effort to analyze the Wilkes Expedition was made by the American Philosophical Society in 1940, when it celebrated the centenary of the expedition's exploration of Antarctica with a Symposium on American Polar Exploration. The papers read were published in the Society's *Proceedings,* 82 (June, 1940). See especially those by Edwin G. Conklin, James A. G. Rehn, G. S. Bryan, and William H. Hobbs.

Also of some interest are Edwin Swift Balch, "Hudson Land," *Bulletin of the American Geographical Society,* XLIII (1911), 445–46; Balch, "Why America Should Re-explore Wilkes Land," *Proceedings of the American Philosophical Society,* XLVIII (Jan.–Apr., 1909), 34–50; Balch, "Wilkes Land," *Bulletin of the American Geographical Society,* XXXVIII (1906), 30–32; George S. Bryan, "The Wilkes Exploring Expedition," *United States Naval Institute Proceedings,* 65 (Oct., 1939), 1452–64; William H. Hobbs, "Discovery of a New Sketch of Cape Hudson in the Antarctic," *Geographical Review,* XXIV (Jan., 1934), 115–17; Hobbs, "The Eastern Landfalls of Wilkes Within the Australian Sector of the Antarctic," *Geographical Journal,* LXXXI (Jan., 1933), 538–40; Hobbs, "Wilkes Land Rediscovered," *Geographical Review,* XXII (Oct., 1932), 632–55; and Frank E. Ross, "The Antarctic Explorations of Lieutenant Charles Wilkes, U.S.N.," *Proceedings of the Royal Geographical Society of Australasia, South Australian Branch,* XXXV (1933–34), 130–41.

Finally, adding to the literature on Wilkes and his expedition are Louis H. Bolander, "The Vincennes, World Traveler of the Old Navy," *United States Naval Institute Proceedings,* 62 (June, 1936), 823–31; Anna Ella Carrell, "The First American Exploring Expedition," *Harper's New Monthly Magazine,* XLIV (Dec., 1871), 60–64; Louis N. Feipel, "The Wilkes Exploring Expedition: Its Progress Through Half a Century, 1826–1876," *United States Naval Institute Proceedings,* 40 (Sept.–Oct., 1914), 1323–50; Thomas R. Henry, "The Discoverer of a New Continent; Charles Wilkes and America's Greatest Exploring

Expedition," *National Spectator,* I (March 27, 1926), 28–30; Jim Dan Hill, "Charles Wilkes—Turbulent Scholar of the Old Navy," *United States Naval Institute Proceedings,* 57 (July, 1931), 867–87; Mary Hannah Krout, "Rear Admiral Charles Wilkes and His Exploits," *United States Naval Institute Proceedings,* 50 (March, 1924), 405–16; and George W. Littlehales, "The Navy as a Motor in Geographical and Commercial Progress," *Journal of the American Geographical Society,* XXXI (1899), 123–49.

INDEX

Academy of Natural Sciences (Philadelphia), 109
Active, schooner: in U.S. Exploring Expedition, 127
Adams, John, 96
Adams, John Quincy, 160; supports plan for United States occupation of South Shetlands, 32, 33, 34; on Reynolds's movement for government-sponsored exploration, 91; and Exploring Expedition, 94, 96, 97; defends U.S. Exploring Expedition, 125, 126
Adelaide Island, 53
Adélie Land, 165; Dumont d'Urville's discovery of, 150
Admiralty range, 158
Adventure: in Cook's second expedition, 12, 13, 14
Adventure Islets, 131
Africa, 9; Greek theory of, 4; Ptolemy's theory of, 4, 15
Agate, Alfred T.: appointed to U.S. Exploring Expedition, 110
Age of Geographical Discovery: conception of Antarctic regions, 4–5
Alabama Packet, brig: in Fanning fleet (1821–22), 56, 60
Albany Institute, *Transactions* of: Eights's article in, 99–100
Alden, Lieutenant James, 162

Alexander I Land, 49, 130; Bellingshausen's discovery of, 48
American Philosophical Society, 109
American Quarterly Review, 90
Antarctica, 30, 45, 51, 54, 142, 143, 152, 165; description of, 15–17; first known reference to as continent, 55. *See also* Antarctic Continent
Antarctic Circle, 14, 47, 62, 92, 105, 109, 158; first crossing of, 13; first discovery of land within, 48
Antarctic Continent, 2, 44, 59, 87, 158, 159, 161, 165, 167, 168; conceptions of, 9, 15, 55; description of, 15–17; animal and bird life on, 17–18; Palmer's voyage to, 39–40; Bransfield's discovery of, 42–43; Palmer's reported second voyage to, 44–47; Bellingshausen's exploration of, 47–49; Johnson's voyage to, 53; Davis's voyage to, 54; first known landing on, 54; Burdick's voyage to, 55; Wilkes's exploration of, 142–46; Wilkes's recognition of, 144, 145–46; Dumont d'Urville's exploration of, 150; discovery of, announced by Wilkes, 154; Wilkes's concep-